Business Etiquette For Dummies®

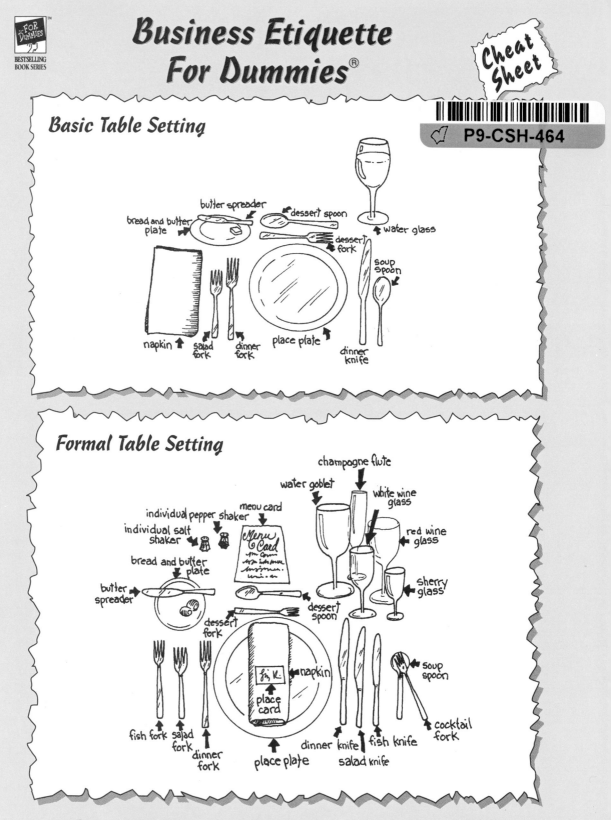

Basic Table Setting

- butter spreader
- bread and butter plate
- dessert spoon
- water glass
- dessert fork
- soup spoon
- napkin
- salad fork
- dinner fork
- place plate
- dinner knife

Formal Table Setting

- champagne flute
- water goblet
- white wine glass
- individual pepper shaker
- menu card
- individual salt shaker
- red wine glass
- bread and butter plate
- butter spreader
- dessert spoon
- sherry glass
- dessert fork
- napkin
- place card
- soup spoon
- fish fork
- salad fork
- dinner fork
- place plate
- dinner knife
- salad knife
- fish knife
- cocktail fork

Business Etiquette For Dummies®

Cheat Sheet

Active Listening

Most of us spend plenty of time talking, but not much time hearing what other people have to say. Here's how to become an active listener:

- ✔ **Set the stage** by setting your phone to "do not disturb," turning away from the computer or other distractions, and facing the person you're talking to. If people have a habit of barging into your office, close the door or find a conference room or a quiet corner of the cafeteria to have important discussions.

- ✔ **Sit in a neutral position.** Sitting on opposite sides of a conference table puts you on equal footing; sitting behind your desk while the other person sits in front of your desk gives you more perceived power. That's just what you *don't* want in this situation, because it immediately puts the other person on the defensive.

- ✔ **Clear your mind of your own point of view.** Your goal is to listen and understand your partner's point of view without considering how it stacks up with yours. During a discussion, we often miss someone else's point because we're busy thinking about what we want to say next. If you're concerned about being able to respond to everything later, take notes. (If you take notes, you may want to explain that you're doing it in order to really concentrate and remember. Otherwise, your partner may think he's undergoing a psychological profile.)

- ✔ **Encourage the other person to keep talking** by nodding your head or asking him to continue, but don't interrupt. Wait until the other person has said everything he wants to say. At that point, you should understand his point of view, even if you still don't agree with it. That's your basis for negotiation and compromise.

Making Great Conversation

If you're in a group of people and need to raise a topic of conversation, try one of the following topics:

- ✔ **Sports that are of national prominence:** Examples include the Super Bowl or the Olympics.

- ✔ **Current events:** Make sure to read the newspaper or a news magazine the day of the event. Appropriate current events include business news, personal interest stories, stories about nature, and stories about local civic accomplishments.

- ✔ **Positive items of interest to everyone in the company:** The new advertising campaign or the redesigned corporate cafeteria, for example.

- ✔ **Bestselling books.**

- ✔ **A compliment about the event, host, food, wine, or the venue.**

For Dummies: Bestselling Book Series for Beginners

Praise for Business Etiquette For Dummies

"*Business Etiquette For Dummies* is a great reference guide for business protocol. This book packs 20 years of business etiquette into 360 pages. *Business Etiquette For Dummies* answers all the questions even the most seasoned business person is afraid to ask."

— William Minor, Vice President HR, Lam Research

"Good manners still play a central role in the job-hunting process. Whether joining the mailroom or the executive suite, a job seeker wants to make his future colleagues comfortable while getting his points across. *Business Etiquette For Dummies* is an essential reference tool."

— Anne Gregor, Editorial Director and Executive Producer, CareerPath.com.

"Life is too short to deal with jerks. Read this book if you want people to like doing business with you, or give it to others you have to do business with."

— Guy Kawasaki, CEO, Garage.com

"Pay attention to what Sue Fox says on etiquette! She's an expert who knows how the social rules have changed in a networked world. Her helpful advice has the potential to catapult your career. Better yet, *Business Etiquette For Dummies* makes it easy to 'do the right thing' in every business setting."

— Raymond G. Nasr, Director, Corporate Communications, Novell, Inc.

"With *Business Etiquette For Dummies*, even the clueless can learn to be courteous. That can be critically important for someone entering the business culture from engineering or academia."

— Larry Tesler, CEO, Stagecast Software, Inc.

"Doesn't matter if you run a small business or a big company, Sue Fox's guidelines will help you stand out in this competitive world. *Business Etiquette For Dummies* covers from the basic rules to the new corporate etiquette rules. A must for anyone in the Business World!"

— Dr. Ilsa Andujar, Etiquette Consultant, Puerto Rico

"Bravo to Sue Fox for recognizing the need and authoring a book to bring etiquette back to business. Etiquette is as essential in business as it is in our personal lives. Etiquette is a matter of style and balance, it's about getting where you are going and doing it the right way. It's about sending the right signals, having empathy for our associates, and developing successful relationships. With new technology, much has changed, but have we? I have to believe that no one truly wants to make a bad first impression if it can be avoided. All of us still prefer to put our best foot forward. As a marketing consultant in Silicon Valley, I am constantly confronted with new and unusual circumstances challenging my 'etiquette I.Q.' *Business Etiquette For Dummies* provides a much-needed, ready reference for all of us who would rather have it and not need it than need it and not have it!"

> — Valerie Foster, Executive Vice President,
> Splash Marketing Group

Business Etiquette

FOR

DUMMIES®

by Sue Fox

Wiley Publishing, Inc.

Business Etiquette For Dummies®

Published by
Wiley Publishing, Inc.
909 Third Avenue
New York, NY 10022
www.wiley.com

About the Author

Sue Fox is President of Etiquette Survival, LLC, a California-based professional development and publishing company. Fox has provided contemporary etiquette training to business professionals, celebrities, corporations, and educational institutions since 1994. Previously, she was employed in the high tech industry, with ten years experience in sales and marketing at Apple Computer, Inc.

Etiquette Survival provides products, training systems, self-study courses, and business opportunities to individual interested in starting their own etiquette consulting businesses. They also offer educational material for teaching professionals and corporate trainers that would like to incorporate etiquette training into their current classroom curriculum.

Fox is the author of *Etiquette For Dummies*, published by Wiley Publishing, Inc. She is the executive producer of the Etiquette Survival Video and Interactive DVD Series, featuring dining and social etiquette and proper table settings for adults and teens.

Sue Fox and Etiquette Survival have been featured in many publications, including *The Saturday Evening Post, Woman's Day, Vogue, Ladies Home Journal, American Baby, Newsweek, Fortune, Seventeen, Entrepreneur, Self, Real Simple, Los Angeles Times, New York Times, New York Post, Wall Street Journal, Miami Herald, San Jose Mercury, San Francisco Chronicle, Chicago Tribune, Boston Globe, Sunday London Times, Australian Financial News, Folha de S. Paulo, Images of Canada, Associated Press, Nekkei Marketing Journal Japan,* and *Times of India.*

Etiquette Survival media credits include radio interviews and featured stoires by CNBC TV, ABC World News, KRON TV San Francisco, KOVR TV Sacramento, Knowledge TV San Francisco, Mornings on 2 San Francisco, ABCNews.com with Sam Donaldson, CNETNews.com, CBSMarketWatch.com, KQED San Francisco, and KABC Los Angeles.

Fox has established a number of Etiquette Survival consultants across the country, and internationally in Canada, Australia, India, China, Japan, Singapore, Puerto Rico, and Malaysia. Her website is www.etiquettesurvival-inc.com.

She has traveled extensively and is well acquainted with Asian and African cultures. She has an additional background in image consulting and make-up artistry, with twenty years of fashion modeling experience.

Fox resides in Los Gatos, California, and is the mother of two grown sons, Stephen and Nathan.

Authors' Acknowledgments

I'd like to express my appreciation to the wonderful team at Hungry Minds, Inc. My continued gratitude goes to my acquisitions editor, Holly McGuire, for her ongoing support and belief in the value of this book. Thank you to my project editor, Tim Gallan, copy editors Ben Nussbaum and Tammy Castleman, illustrator Liz Kurtzman, project coordinator Nancee Reeves, and cartoonist Rich Tennant, and publicity director Lindsay MacGregor.

I wish to offer my respect and appreciation to writers Perrin Cunningham and Laura Johnston for their creative contribution, intelligence, and dedication; and to my friend and colleague Joie Gregory for her valuable suggestions and outstanding technical editing.

My deepest gratitude goes to my amazing family and my big-hearted friends! Thank you from the bottom of my heart for your loving support, respect, and especially for your constant encouragement. I love you all.

Finally, I am grateful for the ever-growing network of wonderful people I meet along the way who respond with such warmth and enthusiasm to my books, courses, and business. Tom y reader, colleagues, clients, students, and Etiquette Survival consultants, thank you for reminding me that the best way to teach is by example.

— Sue Fox

Publisher's Acknowledgments

We're proud of this book; please send us your comments through our online registration form located at www.dummies.com/register.

Some of the people who helped bring this book to market include the following:

Acquisitions, Editorial, and Media Development

Senior Project Editor: Tim Gallan

Acquisitions Editor: Holly McGuire

Copy Editors: Ben Nussbaum, Tamara Castleman

Technical Reviewer: Joie Gregory

Editorial Manager: Pam Mourouzis

Acquisitions Coordinator: Tonia Morgan-Oden

Editorial Assistant: Carol Strickland

Production

Project Coordinator: Nancee Reeves

Layout and Graphics: Amy Adrian, Jackie Bennett, Jill Piscitelli, Brent Savage, Jacque Schneider, Jeremey Unger

Illustrator: Liz Kurtzman

Proofreaders: Laura Albert, Henry Lazarek, Susan Moritz, Marianne Santy

Indexer: Rachel Rice

Publishing and Editorial for Consumer Dummies

Diane Graves Steele, Vice President and Publisher, Consumer Dummies
Joyce Pepple, Acquisitions Director, Consumer Dummies
Kristin A. Cocks, Product Development Director, Consumer Dummies
Michael Spring, Vice President and Publisher, Travel
Brice Gosnell, Publishing Director, Travel
Suzanne Jannetta, Editorial Director, Travel

Publishing for Technology Dummies

Richard Swadley, Vice President and Executive Group Publisher
Andy Cummings, Vice President and Publisher

Composition Services

Gerry Fahey, Vice President of Production Services
Debbie Stailey, Director of Composition Services

Contents at a Glance

Cartoons at a Glance

By Rich Tennant

page 7

page 137

page 279

page 317

page 257

page 69

page 189

Fax: 978-546-7747
E-mail: richtennant@the5thwave.com
World Wide Web: www.the5thwave.com

Table of Contents

Introduction

As we enter the new millennium, is there any reason to know about etiquette and protocol? Absolutely! The need for etiquette has not disappeared just because we live and do business differently than we did a thousand years ago. In fact, knowing how to treat each other well is more important now than ever. In the last thirty years, fundamental changes have occurred in the makeup of the work force and the way we do business, and some of the rules have changed forever.

By examining how good manners apply to the work world, we will benefit ourselves and everyone around us. After all, who you are shows in how you behave and in how you appear to others. How you look, talk, walk, sit, stand, eat — in other words, how you present yourself — speaks volumes about who you are and creates the impression you have on others. This is true not only in your personal life but in your professional life as well.

A successful career does not always come to those who work the longest or the hardest, nor even to those with the most impressive technical skills. In the new economy, creating a culture of civility at work is important. Casual does not mean rude, and formal does not mean stuffy. Whether your company is dress-down or blue-chip, self-restraint and respect for others go a long way. This is the new competitive edge!

While the basics of etiquette remain the same — you do remember all the basics, don't you? — there are many situations that now need redefinition and rethinking. How do you promote the right sort of relationships in the global office? How do you foster general good will and success with your peers and managers? How do you handle gender, race, and sexual orientation in the boardroom and in the workplace? What are the new rules for interviewing, supervising, and changing jobs? Are there new rules for the way we dress and converse with colleagues, clients, and bosses? What about new rules for business entertaining, conferences, trade shows, and travel?

Think, too, of the enormous impact computers and the Internet have had on the way we do business! Whether you work in the vortex of Silicon Valley or do business far from the high-tech tornado, the information age and its technologies have permanently changed most business. What are the rules for online etiquette and the use of cellular phones, laptops, pagers, Palm Pilots, and videoconferencing? These are new technologies that require new etiquette rules.

The essential soft skills of good manners are critical to advancing your career. Not only do they give you added credibility, they also ensure that you are an exceptional representative of your company. Having these skills often means the difference between being pigeonholed in your current position and being offered an attractive promotion or the opportunity to start your own company. You may even find yourself becoming a model for others in your business by setting a standard of respectful behavior and kindness toward others. People around you will appreciate it and follow your lead.

Not only is proper etiquette now understood to be vital to our careers and professional growth, it is important to personal growth as well. Integrating civility into our behavior allows us to stop worrying about what to do in complex social and business situations. Once good manners become part of who we are, they provide a foundation that we can take for granted when we encounter stress and anxiety. More than that, etiquette helps us recognize the importance of others and the ways in which we can be a presence without being a burden.

For the last seven years, we've been racing to provide contemporary etiquette training for people in virtually every situation in work and life. Our clients come from start-up companies, large corporations, and public and private schools. We have rural and urban clients and have taught groups of business people and students from all over the world. Times have changes drastically during the past few decades, and social and business niceties aren't nearly as pervasive or clearly defined as they used to be. Knowing how to behave courteously and professionally is far from trivial. Etiquette and protocol really do count in the business world. No matter how brilliant an employee may be, his or her lack of social grace will make a bad first impression on clients and business associates.

Sue is President of Etiquette Survival, author of *Etiquette For Dummies* (published by Wiley Publishing, Inc.), and executive producer of *The Etiquette Survival Kit,* a series of education videos and classroom curricula that feature dining and social etiquette.

About This Book

Business Etiquette For Dummies will guide you through the new rules of business etiquette. You'll soon find that good manners are far more than superficial observance of social customs. You'll see that graciousness and civility are sincere and come from the heart.

Our intention for this book is not only to answer the technical hows and whys of etiquette and protocol, but also to show that the core of etiquette is really a way of life, one that emphasizes attention to the needs of others and recognizes the diversity of persons. A person with good manners is someone who always tries to be generous and attentive.

So download some manners — and upgrade your career! Read on to rediscover the good manners you may have misplaced. Perhaps you'll learn a few new tips that you can incorporate into the way you work. And, as you read through this book, grade yourself on how you conduct yourself at work right now, noting where you can improve.

It's never too early or too late to learn about etiquette. Everyone has to interact with others to succeed. This book is great for new players in the working world, but it's also great for those who have been in the workplace awhile and want to clear up confusions about the complexities of social interaction in modern business.

You may use this book as a reference guide, reading any section that interests you. You can start at the back or in the middle. I hope I have avoided dogmatism, but there are some things I think are really important, and I have repeated and overstated them for emphasis. This book discusses some difficult parts of life. The tough issues can't be trivialized, but neither do I wish to be overly serious when it's not necessary. Remember: "Life has to be lived forwards, but it must be understood backwards."

The book is wider than it is deep. In the effort to portray a whole panorama of what business etiquette is all about, I have tried to include virtually all the topics that affect it. Yet no single book can provide every detail. I encourage you to join me in learning about these rules of etiquette, and perhaps you will be encouraged to explore the many other excellent books on this subject.

How This Book Is Organized

This book is divided into seven parts, with 25 chapters and an index. Cross-referencing is provided between the chapters.

Part I: Conducting Yourself with Care in the Business World

What's all this fuss about business etiquette? Can it really help you get ahead in business? In Part I, we explore these basic questions and learn the secrets of contributing positively to the office environment and building good relations with others above and below you on the corporate ladder. We also navigate cultural diversity in the workplace. Finally, we talk about appearance, how much it matters, what people read into your style of dress and body language, and what you can do to give yourself every grooming and style advantage.

Part II: Opening Doors to Communication

"What we have here is a failure to communicate."

How often have you heard those words? Communication is key in business, just as it is in personal life. In Part II, we help you get started by tackling one of your most frequently encountered challenges: meeting and greeting other people. Many of us get tripped up on introductions, so we set you on the right path of who to introduce to whom, how to use titles, and the all-important firm handshake. Then we give you tips on making sparkling business conversation that everyone will want to be a part of.

Speaking on the telephone is another time when manners seem to slide, so we cover how to speak and listen considerately on the phone. You'll explore new tactics for handling voice mail, call waiting, caller ID, speaker phones, cell phones, and beepers. Next, we look at the written word. We close with brand-new advice on navigating cyberspace.

Part III: Overcoming the Big Etiquette Challenges at Work

Every office has at least one — the difficult person. How do you handle that person and wind up on the high ground? What are some tactics for dealing with difficult people? In Part III, we offer tips and strategies to help keep you sane. We also cover office conflicts and help you decide when and how to get involved. Then, we tackle the subject of stress and how to keep your cool under pressure. We discuss some ethical dilemmas that occur at work and use real-life scenarios to illustrate the right and wrong ways to handle them. We close with a discussion of office romance and sexual harassment — and how to draw the line between the two.

Part IV: Entertaining for Business

Business entertaining has expanded far beyond the traditional business dinner. What about golf games, rock climbing, and hang gliding? In Part IV, we put you through a real etiquette workout, reviewing everything from table settings and wine choices to buffet lines and company retreats. Then, we figure out the office party minefield. Should you give a gift? And if so, what? We close with a reminder about combining alcohol and work functions and we give you some tips for handling them both gracefully.

Part V: Meeting Etiquette and Boardroom Protocol

Meetings are a chance for people to size each other up, make judgment calls, and decide whom they want on their team. In Part V, we help you shine in the boardroom. From seating arrangements to chairing a meeting, we hit the potential highs and lows of group gatherings — including the latest information on video- and teleconferencing. Then we give you words of wisdom on surviving trade shows and conferences and on representing yourself and your company to your best advantage. Finally, we show you what to do if the responsibility for planning a special event falls to you. We'll give you checklists, creative ideas, and all the information you need to make your event a success.

Part VI: Going Global: Manners for a Small World

As communication and travel increase, we're working more and more with colleagues overseas. You have to know how to get along in Boise *and* in Bombay. Having to know so much can be intimidating, but in Part VI, we give you some universally helpful pointers. From surviving airline travel to knowing what to pack and how to speak when you get there, we get you through international business travel with dignity.

Part VII: The Part of Tens

This is where you'll find our best advice, concisely given. We've interviewed ten business executives about etiquette, and we offer you their comments. We also provide ten tried and true communication.

Icons Used in This Book

We use little pictures, called icons, to flag bits of information throughout the book. Here's what they mean:

Indicates a story that helps tell the story.

When you see this sign, pay attention.

Beware of these potential missteps.

Take-home messages to last a lifetime.

Small hints that will help make the bumps easier.

Where to Go from Here

The introduction is the end of the beginning and a broad template of the rest of the book. I hope that as you read you may pick up ideas and information that will allow you to be yourself while being considerate of others. Start by becoming aware. So keep reading!

Part I

Conducting Yourself with Care in the Business World

The 5th Wave   By Rich Tennant

"Does our insurance cover a visit from Mike Wallace?"

In this part . . .

We explore these basic questions and learn the secrets of contributing positively to the office environment and building good relations with others above and below you on the corporate ladder. We will also navigate cultural diversity in the workplace. Finally, we'll talk about appearance, how much it matters, what people read into your style of dress and body language, and what you can do to give yourself every grooming and style advantage.

Chapter 1

Good Manners Are for Company — Your Company!

· ·

In This Chapter

▶ Getting acquainted with the etiquette of today's business

▶ Displaying good manners in the workplace

▶ Being a good representative for your company

▶ Modeling manners

· ·

Good manners are important in the workplace for the same reason good manners are important anywhere: Good manners demonstrate that you possess self-control, that you are civilized, and that you care about and are capable of respecting others. Imagine a company culture based on civility!

It doesn't matter whether your company is a highly caffeinated start-up, a small gift boutique, or a good ol' boy law firm, good manners are important because they emphasize your willingness to control your own behavior for the benefit of others. Social relations between people evolve. Criminal and civil law codify the most serious boundaries of behavior. The accepted guidelines for getting along with others — etiquette — cover less grave behaviors.

Etiquette and good manners set out the "grammar" of social interaction. Grammar helps you get your words and sentences in the right order so that people can understand what you are saying. It helps others understand the content of what you mean without having to worry about the form. The same is true of etiquette. Etiquette helps you get your behavior in expected order so that others can focus on the content of what you're saying rather than on the form of your behavior. In that sense, good etiquette, like good grammar, becomes invisible.

New Business, New Etiquette

Forty years ago, American business etiquette included a chivalrous attitude toward women and often masked a prejudice toward people of color and those of foreign birth. Those attitudes are unacceptable. In addition, some baby boomers grew up thinking that etiquette was incompatible with "being real" and authentic. The result was that, throughout the 1970s, 1980s, and 1990s, people were really confused about what business etiquette required or even whether it was required at all. In the last few years people have realized that business etiquette is still necessary and that it can be formulated without chivalry and prejudice.

The new business etiquette retains vestiges of its origins in military protocol but ignores gender and race. In addition, business etiquette now incorporates a global perspective. The result is a complex web of protocols (which we untangle throughout this book) governed by one simple principle:

> *Respect others and help them feel comfortable by behaving in the least offensive manner possible.*

The following anecdote, based on a true story told by a Denver executive, illustrates the problems people sometimes get themselves into by forgetting business etiquette.

Military protocol and business etiquette

Business etiquette has its roots in military protocol. As in the military, the role of rank in business has been fundamental to corporate organization and culture. Even when, as in many of the "new economy's" companies, rank is intentionally minimized, that change is against the backdrop of its customary importance.

Rank in business goes hand in hand with experience, seniority, and promotion. We all assume that, as you get more experience, your judgment improves, and with improved judgment comes greater executive responsibility. And, just as in the military, greater executive responsibility engenders deference and respect from those junior in position. It is not at all unusual for subordinates to call their supervisors and managers by 'Mr.' or 'Ms.', just as, in the military, one calls superior officers by their title.

But the military roots of business etiquette go deeper than calling people by their proper titles. In most businesses, along with executive responsibility comes certain perks that junior employees do not have. Senior executives typically have greater discretion over the structure of their day; they typically have access to clubs, corporate boxes, and pampered travel arrangements; they typically are exempt from making picayune decisions. All of these perks mirror those found in the military.

Working as an engineer for an international company, Scott was invited to lunch at an upscale restaurant by his boss to meet three of their company's best clients: one from Bombay, one from Jakarta, and one from Boston. Scott arrived wearing a T-shirt, jeans, and running shoes, greeted the clients with a slap on the shoulder, called everyone "my man," interrupted others while they were talking, and ordered two martinis before launching into a huge, rare steak. The next day, Scott was no longer an engineer for an international company.

In business, it's your responsibility to anticipate your customer's values, as well as some of the nuances of the customer's cultural expectations. Most Indians consider the cow to be a sacred animal, most Indonesians don't drink alcohol, and most Bostonians expect a handshake and a name. It's your responsibility to ask your boss what she's wearing to lunch and following suit. Don't let your behavior damage your company's relationship with its clients — and cost you your job.

Or consider this story from an attorney that illustrates some of the generational differences prevalent in business.

Josef was a receptionist at a mainline Philadelphia law firm when one of the firm's oldest clients entered the office. Rather than greet her with, "Good morning, Mrs. Blueblood," as everyone else had for years, Josef decided to be friendly and said, "Hi Muriel, how's it going?" Mrs. Blueblood promptly decided to retain the services of a different law firm, explaining to one of the partners that the receptionist was improperly trained.

Most etiquette breaches do not immediately result in such drastic consequences, but the cumulative effect of repeated faux pas can be loss of respect, loss of reputation, and loss of business.

A few generations ago, large corporations and elite universities groomed their employees and students in etiquette. As part of management training, corporations required an etiquette course where executives practiced and refined their abilities to master introductions, dining skills, business dress, and correspondence. Most Ivy League students were groomed in etiquette through dining houses, fraternities, and sororities.

In the 1970s and 1980s, etiquette courses were rarely included in management training and were much less frequently found on college campuses.

But this trend is changing. As the business world becomes increasingly diverse, there has been a realization that etiquette training increases productivity, worker satisfaction, worker retention, and business growth by helping everyone get along.

In today's business world, 25-year-old CEOs are negotiating with 48-year-old CFOs and 72-year-old Presidents, often with a wide variety of cultural backgrounds. The need for good manners has never been more pressing. The new sensibility of respect for others means that not just the new employees, but everyone — from the most senior executive to the newest sales recruit — has to master the new business etiquette.

The Importance of Manners in the Workplace

Business etiquette is vitally important for creating a harmonious work environment and for representing your company in the best manner possible. Although many people consider their technical skills and intelligence to be their most important job qualifications, many employers consider the ability to get along well with colleagues and clients even more important. As John Rockefeller once said, "I will pay more for the ability to get along with people than for any other ability."

Having good manners doesn't mean acting like Niles Crane or correcting everyone else. Being well-mannered means one thing above all else: respecting others and treating them with courtesy and kindness.

In the workplace, manners get realized in a lot of different ways. You should do the following:

- ✔ Respect the company's culture. If your company's culture is laid back and casual, don't wear your expensive Italian suits.

- ✔ Respect rank and treat it appropriately. Most companies have a hierarchy. Learn what it is and what each level requires from you.

- ✔ Respect others' privacy and be courteous to them. Although you work with other people, you need to acknowledge their personal boundaries and not overstep them with unwanted intimacy.

- ✔ Respect others' views and handle disagreements gracefully. People's religious, political, moral, and lifestyle opinions differ. Acknowledge that and refrain from imposing yours on them.

- ✔ Handle job stress without imposing yourself on others. Stress is unavoidable. However, your response to stress can be changed so that you do not yell at others.

- ✔ Extend courtesies to all members of the company. Just because you're a middle manager doesn't entitle you to treat the shipper with contempt. Everyone deserves courtesy.

> ✔ Be courteous when using shared company equipment. Recognize that company equipment is owned by the company for the benefit of many. Treat the company car kindly and don't hog the copier for making copies of your daughter's birthday invitations.

The Importance of Being a Good Representative

As a representative of your company, you stand not only for yourself but also for the company as a whole. If you are poised, courteous, and respectful to your company's clients, they will extend their approving judgment to other employees of your company. If you are inconsiderate, insolent, and rude to your company's clients, you will be out of a job shortly.

Being your company's representative doesn't mean that you should be obsequious to your company's clients and customers. Instead, you can be professional and courteous by following these tips:

✔ Respect your client's time by being punctual to meetings and meals.

✔ Respect your customers — even the rude ones! Don't repay rudeness with rudeness.

✔ Respect your client's privacy. Avoid prying into private affairs unless invited to do so.

✔ Handle yourself in a gracious and courteous way during business meetings.

✔ Write follow-up letters and thank-you notes to clients.

✔ Remember that you are an employee at all times when at conventions and trade shows — even in the evening!

Modeling Manners for Others

By learning business etiquette, you become a model for others. Your considerate behavior in the office and with clients is instantly recognizable and beneficial to you and to your company. When a courteous employee works with others, her grace lends an air of professionalism to the workplace that others emulate and that employers reward.

Being courteous and being rich are not mutually exclusive.

Being a well-mannered business professional is harder than memorizing a bunch of stuffy rules. The greatest challenge is to incorporate the rules of good behavior so readily that you don't have to think about them at all. The trick is to incorporate etiquette into your daily behavior at home and at the office so that behaving well doesn't add extra stress. This way, you can focus on important things, such as making a deal and doing your job. If you practice the guidelines in this book — and practice, practice, practice! — eventually you won't have to think about any of these rules. Paraphrasing the philosopher Wittgenstein, etiquette is a ladder that once climbed can be thrown away.

Chapter 2

Moving Gracefully in the Business World

*E*ntering the business world for the first time requires patience and an open mind for the many subtle differences between student life and business life. Prior to starting your job at First Mighty Proper Bank, you may never have had to call anyone "Mr." or "Mrs." And, while your friends may all have similar backgrounds and tastes in clothes and music, the office you're now working in may have all kinds of people in it with whom you have to get along.

In this chapter, you are introduced to the skills required to be respectful and polite in your professional life, from your job interview to everyday life in the office. Among other things, you discover how to respect others' privacy, how to handle criticism and compliments, and how to be a good visitor and host. By the end of the chapter, you'll know what it takes to be a gracious and generous colleague.

Braving the Job Interview

So, after days of networking, you have an interview with the company you most want to work for. Congratulations! Your next response is likely dread. How can you make the best possible impression? You want to be polite and charming, but you don't want to come across as a spineless sycophant. You want to negotiate a great starting package, but you don't want to seem like a greedy, arrogant twit. Bottom line, you want them to like you, and you want them to convert their affection into cash while you both maintain professional decorum.

Aaagghh!

If you're like most people, job interviews are on your list of least-favorite activities. Just as you're meeting a whole group of people for the first time, you're also trying to assess them as potential colleagues and determine whether all those nice things they're saying about the company and how much they love it are really true. You're also trying to assess the job, the position, and how it compares to your other opportunities. As though that weren't enough, you suddenly need to brag about your many accomplishments — something your mother told you never, ever to do. All this pressure is enough to send you around the bend. The sweat begins to form on your palms, you start to look like a deer in a car's head lights, you worry about having a tear in the seat of your pants, and you're convinced that when you open your mouth nothing but a squeak will emerge.

Relax. This section doesn't guarantee you the job, but it can help you maintain your dignity.

Soul searching before job searching

First of all, you need to put some serious effort into deciding what kind of job you really want. A lucky few just know they want to play the oboe for a medium-sized symphony in a Midwestern city. Most people — especially those who've just graduated with a degree in French literature — need a little more help clarifying their skills and goals.

You're in luck. An entire industry is dedicated to helping you find the perfect job. Start on the Internet or at your local library or bookstore. You can also check out www.monster.com, not only for guidance about different lines of work, but also for interviewing tips and outstanding advice on composing an effective résumé.

After you secure an interview — or even before — do a little reading about the company. The Internet has made this research much easier than ever before. Your parents had to go to the library to dig up annual reports before the big interview, you have only to fire up your browser to gather loads of information.

In the unlikely event that the company doesn't have an online presence, or that their site isn't very informative, start with what you know:

- **Grill the person who referred you to the company for information.** Does the boss have any pet peeves? What are they? Is the company formal or casual? What should you wear to the interview?

- **Do a news search for the past few months and see what you can find.**

- **Track down the friend of the friend who used to work there.** Most people like to talk about their careers, and almost everyone is pleased to help a job-hunter.

Honing your telephone skills

You've been using the phone since you were five, right? You have one in every room of the house. But do you know how to act when you're calling a company for information?

- **Always introduce yourself first:** "Hello, this is Bootsie Nibblins. I'm calling for Harold Huggins," or "I'm calling to find out the name of your Vice President of Marketing."

- **Be patient:** Receptionists often must put you on hold momentarily in order to address other incoming calls.

- **Provide additional information politely if the person with whom you're speaking with requests it:** Most receptionists and assistants try to eliminate junk mailings, but they should have no problem with providing the information you need to send a résumé.

- **Explain the subject briefly when making follow-up calls:** "I had sent Mr. Huggins my résumé, and I'm calling to be sure he received it."

- **Leave a brief message if you get voice mail:** Include your name and number, explain your reason for calling, and at the end of the call, repeat your name and number.

- **Find out the name of the person who has helped you before hanging up, in case you need to call back.**

- **Always say thank-you!**

Writing appropriate letters and résumés

When you send your résumé to a company, either via e-mail or in hard copy, you will likely attach a cover letter. The cover letter should be on personalized stationery with your address, telephone number, and e-mail address (if you have one) on the top of the page. Include this basic information even if the letter is an e-mail or e-mail attachment.

Stick to the communication medium you start with until the employer changes it. If you begin the correspondence on the Internet, you may continue on the Internet. If the company starts to call you, then you call them back.

Correspondence is an extremely important way to demonstrate your grace and professionalism both before and after an interview. Whether you're responding to that cryptic e-mail address that was in the newspaper ad, composing a letter to the CEO on your best stationery, or sending your prompt thank-you note (don't even THINK about skipping this step!), your written words have the potential to leave a lasting impression. Make sure that your letter is the one that reminds the interviewer how smart and poised you were, instead of the one that gets e-mailed around the company as a source of amusement.

Speaking of attachments: If you want to send a large one, ask someone — a receptionist, the person who will interview you, someone in Human Resources, your potential boss — first. Simple text résumés and cover letters are generally fine. Graphics files or longer documents may not be. You may have the latest and greatest technology and a fast Internet connection, but if your prospective boss is out of town and trying to download your graphically interesting portfolio through a hotel room phone, she will be thinking dark thoughts about you.

Unless you have already cleared it, do not e-mail large or complex attachments with your résumé. Although attachments may be appropriate if you're applying for position as a Web designer, never assume that the other person has time to download your creation.

Your cover letter should follow these guidelines:

- ✔ **Keep the cover letter short and to the point.**
- ✔ **State your interest in the job, briefly highlight your qualifications, and provide contact information:** If you have names to drop, now is an appropriate time. ("Our mutual friend, Lord Whiffenpoof, told me you have been golfing together for years, and he suggested I get in touch with you about entry-level accounting positions.")

✔ **Don't go into unnecessary detail:** You don't need to blather on about your interesting collection of license plates (unless this interest has a direct bearing on your ability to succeed in the position). Until you're in an actual interview, potential employers are unlikely to be interested in this kind of information.

✔ **Avoid grammatical and typographical errors in your résumé and cover letter at all costs:** Your sloppiness, however unintentional, may be interpreted as a character trait. Use spell checking and grammar checking software, and have at least two people you trust proofread both résumé and letter before you send them.

Your résumé should be long enough to include all pertinent information, but not long enough to include your good dental hygiene citation from eighth grade. One page is just fine if it allows you to present a complete picture. If not, don't be shy about adding an extra sheet. One reliable format is a modified chronology, with skills first, then work experience in reverse chronological order (most current first), and then education.

Again, information should be specific. "Seeking a growth position with an exciting company" tells potential employers that you don't know what you want. For more complete résumé advice, refer to one of the many excellent books on the subject, see a career counselor, or visit www.monster.com.

Deciding what to wear

Dressing for a job interview used to be very simple — navy suit, white blouse or shirt, and well-polished black shoes. If you're interviewing in a traditional office and/or industry, these rules still apply. Pick a conservative tie or scarf to match your navy suit ensemble, snip off errant price tags, lose the flashy jewelry and excessive perfume or aftershave, use a comb, brush your teeth, and you're home free.

In recent years, however, dress codes have become much more relaxed at many companies and nonexistent at others. In this case, your decision is a little more difficult, and it may require some (easy) research.

Many employers explain that their casual dress policies recognize that job performance is more important than appearance. At the same time, most of the people who will interview you — whether they admit it or not — would like to see some sign that the interview was worth some special effort on your part. Dress is one way to convey that impression.

Information, please . . .

"Informational interviews" are just fine between consenting adults. If you call your friend's uncle and say that you understand he isn't hiring, but you would really like to find out more about ostrich ranching, your intentions are very clear.

Odds are that he'll be delighted to spend an hour telling you everything you want to know. If he's not interested, he can make up a polite excuse. Either way, you have both followed the rules of business etiquette.

Still, you may have a dilemma. On the one hand, you don't have the job yet, so you may not be entitled to dress like an employee. You want your dream company to know you're professional and interested. On the other hand, you don't want to look like some uptight weenie who won't fit into their hip-yet-casual atmosphere. Your best bet is to determine the standard dress code there, and then exceed it just a little. At a company where employees are casual but neatly pressed, you may want to dress it up a little with a coat and/or tie. If they're wearing flip-flops and cutoffs, your khakis and clean shirt could be just the ticket.

One way to find out how people dress is to hang around the entrance when people are coming in and out. (Try not to appear suspicious to the security guards.) Another way is to ask. When you're setting up the interview, you could ask the manager or recruiter, "Does Swell Company have a traditional dress code, or a casual dress code?" By phrasing your question this way, you won't raise any red flags at a company with traditional dress. Chances are the other person will realize that you're trying to figure out what to wear to the interview and will advise you accordingly. If you're reluctant to ask the manager who will be interviewing you, try calling the receptionist. Just keep in mind that he or she probably won't be deciding whether to hire you. For more tips on dressing professionally, see Chapter 4.

If your hands have a tendency to sweat, apply an antiperspirant to your palms the night before an interview and again in the morning.

Getting yourself ready to interview

Careful thought about your job search will keep you from wasting others' time. Doing practice interviews is an excellent strategy — but you should do them with friends, family, friends of the family, or at least companies you have some interest in, even if you consider them a last resort. If you can't get anyone to listen to your interview, do an interview with yourself and videotape it. Whatever you do, please don't interview with a company if you're sure you don't want to work there. You'll be wasting the time of a very busy person who is already short staffed. You also may be taking time away from someone who very much wants to interview. Besides being impolite, this is bad career karma.

That's not to say that you must know exactly what job you want before doing any interviews. Some people are nearing retirement and still haven't quite finalized a career path. You should, however, have some solid ideas on the subject and be ready to articulate them. Submitting a résumé to one firm saying you're interested in "human resources management at a small company" and to another seeking "a recruiting position with a multinational firm" is quite acceptable. As long as both of these positions are within your universe of attractive jobs, you owe it to yourself to explore them. What is unacceptable is to interview for a systems analyst position just for the experience, and then confess halfway through that you really want to be an actress.

Making a splash on the big day

Everybody's been there. First, use a good antiperspirant/deodorant. Next, **RELAX!** That's right — relax. If that seems impossible, just concentrate on breathing deeply. The idea is to keep oxygen flowing to your brain so that you can remember all the reasons why you deserve this job. Deep breathing also prevents you from losing consciousness and waking up underneath that big ficus in the lobby.

Of course you have a great deal on the line in a job interview, but your display of nervousness may thwart your ability to negotiate the best deal and may even harm your chances of getting the job. That doesn't make you feel any better? Take more deep breaths.

Arriving at the office

Here are a few pointers to get you started:

- **Be on time:** If you get lost easily, or even if you don't, leave a few minutes for construction delays, traffic, and a pit stop. If you've never been to this building before, get specific directions, including where to park, which entrance to use, and where to go once you get inside. Write the information down and look at the map. Better yet, drive over a day or two in advance so that you'll know exactly where you're going.

✔ **Get the the correct pronunciation of your interviewer's name:** You can ask for this information when you're asking for directions. If the name is difficult, practice.

✔ **Know your interviewer's title, if any, and use it until asked to do otherwise.** You do not call your interviewer by her first name until you've been informed by your host that you can drop the titles and surnames.

✔ **Bring a folder with a few clean copies of your résumé, some paper to write on, a good fountain pen with quick drying ink and a tissue or two:** A leather portfolio adds a nice touch. Avoid bringing enough luggage to take you to Kuala Lumpur.

✔ **Be pleasant to the receptionist, security guard, or whomever else may be helping you find your interviewer:** If this person is on the phone, be patient. Find something else to look at until they finish, and don't tap your fingers on the counter or succumb to other nervous tics. At the very least, this person is another working professional who deserves your respect. At the most, you will be working here in a few weeks, and you don't want to be nicknamed "Mr. Itchy" before your first day on the job. If the receptionist appears frazzled and can't get to you immediately, you should have arrived earlier! Arrive early enough that you aren't faced with this problem.

On the other hand, you don't want to be overly friendly. Take your cue from the employee. If he strikes up a conversation, go with it. If he seems busy, don't bother him. Now is not the time to line up a date. (If you don't get the job, you can always call back.)

✔ **Be patient while waiting for your interviewer:** Yes, she should be on time, but a million things could have thrown her off schedule. Because you have cleared your calendar for the afternoon — haven't you? — you should have no problem spending a few minutes reviewing interview answers in your head or looking at the industry awards hanging in the lobby and thinking of a way to work them into the conversation.

✔ **Don't chew gum, smoke, eat, or drink on company premises unless refreshments are offered:** Your water bottle, handy though it may be, does not belong on the interviewer's desk — even if you're very thirsty, and even if your doctor has advised you to drink lots of water.

One manager loves to recount the story of a young woman who arrived for her interview and pulled a brownie out of her purse, explaining that she needed to eat frequently to maintain her blood sugar. Though she offered to share, she didn't get the job!

During the interview

If you've been practicing your etiquette, then good behavior has already become habit. If you have not been practicing, you may want to skip around to other pertinent chapters of this book to refresh your memory.

Remember to do the following:

- ✔ **Start with a smile and firm handshake — obviously!**

- ✔ **Stand up when your interviewer approaches.**

- ✔ **Greet him by name, look him in the eye, and thank him for this opportunity:** Refer to the interviewer as Mr. Nguyen if you have never met; Duc if he has previously indicated that calling him by his first name is okay.

- ✔ **Leave unnecessary items in your car:** When the interviewer shows you to her office, you don't want to spend time packing for the trip. Women, in particular, sometimes find themselves loaded down with purses, tote bags, briefcases, and enormous zippered day planners. Men are rapidly catching up, but instead of carrying purses, they stuff their pockets and surround their waistlines with electronics. Try leaving all but the most important items in the car.

- ✔ **Give the interview your full attention:** This opportunity may be your best chance not only to sell yourself but also to notice important details about the interviewer and the company. Minimize possible distractions by turning off pagers, cell phones, watches, and other beeping gadgets. If you must set your pager on "vibrate" mode, resist the temptation to read messages that come in during your interview. Unless you're a transplant candidate waiting for an available organ, the messages can wait. This simple courtesy lets the interviewer know that you're organized and professional.

- ✔ **Watch your language:** Swearing is rarely appropriate at the office and never appropriate during an interview. Even if the interviewer swears, you don't have to.

- ✔ **Be as specific as possible in answering the interviewer's questions:** Anticipating possible questions in advance (again, with the help of the many available resources) is helpful and allows you to prepare your answers. Whenever possible, cite actual examples from your experience. Give yourself time to think about your answers before you speak — they don't have to be automatic. If you get a question you didn't anticipate, don't panic. If you've spent time preparing for the interview and understand your own needs and interests, you can answer just about any question with some degree of success.

✔ **Add other comments and ask questions at the end of the interview:**
Once the interviewer has finished answering questions, she will almost
always give you the opportunity to add other comments and ask questions. If you feel that the questions she has asked haven't allowed you to
explain why you're the right person for the job, now is the time to volunteer that information. Not everyone is a good interviewer, but you can
help bring out the important information about yourself.

You should always have some questions. Even if you feel you know everything already, ask something like, "What is your favorite thing about working
here?" or, "What are the greatest challenges your company faces right now?"
Avoid questions that you can easily answer through a Web site or annual
report — if you ask them, the interviewer may conclude that you didn't take
the time to research the company.

Closing the interview

When the interview is over, do the following:

✔ **End as you began, with a firm handshake and a big smile.**

✔ **Tell the interviewer now that you'll call him to follow up, and specify a
time period that's reasonable based on your discussion:** For example, if
he's indicated that they'll be interviewing for another three weeks before
making a decision, tell him you'll call near the end of the three weeks.

✔ **Thank him again for his time.**

✔ **Walk out confidently:** You did it!

Following up

You must always, always write a follow-up note immediately after an interview. Compose your note in your very best handwriting in black or blue ink
on a quality cream or white paper — no lovable basset hounds, Looney
Tunes pals, or grocery-store thank you notes, please. Buy this paper and
some stamps before the interview so that you can write the note as soon as
you get home, while everything is fresh in your mind. If you're unsure about a
title or spelling, call the company to find out. After all the effort you've put in,
this is no time to cut corners!

And yes, if you interviewed with several people, each person gets a note. You
should make an effort to vary the wording a little, just in case these people,
well, compare notes!

Your note can be very simple: a salutation, a thank-you, a specific point of some kind, and a closing. Here's an example:

Dear Ms. Moneypenny (or Dear Frieda),

Thank you very much for taking the time to meet with me this afternoon. It was a pleasure to meet you, and your observations about the effect of the lunar cycle on savings rates were fascinating. I hope that my minor in astronomy, in addition to my summer internship at Big Big Bank, will persuade you that I am the right candidate to fill the Junior Loan Officer position. I will give you a call after the full moon. I look forward to speaking with you again.

Best regards,

Raoul Pennypacker

Even if your handwriting is atrocious, a handwritten note has far more impact than an e-mail or no note at all. At the very least, the interviewer will put you on the list of people who took the time to follow up. If it's a close contest between several candidates, your graceful good manners could give you the edge.

In some instances, you may apply for a job over e-mail or a Web site and then be interviewed via e-mail or Web chat without ever speaking to a human being. In that case, you may e-mail your follow-up note, in keeping with the "cyberness" of it all. If you've had a telephone interview, however, your note should still be handwritten.

You even send a short thank-you note to someone who gives you a screening interview. You may not even get beyond the screening interview, but your good manners will be remembered in the future if any other job for which you're qualified comes up.

Lastly, follow up by phone as you said you would. If you don't get a return call right away, don't be a pest. Let a couple of days pass between each call, or alternate between telephone and e-mail. Most people are busy but committed to getting back with you. If someone refuses to call you back, you're probably lucky not to be working with that person!

One principle of etiquette is to help the other person feel comfortable, but sometimes etiquette also helps you feel comfortable because you are confident that you know what to do in every situation. However, if, despite your graciousness, you feel uneasy during an interview and are uneasy the entire time you're in the building, don't accept an offer. Trust your gut instinct.

Being a Positive Part of the Office Environment

Everyone knows people who are easy to work with and people who are, well, not so easy to work with. Whether you're just starting a new job or have been with the same company for years, you're likely to ask yourself at some point just why some people are so much harder to work with than others. Psychological explanations may help you understand, but they don't always help you work with difficult individuals. For that, you need patience, respect, and consideration. In short, you need good manners.

Having good manners in the workplace means working with others so that you're a positive part of the work environment, even when the environment is stressful and even when others aren't being helpful, even when some people are being out-and-out rude.

One thing to remember is that problems that start off small can become big if you let them go on very long. Small slights, swearing, peevishness, and forced smiles have a way of getting under everyone's skin. More outrageous behavior, such as temper tantrums, yelling matches, crude displays of power, and harassment of any kind, simply shouldn't be tolerated by anyone.

Of course, everyone has bad moments. Some people have bad days or weeks! The well-mannered person apologizes if he's having a bad day, and he tries to do better. If someone else's temper has to be mollified, the well-mannered person tries to facilitate smoothing the ruffled feathers by whatever means are appropriate.

Developing good relations with your peers: General office etiquette

You can do many things in an office environment to irritate other people, just as you can do many things to make yourself a prized office worker.

The prime directive in office etiquette is respecting other people. That means acknowledging that others have rights, are entitled to private space, and deserve consideration.

Personality types

Part of respect is knowing enough about others to know what they're likely to like and dislike. The polite person is sensitive to differences in personality types and acts on that knowledge. An office has lots of personality types. Watch for the behaviors that each personality type exhibits and appreciate the diversity. People's quirks are inherently interesting and acknowledging them can help increase office harmony.

- ✔ **The control freak:** This personality wants to do it all herself. She doesn't easily trust others but will do a great deal of work. You can identify a control freak by her impatience with others on tactical and strategic decisions and by her constant desire for more challenges.

- ✔ **The appreciation fan:** This person wants to be recognized by others. You can identify him by his self-promotion and his promotion of his team. He gets sulky if his hard work isn't publicly recognized on a regular basis.

- ✔ **The obsessive:** This person wants to get things right. He is an information junky and is often a loner. You can identify this person by the way he devours information — the more the better! He'll do outrageous amounts of work, but he doesn't like to make decisions because he is afraid that the decision he makes may be wrong.

- ✔ **The consensus builder:** This person wants everyone to get along. Not prone to quick decisions — how could there be such a thing, everyone has to agree! — the consensus builder is inclusive and compassionate. He enjoys working with others but gets nervous when asked to take initiative by himself.

- ✔ **The socialite:** This person wants everyone to have a good time. You can identify him by his preference for chatting while others are around and having fun. Although he works best after hours or at home, the socialite generally improves other people's motivation.

- ✔ **The steamroller:** This person wants to get things done now. You can identify him by his willingness to make decisions, even when information is incomplete. On a team, the steamroller keeps the group moving at full speed and won't tolerate seemingly meaningless discussions.

Most people are combinations of these basic types, and each of these personality types is helpful in particular situations. Need a quick decision? Go to the steamroller. Need to put a team together for a project? Make sure that you include a consensus builder. Need someone to sift through a long report? The obsessive person is your choice.

Office manners

The idea behind looking at personality types is not to pigeonhole people but to recognize certain strengths and weaknesses. One of the keys to etiquette is paying enough attention to others to be able to modify your behavior to accommodate them. Appropriate responses to particular personality types are helpful for anyone who wants to be an effective colleague.

Of course, all these different personality types have to live together in a small space. Keep the following tips in mind for surviving life in a workplace environment:

✔ Dress in a manner consistent with company culture and make sure your clothes are always clean.

✔ Stand up straight and sit with legs together to avoid displays.

✔ Treat a cubicle as though it has a door and a ceiling. Speak calmly and with an even cadence, in person and on the telephone. Personal telephone conversations should be kept to a minimum if you inhabit a cubicle. No one wants to hear your arguments with your spouse.

Confidential business conversations should also be kept to a minimum if you're in a cubicle for similar reasons. You don't want to prematurely spill the beans on some important deal.

✔ Face forward in the elevator.

If you're getting off near the top of the building, move to the rear of the elevator. If you're getting off on a lower floor, stand close to the front.

✔ Say "hello" or "good morning" to those you encounter in the morning and "goodnight" to those you encounter as you leave.

✔ Shower or bathe *every* day.

✔ Brush your teeth *every* morning after breakfast.

Avoid these faux pas:

✔ Aggressive behaviors such as leaning into people, pointing at others, and herky-jerky arm movements.

✔ "Adjusting" in public.

✔ Snorting, spitting, or picking at any part of yourself.

✔ Interrupting others.

✔ Crowding others.

✔ Bringing odorous food to the office.

- Playing loud music in the office.
- Interfering with people in the cafeteria, at the water fountain, or at the coffee machine by getting in their way or preventing them from doing what they are there to do.
- Heavy use of perfume or cologne.

Creating and keeping good relations with your staff

Your staff helps you do your work. They're not your slaves, and they're not drones; they're people who deserve your respect. Praise them when their work is excellent. Criticize their work when it needs improvement. Above all, acknowledge their existence and their hard work and treat them with courtesy. Without them, you wouldn't get your work done.

The best way to earn respect is to treat others with respect.

As the boss, the things you say and do have consequences for others. Do your best to make these consequences positive:

- Ask others to do things rather than tell them.
- Be clear.
- Be polite.
- Learn people's names and use them.
- Recognize that everyone has a life outside work.
- Don't pry, but be accommodating.

A doggone good manager

Treating employees with respect looks simple, but the way some people treat others is amazingly poor. Following is an example of how to do it right!

Tina was an accountant who had no family but shared her life with three dogs. She lost one of her dogs to a long battle with cancer, and was devastated. Other members of her firm treated her loss as sad but unimportant. Her supervisor recognized the dog's significance to Tina, sent her a handwritten letter of condolence, and quietly arranged for her to have a week off.

By recognizing the emotional importance of this event, the supervisor showed appropriate respect for his employee. Tina was immensely grateful for this act of kindness and, when next asked, worked overtime on a big project.

Names

Get names right. Learn other people's names and how they prefer to be addressed. Memorizing names is hard for some people, easy for others. If it is hard for you, admit it up front. If you make a mistake and call someone by the wrong name, apologize and blame yourself. Say something like, "I'm terribly sorry, Juan, I'm so bad with names sometimes. I'll get it right from now on." Then make an effort to get it right. Repeat the name to yourself. As soon as possible, find a pen and write "Juan in Information Technology" thirty or forty times.This trick works!

As far as your own name goes, let your staff know how you prefer to be addressed. Say your name slowly and clearly when you meet new employees so that others will understand the proper pronunciation. Spell your name if you think it will help. Your assistant should be able to field most questions for others. But if a new sales rep insists on calling you "Rita" and you prefer to be called by your surname, then simply say, "Would you please call me 'Ms. Jones'?" and move on.

Working relations

An oppressive boss is a nightmare. Someone who thinks her employees need to be blamed for her mistakes or someone who thinks his assistants should understand that his violent temper is simply part of his creativity is a notorious figure.

Peggy, a corporate loan officer, habitually "forgot" to inform her employees of important deadlines and managerial requests. Then she routinely blamed her employees for the multitude of problems created by her own incompetence. When her negligence was exposed, Peggy hurled a barrage of insults and a notebook across the room. She concluded the performance by bursting into tears, running out of the conference room, and slamming the door to her office. Within a week, more than half of her department had either quit or asked to be transferred. The unit was a shambles.

You don't want to be that figure. You want your employees to respect you, and you want them to be willing to give their best for you and the company. You will get both only if you treat them with respect and hold yourself to the same standards to which you hold them.

The way you formulate a request makes a difference. Saying to your floor manager, "Mr. Hyper, would you straighten out Ms. Noenergy's chronic tardiness?" is certainly better than "Mr. Hyper, you better get Ms. Noenergy to work on time immediately or you're out of the merit pool!" but it is not as good as "Mr. Hyper, Ms. Noenergy is chronically late and it's having a negative impact on the entire unit's performance. Would you please impress on her the importance of being on time? I'd like this problem solved by next week. Thanks."

Secondly, keeping an even tone in your voice helps everybody do his job efficiently. Dictating a dismissal letter in a calm manner is better than venting your rage while you dictate. Correcting errors is best accomplished privately, politely, and precisely. Yelling at people — even people who deserve it — is rarely effective.

Third, try to give precise and clear instructions for work. Vague and ambiguous instructions are stressful for anyone trying to fulfill them. Rather than say, "Do you understand?" say, "I'm not sure I've covered everything. Can you think of anything that I've left out?"

Of course, no one is perfect. If you make a mistake, admit it. If someone else makes a mistake, remember that *your* irritation is rarely *another* person's motivation. Instead, focus on the problem and its solution.

Creating and keeping good relations with your superiors

Unfortunately, plenty of bosses expect a level of servitude that is utterly unreasonable. Whether you're in business, entertainment, academia, or banking, you find oppressive superiors who enjoy watching people squirm. We'll talk about what to do with some kinds of bad bosses later in the book. Here, we discuss general guidelines for appropriate behavior toward those who are higher than you in rank.

Follow your boss's lead.

Newcomers at a company often believe that they can establish themselves in a company's culture by being unfailingly outgoing and friendly. The trouble is, business culture is based on rank; friendliness, even if well-intentioned, is sometimes at odds with rank. Your primary function at work is to do your job. Too much friendliness can actually hurt your effectiveness.

One way that friendliness unleavened with manners can be unproductive is in your relations with your superiors. Slapping them on the back and assuming that they're interested in your latest adventure may get you nowhere fast. And talking to them as though you are their equal may be seen not as friendly but as bumptious and pushy.

At a business dinner, the president of a computer hardware company offered a toast to the vice president of sales and marketing. Although funny, the toast was positive and appreciative of the vice president and of the entire division. A new sales rep, after too many cocktails, mistook the *toast* for a *roast*. He stood up and delivered an off-color discourse on the vice president based on the one time he had played golf with her. His attempt at humor was met with cold stares and dead silence. Luckily, the waiter arrived just then with the soup!

So curb your chumminess and check your sense of humor enough to avoid humiliation. Take the following tips as your first lesson in cultivating good relations with your superiors:

- ✔ Do your job.
- ✔ Treat your boss with respect and understanding.
- ✔ Call your boss "Mr. Garcia" if everyone else in your position does so. Don't assume that you have the right to call him "Spike" unless he asks you to do so.
- ✔ Dress in a style similar to your boss.
- ✔ Don't assume that your boss is your friend. Don't venture into your boss's private life unless invited.
- ✔ Don't confuse business entertaining with social events.

Interacting with superiors requires that you be aware of certain subtleties. Although your company may have a friendly "backyard barbeque" culture, your boss should be the person to introduce more personal subjects. If you're in a social situation with your boss, general small talk topics are permissible until your boss takes the lead and introduces other topics.

Offering compliments and criticism

Compliments and criticism are unavoidable in the workplace. We cover both in this section.

Praise and criticize the work, not the person.

Compliments

Compliment others when they've done exceptional work, when they've done more than you've asked them to do, and when they've done you a favor. Don't cheapen compliments by offering them willy-nilly, like a kindergarten teacher. Give compliments when people deserve them. Think of them as little gifts.

Compliments are directed to a person's work and professional conduct, not to a person's personality or body. (We cover some of the difficulties that can occur with compliments in Chapter 14, on sexual harassment.)

Delivering compliments in person or in writing is largely a matter of personal style. Some people prefer face-to-face, some e-mail. One nice thing to do is to compose a handwritten note, seal it in an envelope, and deliver it to the person with a handshake and a quick "good job." A handwritten note from a superior is a pleasant surprise that is long remembered.

Giving compliments

Giving compliments should be easy, but, surprisingly, most people need practice to do it right.

A compliment shows appreciation for someone else's work. Focus the attention on the other person, not on yourself.

An assistant professor recently received tenure and promotion to associate professor. His chair, who had been made full professor the previous year, complimented him as follows: "Congratulations on getting tenure. Of course, being named full professor is better." Compliment grade? D!

Always compliment:

- ✔ **Politely:** Be sincere and use a genuine tone of voice. Insincere or snarling compliments are pointless.

- ✔ **Precisely:** Be precise and detailed. For example, "Jane, you did an excellent job on the Millman project. It was accurate, extremely well-written, and I really appreciated receiving it before the deadline. Thank you for such a great effort."

- ✔ **Promptly:** Be timely. No one wants to hear "Oh, by the way, Ralph, the work you did on that contract for what's-his-name last year was good."

- ✔ **Publicly:** Usually, it's best to praise in public. But shy people and those with cultural prohibitions against public praise are best praised in private.

Receiving compliments

Receiving compliments is even easier, but done poorly even more frequently.

There is one and only one rule for receiving a compliment. When getting a compliment, always say "Thank you."

That's it! Be genuine. It's hard to accept praise. But, remember, it may help to think of a compliment as a small gift.

Don't apologize, belittle your accomplishment, or amplify on the compliment by adding your own self-praise. If you apologize or belittle your accomplishment, the person giving the compliment will think you're fishing. If you congratulate yourself after someone else has, you appear to be an arrogant so-and-so who doesn't deserve compliments at all! Just say "Thank you," perhaps smile, and be done with it.

Criticism

Giving and receiving criticism is difficult. Unfortunately, it is a necessary part of working. Get used to it. Luckily, the following suggestions can make criticism easier to handle.

Giving criticism

If you have to give criticism, avoid anger and irrelevant detail. If you need to give praise *and* criticism, give the praise first.

The *only* reason to give criticism is to improve performance. Criticizing is not complaining and it's not attacking.

Always criticize:

- ✔ **Privately:** Criticize only those who need to be criticized and do so away from all others. Nobody else needs to hear what you have to say.

- ✔ **Politely:** Assume that the other person has feelings that will be hurt when they hear your criticism. Focus your criticism on the problematic work and not the person. Avoid identifying what he did as "stupid," "brainless," or worse. And never call anyone names.

- ✔ **Precisely:** Criticism should be specific and constructive. Identify the problem and look for a solution. For example, "Chris, last week's order for Arete Systems was shipped to Hexis World instead. This is the third time this month that one of their orders has gone astray. Let's discuss what happened and figure out how to prevent this problem in the future."

- ✔ **Promptly:** Hand out criticism as soon as possible. If you're mad, take a few deep breaths and count to ten. Repeat as necessary! If you need time to formulate your criticism, take it. But procrastinating only increases the chances that the problem will be repeated and make you feel worse. Deal with it now.

Receiving criticism

Being criticized is difficult. When someone is criticizing you, follow the four cardinal rules and always take criticism:

- ✔ **Professionally:** If the criticism is appropriate, accept responsibility. Avoid excuses or blaming others. Apologize, assure the other person that the mistake won't happen again, and then live up to your word.

- ✔ **Politely:** Assume that the other person doesn't mean to insult you when she gives criticism. If she calls you names or is rude, redirect the discussion to the work itself. Avoid retaliating in like manner — you'll almost always make the situation worse. If necessary, you may say something like, "I can see the problem here. Please accept my apologies. I'd like to think about what you're saying and think of a solution. May we talk again after lunch?"

- ✔ **Positively:** Assume that the other person has something helpful to say. Listen. Try to understand the issue. If you're too mad to understand, count to ten. Repeat as necessary! Ask for clarification. Ask for assistance.

- ✔ **Appropriately:** If the criticism is unfair or misplaced, say so, so long as you're polite and do so in private. The workplace is neither a family nor a therapist's office. You're no one's punching bag and you're not responsible for accepting other people's mistakes or poor performance.

Handling Office Visits

When you leave the office to visit colleagues and other associates, your behavior reflects not only on you but on the people you're visiting. And how you handle visitors in your own office speaks volumes about your social skills. The following sections show you how to be both a good visitor and a good host.

Visiting an office

Visiting someone else's office is generally not a complicated affair, and the rules are fairly simple. Nonetheless, tales of churlish behavior by visiting colleagues have inspired these tips:

- ✔ **Make an appointment:** If you choose not to make an appointment, leave quietly and cheerfully when your colleague doesn't have time to see you.

- ✔ **Look up your destination on a map before departing:** Better yet, call the office and talk to an expert — someone who drives to work there every day. That person can also tell you where to park, which entrance to use, and so on.

- ✔ **Don't bring any food or drink with you to someone else's office, unless you've been asked to provide food for the meeting:** No one wants to watch you eat or dispose of your lukewarm latte after you leave.

- ✔ **Be polite to everyone at the office:** If the office has a reception desk, state your name, whom you're visiting, and the scheduled time of your appointment. If the receptionist is on the phone, be quiet and wait your turn.

- ✔ **Don't touch things in someone's office without asking, even if they look like toys.**

One CEO sets an intriguing black lacquer box on the edge of his desk. When people open the lid, out springs a jack-in-the-box holding a sign that says, "Don't touch my stuff." He never has to repeat that message.

Hosting visitors in your office

Trite but true, the good old Golden Rule applies when you have guests at the office. In case you're not sure what you would have them do unto you:

- **Provide clear directions:** Getting lost puts people in a bad mood. If you're not good at giving directions, have someone who is write them out and keep them on hand. Or print them out from the Internet. Yahoo.com has a directions service.

- **Be on time:** Your lobby isn't that interesting, and your visitors' time is as important as yours.

- **Always stand up to greet and shake hands with visitors entering your office.**

- **Clear a comfortable space for your visitors to sit, as well as some writing space on the desk, if needed — especially if your office is a "pile file."** A conference room is always preferable, if one is available. Have some hangers on hand for coats.

- **Offer your visitors something to drink, such as water, coffee, or other more exotic beverages you may have on hand.**

- **Make your time limitations clear up front:** "I have another meeting at 3:00, Peg, but I know we can get a good deal accomplished in the half hour we have."

- **Escort visitors out instead of letting them wander, especially if your office layout is confusing.**

Train your front desk staff to make eye contact with visitors, even while on the phone. Although visitors should be reasonably patient, they shouldn't be made to feel secondary to telephone callers.

Chapter 3

Working in a Diverse Environment

● ●

In This Chapter

▶ Physical differences

▶ Racial and ethnic differences

▶ Gender and sexual differences

▶ Showing others how to offer respect

● ●

*T*he fact that people are different isn't a news flash. Why then do people spend so much time belaboring the obvious? People love to talk about other people. Perhaps curiosity makes others a natural topic of conversation. Perhaps differences are an easy source of cheap humor. But this kind of cheap humor can get you into trouble, especially in the workplace.

Stereotyping, ridiculing, demeaning, or insulting other people is always a mistake. At work this behavior can be disastrous. You should not assume that the women in the room are secretaries or nurses, or that the men are bosses or investors. Nor should you assume that the person on the other end of the phone shares your ethnicity. The man using the wheelchair may be the CEO, and your potential client may be gay.

In and of themselves, these differences are simply not always that interesting and shouldn't be the subject of comment. Even where the story behind the difference may be interesting, it is important to remember that it is rude to pry unless you're invited to do so. Regardless of individual particulars, you have a job to do that brings you together. Focus on the job and treat other people as important. In other words, treat them with respect.

By the way, most folks are not the voice of their people. Questions like, "So, Bob, how do your people feel about Sudsy Flakes?" and "Mary, what's the black perspective?" are racist and offensive. Treat people as individuals, not as poster children.

In this chapter, you find out how to be a respectful colleague to people who are physically, ethnically, and culturally different from you. You'll also be introduced to some straightforward principles that protect your and other's privacy from unwanted prying.

Respecting Physical Differences in the Workplace

The United States is home to more than 50 million people with disabilities, and more than half of all Americans say they're a bit unsure around people with disabilities. Pretty clearly, life at work can be tough if you're among the 50 million, and getting over your uncertainty about people with disabilities is a matter of urgent importance if you're one of the others. If you are nondisabled, the tips in this section will help you work more comfortably with your colleagues or clients with disabilities. If you have a disability, take the initiative and give your coworkers, employees, or boss some guidelines for working with you.

Federal law requires that employers make reasonable accommodations for those with disabilities. For example, no employer with more than 15 employees can discriminate against qualified people who have disabilities. Any employer who hires someone with a disability is expected to accommodate the disability, unless undue hardship is the result. These accommodations include providing auxiliary aids for those with vision or hearing disabilities, and making sure that physical barriers are removed if they can be. If they cannot, employers must provide alternatives.

Really, these legal requirements are no more than what common courtesy dictates. If you hire someone who uses a wheelchair but have no way for that person to enter and exit the building, you haven't considered his or her comfort.

When you work with someone who has a disability, you may feel that he or she should be treated differently. This thinking is, for the most part, a mistake. People are people first and disabled or nondisabled second.

A good place to start treating those with disabilities with respect is with the language you use. Your choice of words has an enormous impact on the way you interact with others:

- ✓ **Avoid using words such as "handicapped," "crippled," and "invalid" to refer to those with disabilities:** Saying "Tom has epilepsy" is preferable to "The epileptic guy? His name is Tom."

- ✓ **Avoid using words such as "healthy" or "normal" to refer to those without disabilities.**

- ✓ **Talk to everyone in a medium tone of voice:** Don't talk too loudly to anyone with a disability.

- ✓ **Avoid getting overly concerned with phrases of speech in the presence of people with disabilities:** For example, you can say, "I see what you mean!" to someone who has a visual impairment and you can invite someone who uses a wheelchair to go for a walk.

Avoid the mistakes of staring, averting your gaze, and "helping" a person with a disability who hasn't given you permission to do so.

For anyone who is interviewing or employing a person with a disability, certain rules of etiquette can help you deal appropriately with those people who have disabilities:

✔ **As an employer, train your staff to anticipate and accommodate those with disabilities:** Know where the accessible parking, elevators, rest rooms, and drinking fountains are in your building. Be prepared to give clear directions to those with visual impairments.

✔ **Educate yourself about the assistance technologies people with disabilities are using:** These include wheelchairs, hearing aids, enhanced and auditory computer screens, transcription devices, walking aids, and guide animals.

✔ **Offer to shake hands.** If the other person extends the left hand, shake the left hand. If shaking hands isn't possible, a nod of the head or a light touch on the shoulder or forearm to acknowledge the person is appropriate.

Dealing with specific disabilities

Some rules of disability etiquette are firm, others aren't. You should never feed a guide animal, but whether you should help those who have visual impairments cross the street depends on their interest in having your assistance.

Look everyone in the eye

Staring and averting your gaze are equally hurtful to a person with a disability. As everyone knows, having someone stare at you makes you wonder what is so strange. But averting your gaze may actually be worse because it can make you feel that you are so hideous that other people can't stand to look at you. Either way, you feel awful. Not surprisingly, then, our advice is simple: Interact with a person who has a disability with respect and as you would interact with those who do not have a disability.

"Helping" someone who has a disability is also discouraged, unless the person has given you permission to do so. People who have disabilities are not incompetent. Just as you would be offended by others who routinely offered to carry your briefcase because you're so small or offered to make your phone calls for you because your voice sounds like a bullhorn, so too people with disabilities are offended by patronizing offers of assistance. If you are asked to help, ask how to help. Otherwise, assume that the person is no less able to care for himself than you are.

Far too many nondisabled people worry needlessly and harmfully over their interaction with people with disabilities. Remember, people are people first. Address the person to whom you are speaking, not technologies or assistants. Don't stare and don't shy away.

If someone asks for your assistance, ask for specific instructions and follow them carefully. Refraining from helping someone can sometimes be painful. However, as painful as it may be to watch someone struggle, a decision to decline your assistance must be respected.

Hearing impairment

Hearing disabilities range from the mild to the severe. They're usually hidden and often hard to detect. If you're having difficulty getting a response from someone you are speaking to, he may have a hearing disability. He is probably not rude.

If someone is hearing impaired, the best way to get her attention is to move so that she can see you or to touch her lightly on the shoulder or forearm.

If the person with a hearing disability would like to use American Sign Language (ASL) and you know it, by all means use it. If you don't know how to sign, admit it and either find someone who does know or use writing. Although some people would love to teach you a new language, insisting that a person with a hearing impairment teach you ASL is rude. If you want to learn it, go buy a book or take a class.

If the person has an interpreter, here are a couple of tips:

- ✔ **The interpreter sits or stands next to you, facing the person with the hearing disability.**
- ✔ **Always talk to the person, not to the interpreter:** In a business situation, never consult the interpreter. The interpreter's job is to facilitate conversation, not to make business decisions.
- ✔ **Pause occasionally if the interpreter falls behind.**

Although interpreters are common in some circles, particularly political and diplomatic ones, they're not universal. Those with hearing impairments often use sign language or read lips. If the person you're talking to can read lips, here are some tips:

- ✔ **Face your conversation partner:** Don't walk around.
- ✔ **Speak clearly and slowly, but naturally:** Exaggerating your lip movement only makes lip-reading harder.
- ✔ **Don't eat or smoke while talking and don't talk with your hands near your mouth.**

Avoid these embarrassing mistakes:

- ✔ **Never shout:** It won't do any good, even if the person has only partial hearing loss. Shouting is distorted, it can hurt, and it makes you look ridiculous.
- ✔ **Never simplify what you say:** You're talking to an adult, not a child.

Visual impairment

As in the case of hearing impairment, vision impairment comes in a wide variety of kinds and degrees. Some visual impairments include tunnel vision, in which one only sees a small, central, part of the visual field; partial vision, in which one sees a portion of the visual field, usually one side; and total vision impairment, in which one sees nothing.

Use words with someone who has a visual impairment.

Here are some tips to keep in mind:

- ✔ **Announce yourself and whoever is with you to the person with a visual disability:** For example, "Hi Juan, it's Sally. I have Wanda Lee with me."
- ✔ **Say "Hello" and "Goodbye" and tell the person when you're moving around the room.**
- ✔ **In meetings, use names with exchanges between people to help the person with the visual impairment follow the conversation:** "Valerie? John here. Can you give us the latest on the Lohman account?"
- ✔ **Offer to read instructions or other printed material aloud.**
- ✔ **Where danger looms, voice your concerns politely:** For example, "Ben, there's a chair directly in front of you. Would you like me to move it?"

You can really inconvenience someone if you make the following blunders:

- ✔ Never touch or move *anything* in the office of a person with a visual impairment.
- ✔ Never move furniture elsewhere in the office without informing someone with a visual impairment.

People with visual impairments often use a variety of technologies to navigate through the world. Some carry canes, some are accompanied by guide dogs. Offering assistance to someone with a visual impairment is always appropriate, but if he or she refuses the offer, accept it politely. And keep the following in mind:

- ✔ **If you're asked to guide, offer your elbow:** Describe your route, announcing upcoming transitions and changes. When you reach your destination, avoid leaving the person in empty space. Find a chair, table, or a wall. Place the person's hand on the back of the chair, on the table, or on the wall for orientation.

- ✔ **At meals, describe the location of the food on the plate using clock time.** "Shrimp at 7 o'clock; peas at 3." Offer to help cut food.

- ✔ **When exchanging money, place bills in separate stacks and present each stack:** For example, "You're change is $47.54. Here are two twenties; one five; and two ones. And here is the 54 cents."

- ✔ **When signing documents, offer to guide the person's hand to the correct position and offer a straight edge, like a ruler, for alignment.**

When dealing with guide animals, never touch a guide or service animal unless the handler gives you permission, and never call out a guide animal's name.

Committing these faux pas is dangerous, not only to the animal and its handler, but also, potentially, to you. If you touch a guide animal, you may inadvertently be giving it a signal to do something, something that its handler doesn't want it to do. And calling out a guide animal's name can divert its attention from assisting its handler.

Mobility impairment

Mobility impairments vary from walking with difficulty to walking with a cane to using a wheelchair. As always, treat those with mobility impairments with respect.

People with mobility impairments often cannot go where those without those impairments can. Be gracious in picking out routes to destinations, taking their impairment into account.

If someone uses a motorized wheelchair, wait until the wheelchair is powered down to shake hands. When having a conversation with someone in a wheelchair, move so that the two of you are at the same eye level.

Don't let yourself make the following gaffes:

- ✔ **While you put a client's coat in the closet, never move mobility aids out of reach.**

- ✔ **Never "try out" another person's mobility aids — they're part of his or her personal space.**

- ✔ **Never push a person in a wheelchair without permission.**

- ✔ **Never lean on or hang on a person's wheelchair.**

Going the extra mile

If you don't have a disability, you are likely to work with people with disabilities at some point in your career. By combining the business etiquette tips in this book with a healthy dose of common sense, you'll do fine.

If you have a disability, taking the initiative yourself is perfectly acceptable. For example, you may call ahead for travel information to companies where you have an appointment. At the workplace, you may say, "Jaegwon, I don't know whether you've ever worked with a person with a mobility impairment before. Here are a couple things that will make working together easier for us."

As a colleague or an employer, educate yourself about the assistance technologies that your coworkers use, and adapt your presentations and communications to accommodate them. People with visual impairments use scanners to move text from page to computer screen-reading software to synthesize the words on the screen. People with hearing impairments use telecommunications devices for the deaf (TDDs) or similar tools. High-tech devices of all kinds are available to individuals with limited mobility.

For an interesting primer on assistance technologies, consult Apple Computer's Disability Resources page at: `www.apple.com/education/k12/disability/`

For more information about disability issues, contact the National Organization on Disability at: `www.nod.org` or contact them via snail-mail at National Organization on Disability, 910 16th Street NW, Suite 600, Washington, DC 20006.

Respecting Racial and Ethnic Differences in the Workplace

Along with the cultural diversity inherent in the global marketplace comes confusion about how to behave. People don't always know how to interact with others from different ethnic and racial backgrounds. In fact, people don't even know whether their behavior *should* be different. This section clears up some of the confusion.

Race and ethnicity are less important than your beliefs and attitudes about these things. Don't typecast or stereotype because of physical or cultural features. The paramount rule of etiquette — respect for others — rules out such behavior. Nevertheless, differences do exist, and you need to know both how to respect them and how to "code change" appropriately, that is, you need to know the etiquette of particular situations and how to adjust your verbal and nonverbal behavior for those situations.

Within the United States, numerous races and ethnicities are represented. Over time, however, a standard code has emerged to allow people to get along with one another in business and to know what to expect from each other.

The code of business in the United States is racially and ethnically neutral. Translated, the code of business is really a modified version of the straight white male code. Standard American English is the international language of business and standard Western manners are the official protocol in the United States.

For better or worse, if you don't speak or behave according to these standards, you immediately set yourself up for criticism. But by the same token, if you don't recognize and respect those who follow other traditions, you may also get yourself in a jam.

A paradox lurks here. The standards of business etiquette in the United States require Standard American English and Western manners. But Standard American English may not be your native language and you may be a member of a tradition whose codes of manners are different from Western manners. Luckily, you have a way out: When in the United States, do as the Americans do.

Of course, you don't have to adopt American business etiquette around the clock. At times business etiquette is entirely inappropriate, and your role as a professional need not consume your life entirely. U.S. business etiquette applies when you're doing business in the United States. When you're not doing business or when you're not doing business in the United States, other codes of etiquette apply. This is code change.

In addition, knowing more than one language helps almost everyone in the business world. Learning even a few words and phrases can be a real plus. In certain businesses — the music industry, for example — slang and jargon are useful. But for almost all other situations, speaking and writing clearly and grammatically is paramount.

Now that you can communicate, how do you behave? Respect dictates that you take it upon yourself to learn about other cultures. If your business regularly takes you to other parts of the world, take a course in protocol or read about those parts of the world.

Be wary of typecasting. Don't assume that your Chinese client prefers a Chinese restaurant or that your African-American boss wants to be addressed as "Bro!" And unless you're addressing a king or queen, do not assume that an individual speaks for his people.

Respecting Gender and Sexual Differences in the Workplace

Dealing with gender and sex in the workplace can be a mess. In the same way that business is color blind, it is also sex-blind. The way to get along is to assume that everyone has a sex life — and then forget about it! We don't mean that everyone has to act in the same way or that you can't express your individuality. But what people do in their private lives is exactly that: private.

Don't assume that everyone is heterosexual; don't assume that everyone is gay. Assume that other people are interested in love and sex, but that the details are none of your business. Never make jokes or snide remarks about gender or sexual preference. There, now you're fine.

When you're at work, the main objective is to do your job, not to score.

Differences between social and business etiquette

Although you probably realize that there are differences between social and business etiquette, you may not be so sure what they are and when they apply.

Business is gender blind. What matters is title and position, not gender. However, you may be completely stumped when it comes to working with members of the opposite sex. For example, if you're a woman, do you open the door for others? Do you wait for your male boss to open the door for you?

To avoid crashes, here's the rule: In business, the first person to the door opens the door for everyone else, regardless of gender. However, full arms exempt you from door duty.

As with all good rules, this one has an exception. You always open the door for your client or customer!

Use the following common-sense tips as a guide to intergender relations:

- ✔ **Offer to help an overburdened colleague, regardless of gender:** For instance, if your colleague has an arm full of books and papers, offer to take some of them.
- ✔ **The host pays, regardless of gender.**

✔ Help others if they're having a difficult time with a coat, regardless of gender.

✔ Stand to greet someone, regardless of gender.

✔ Women shake hands in business, as men do.

Conversational style

Men and women may have different conversational styles. You may not need to know all about Mars and Venus, but using your antennae is helpful.

Many empirical studies have found that men and women view conversations differently. The "let's get down to brass tacks" attitude adopted by many men may be irritating to some women. Likewise, the detailed descriptions offered by many women may be tedious for some men.

To even things out, some companies use a "Five Minute" rule in meetings. Speakers have a maximum of five minutes to make their point — no more! This way, everyone has a turn to speak in his or her own style, but no one monopolizes the conversation. And Mr. Buttinski may be politely restrained.

Be patient. Tolerate differences in conversational style. But be fair — no interrupting and no rattling on and on. And keep the following in mind:

✔ **Face each other when talking.**

✔ **Maintain eye contact.**

✔ **Avoid using "You need to . . ." constructions:** Instead, try, "Will you please start working on that contract by Wednesday?" or "You may want to consider using the MYOB program."

✔ **Respect personal space in conversations:** Don't crowd your partner or point fingers.

Never make snide remarks or jokes about other genders or sexual preferences and never stare at parts of other people's bodies.

Chapter 4

Creating Business Style and Cultivating Professional Presence

*L*ike it or not, most people believe that what you see is what you get. What they usually see first is your clothes. Clothes are a nonverbal code of communication. What you wear signals your image to others. What signals do you want to send? Although Erin Brockovich got away with dressing like Erin Brockovich, most lesser mortals would not. In this chapter, we introduce a simple system for dressing well, even on casual days!

In business, creativity in ideas is often more important than creativity in dress. Derived from the military dress code, the idea here is that if everyone dresses in a relatively similar manner, then the playing field isn't so bumpy. Some restraint is appropriate because you want to emphasize the product or service of your company, not your wacky sense of personal style (that's why you have days off). You are the vehicle for the product or the service, not the center of attention.

Then you have to consider your body language. Comporting yourself with ease and dignity signals to others that you care enough about them and about yourself to pay attention to your physical presence. This chapter helps you be aware of what your body is saying to others.

Create Your Business Uniform

No doubt about it, clothes are a source of anxiety in the business world. So many styles are appropriate in today's business world that getting dressed in the morning can be baffling.

The solution? KISS — Keep It Simple and Sophisticated! You want your confidence to come from your professional abilities, not to be manufactured in Italy. Still, your clothes are important — if you dress with your next position in mind, you're more likely to get there.

Memorize these colors:

- Navy blue
- Charcoal gray
- Black
- Khaki
- White

ANECDOTE

Dressing systematically

Of all the people I, Perrin, have worked with in and out of the fashion industry, one person stands out above all others. This person — now the owner of his own catalogue clothing company — has a *dressing system* that he varies slightly for different occasions. His system is not particularly expensive either: He has two suits, a tweed sport coat, white shirts, blue shirts, black turtlenecks, jeans, khakis, some T-shirts, wingtips, Oxfords, and sneakers, a few ties, and a tuxedo.

Here's how the system works: He wears a two-button, charcoal-gray suit either with white, spread-collar shirts, white Oxford cloth button-down shirts, or black turtlenecks. He sometimes wears an Ancien Madder tie. He has two pairs of glasses: one conservative round wire rims, one hip plastic. Sometimes he wears contacts. For casual occasions, he wears a herringbone sport coat with either a white, button-down shirt or a black turtleneck and plain front khakis. For extremely casual occasions, he rolls up the sleeves of his button-down shirts and wears sneakers. He has two extremely high-quality belts, one black, one brown, and a pair of braces. A few times a year he dusts off the tuxedo.

He *always* looks great, although that's not what you really notice. What you remember is how smart, how witty, and how focused he is. *That* is what it means to be well dressed.

These are the staple colors of every business wardrobe. Regardless of how formal or casual you are, or whether you're male or female, these are the colors you start with. Don't get us wrong, color can look great; for example, a brightly colored shirt can punch up a dark gray suit for both men and women. But in general, you are better off starting with the neutrals just listed and adding color rather than starting with color and trying to find something appropriate to match. You can add a mango shirt, tie, or scarf to a charcoal suit easier than you accessorize a mango suit.

Here are some guidelines for both men and women to keep in mind:

- ✔ **In the suit world, start with the basics:** A navy blue wool suit and a charcoal wool suit, white shirts, black shoes, black belt, and black leather briefcase/notebook computer case.

- ✔ **In the casual world, start with the basics:** Khaki pants or skirts, white shirts, black or brown shoes and belt, and a black or brown leather or ballistic nylon briefcase/notebook computer case.

- ✔ **Add your own touches in keeping with your company's style.**

Of course, this system is rigid, and you certainly don't have to follow it slavishly. But starting with a good foundation of high-quality, neutral-tone clothing allows you to build a wardrobe that minimizes your anxiety and maximizes your investment. With some discipline, you can create a wardrobe that stays current and looks smart without breaking your paycheck.

Dealing with dress codes

Another wrinkle in business clothes is that different businesses and professions have different dress codes. If you're in a traditional profession like law or medicine, you should dress at least as formally as your clients. If you're a Nobel Laureate, you get to wear whatever you want.

Some companies have a dress code, which is often articulated in an official document available from the Human Resources department. Get a copy of it and read it. More frequently, the dress code is unstated but enforced by practice. In these cases, you simply have to watch and learn. Watch the people around you, especially your boss. Whether your boss is a man or a woman, notice the style. How formal is it? Plan your wardrobe in a similar style. If your boss always wear suits, you should buy a suit or two. You don't have to match, but you shouldn't be contrary.

Avoid outdressing your boss. Your custom-made Windsor & Thames, 300-thread count, monogrammed, Egyptian cotton shirt may feel like a dream, but to your boss wearing Eddie Bauer it may scream "pretentious!"

With that said, the following sections look at some of the important choices you have to make and provide some advice on those choices.

Defining "casual"

The casual look has invaded business in a big way. However, dressing casually for business takes a great deal of thought. Causal may allow for something other than a suit, but it doesn't mean that you should go to work in a tube top and Birkenstocks either (unless you work at a surf shop). Business casual isn't the same as other kinds of casual. Business casual wear is its own category.

Just to make everything more confusing, business casual and Friday casual are different. Business casual generally means khaki pants or skirt, a plain shirt or blouse, sometimes a sports coat or blazer, and brown leather shoes. Friday casual includes all that but adds jeans and tennis shoes in some offices.

The basic etiquette principle of not calling too much attention to yourself applies to clothes, too.

Business casual wear can be every bit as much of a uniform as the suit used to be. Before you start jumping up and down protesting that you don't want to wear a uniform because you want to express your individuality and you don't work at Tasti-Cone anymore, remember the one positive thing about the Tasti-Cone experience — at least getting dressed for work was easy!

Taking inventory of your wardrobe

Before you crack out the credit card and head for the mall, take inventory. This task takes all day for some people — take the phone of the hook, send the kids to grandma's, and make your bed. Then follow these steps:

1. Take *everything* out of your closets, drawers, boxes, and laundry baskets.

2. Divide your clothes into piles: shirts, jackets, and so on.

3. Everything with holes, stains, or rips goes into the "Fix or Toss" pile.

4. Everything that doesn't fit *right now* goes into the "Wishful Thinking" or the "Archive" pile.

5. Everything with advertising goes into the "Planting the Peonies" pile.

6. **Everything that may qualify as business attire goes onto the bed.**

7. **Look carefully at the items on the bed.**

   Do they really fit? Try them on to be sure. If they don't, "Wishful Thinking!" or "Archive!" Are they worn out? Are they hopelessly out of date? If they are, "Fix or Toss!"

8. **Divide "Fix and Toss" into things that are beyond repair and things that are not.**

   The beyond repair pile becomes your rag bag; the rest goes to the tailor or to Goodwill. Ditto "Wishful Thinking." If you *really* think you will lose thirty pounds, you may keep it in the "Archive" section of your closet. Otherwise, be generous — donate it!

Now, you should have culled your wardrobe enough to know what you own. Check off any of the following items you already have:

- Black and brown leather belts. Own at least two of each, one narrow, one a little wider. Women may own other belts in addition to black and brown ones.
- Black leather dress shoes
  - Pumps (women). Heel should be no higher than two inches. The more conservative your job, the more traditional the style.
  - Wingtips or Oxfords (men)
- Briefcase, card case, portfolio, and pen
- Brown leather shoes
- Close-to-knee-length skirts (women)
- Dark socks (men)
- Khaki pants
- Leather winter gloves
- Navy blue or charcoal-gray suit
- Oxford cloth or polo shirts (men)
- Silk ties or scarves
- Skin tone and dark blue and black hosiery (women)
- Trench coat with a liner (men and women)
- Twinsets (women)

- ✔ Umbrella, black and large enough to protect two people
- ✔ Watch with black leather band or metal (gold or silver) band
- ✔ White dress shirts or blouses

The preceding list is the start of your business wardrobe. You may not need all of these things if your office is strictly formal or strictly casual.

Casual Workplace Wear for Women

Casual business attire for women requires some thought because you have so many choices. Keep to the KISS principle even with casual clothes: Keep It Simple and Sophisticated. Dark colors convey authority; bright colors convey friendliness. Light colors such as taupe and khaki are generally more casual than black, gray, or navy.

Here are some color matching tips to get you started:

- ✔ Start with the following items: a dark jacket, several high-quality T-shirts, a plain white blouse, several twinsets (cashmere if you can afford it), dark skirts or pants, and two pairs of high-quality leather shoes, one brown, one black.

- ✔ Twinsets or other sweaters — which can be a great place to add color — provide more finish than just a shirt or blouse, but are less formal than a jacket.

- ✔ Ensembles are casual variation on the traditional suit. Many items come in coordinated fabrics that you can mix and match, such as shirt-jackets, A-line skirts, and slim pants. You may wear them together for a more formal look or as separates for a more casual look.

- ✔ Because navy blues are almost impossible to match, black shoes are always appropriate with navy blue.

- ✔ Dark colors are a good first choice for jackets, pants, and skirts because they wear well. Add light colors as appropriate. Add blouses and shirts, scarves, belts, shoes, and jewelry in interesting colors and textures.

Try to avoid these fashion mistakes:

- ✔ Avoid excessive use of bright color and wild patterns.
- ✔ Avoid excessive jewelry and jewelry that signals your arrival with tiny clinking sounds.
- ✔ Your shoes do not need to "match" your blouse.
- ✔ Spiky, strappy, sandals in metallic colors or with rhinestones aren't appropriate for most businesses. Nor are open-toed shoes.

Formal Business Clothes for Women

You're well-advised to stay conservative at your workplace until it is blazingly obvious that you don't have to. And that means that you'll want to have some suits and pantsuits in your business wardrobe.

Suits

The keys here are fabric, fit, and comfort.

For autumn, winter, and spring, wool is still the best choice. For summer, cotton and linen are good choices, especially if blended with a small amount of stretchy fabric. Tropic weight wool is another good option.

Microfibers have come on strong in the last ten years, replacing the first and second generation polyesters. Suits made from a natural fabric interwoven with a microfiber are particularly useful, as they typically require less ironing and pressing than natural fabrics and have the marvelous property of making almost everyone look trimmer.

You can occasionally wear leather effectively, but the key to doing so is to keep it understated and tailored. Any hints of the motorcycle world or other dark regions are off-limits.

Navy blue, black, charcoal, taupe, white, burgundy, and forest green are all acceptable business colors. Although darker colors are typically worn in winter and lighter colors are worn in the spring and summer, this rule is really no longer hard and fast. Some women can wear red, but oranges, yellows, bright purples, and other loud colors are best used in small amounts.

Have the suit professionally fitted. Choose suits with jackets and skirts that are appropriate for your body type. Long jackets that cover the hips are flattering to most women. Buy clothes that you can wear now rather than clothes you may be able to wear if only. . . .

Skirts

The most important things to concern yourself with here are fit and length. Don't make your skirt too tight and don't make it too short. Sit down in front of a mirror — if you're concerned about the view in any way, the skirt is too short. Likewise, if you must walk like a geisha, the skirt is too tight. If you appear to have just arrived from Queen Victoria's court, the skirt is too long! Straight skirts are preferred over full skirts or pleated skirts, all other things being equal. But other things are rarely equal, so if you wear full or pleated skirts, make them longer than straight skirts. Business skirts are typically hemmed just around the knee.

The office is not the place to advertise your fantastic legs. A well-known Chicago attorney appeared on a popular afternoon TV talk show discussing issues in employment law. The first three callers and members of the audience all commented on her beautiful legs without asking any questions! She was mortified. After this appearance, her colleagues called her "Stilts" for a year.

Pantsuits

You find pantsuits, which are flattering for most women, in almost every venue of the contemporary business world. Keep the colors muted: blue, black, charcoal, taupe, burgundy, and some greens are good choices. And make sure that your pantsuit is fitted properly.

Pantsuit jackets should cover the hips for all but the most slender women.

Blouses and shirts

What you wear with your suit or pantsuit is as important as the suit itself. Blouses made of transparent material are inappropriate. High-quality cotton, silk, or a microfiber blend are good choices. Collars on women's blouses and shirts are much more varied than those on men's shirts. Have fun, but avoid the Tinker Bell or Pagliaccio look.

Choose opaque materials for business shirts, and coordinate your blouse color with your suit color.

Stockings and pantyhose

Pantyhose and stockings are both acceptable in the workplace, so long as they're matched to your other clothes, aren't heavily patterned, and don't suggest anything other than a commitment to work. Currently, very sheer skin-toned stockings are the standard, although some people prefer black or off-black with dark skirts. It is, of course, inappropriate to pair stockings and skirts short enough to reveal your garters.

Shoes: Pumps, boots, running shoes

Even if you've never bothered to visit the cobbler, in business we strongly advise you to take care with your shoes. Keep them functional, attractive, clean, and shined.

Keep a black Sharpie marker with you to touch up scuffed shoes.

Most women find that low-heeled pumps are suitable for the vast majority of business situations. They're good looking, comfortable, and are available in sufficient variety to coordinate with anything you may be wearing. Make sure that you have at least a pair of black shoes and a pair of tan or taupe shoes for summer.

Never wear white shoes, except sneakers, before Memorial Day or after Labor Day, unless you're a bride.

Heels can be as high as, say, an inch and a half or two inches, but much higher than that looks unprofessional. And keep the higher heels for your skirts — two inch heels with a pantsuit is too dressy for day.

Open-toed sandals or shoes and mules are popular but inappropriate in conservative establishments. Hiking boots, clogs, running shoes, spike heels, and platforms are appropriate for specialty businesses only.

Don't make these mistakes:

- ✔ Never wear spike heels or tall leather boots for business.
- ✔ Never wear dirty or scuffed shoes.

Accessories

Welcome to the bottomless pit of accessories!

What if you don't know 397 ways to tie a scarf? You can still save your wardrobe by keeping it simple and sophisticated!

Scarves

Scarves are readily acceptable in all but the stuffiest workplaces. They should be made of silk, wool, cashmere, or a blend of these fabrics. Cotton scarves rarely hang properly for long.

Some part of the scarf should match at least some color in your outfit. Although you can wear a scarf in different ways — under a jacket, draped over the shoulder, as an ascot — always make sure that it looks as though it's meant to be there rather than as though you forgot to put your towel back on the rack after your shower. And avoid really loud scarves, metallic scarves, and scarves with obvious topography.

Handbags

Handbags should be large enough to carry make-up and whatever technology you use to plan your week, but no larger. Your handbag shouldn't be able to carry your weekly groceries or your dry-cleaning.

Don't skimp on quality; buy the best handbag you can afford. Dark leather is by far the best choice. Avoid spangles, sparkles, and jewels on handbags unless you work at the local retro fashion shop.

Briefcases

You still find briefcases on the end of most business people's arms. Some women only carry a briefcase, in lieu of a handbag, which is much neater. If you must carry an additional handbag, keep it small.

However, increasingly the briefcase and notebook computer bag are merging into one article. Briefcases are traditionally made from leather and either black or brown. Again, black is the dressier of the two. Don't skimp on quality. Coordinate your handbag color with your briefcase color. If you choose a separate notebook computer bag in addition to a briefcase and handbag, make sure that they all coordinate.

In some professions, canvas or ballistic nylon bags are *de rigeur*. Watch those around you to see whether this alternative is common in your business.

Unless you carry samples, plastic or aluminum briefcases are inappropriate.

Belts

Belts should be leather and from ½ to ¾ inch thick. Coordinate their color to your outfit. Avoid metallic belts, belts covered with studs, bejeweled belts, and belts made of plastic or fur. Buckles should be subdued and smallish, either of metal or leather.

If you're wearing a conservative outfit, match it with a conservative belt.

Jewelry: Earrings, necklaces, watches, brooches, pins, rings

Some women are nuts about jewelry, the more the better. But in business, this enthusiasm is best replaced with another maxim: Less is more. Keep your jewelry simple and understated.

Very delicate jewelry looks best on small-boned women. Clunky jewelry is best on big-boned gals.

- ✔ **Earrings can be of a precious metal, such as silver or gold, and can contain diamonds or pearls:** Hollow hoops, so long as they are smallish, are acceptable as well. Match your earring's size, shape, and color to your necklace (if you're wearing one) and make sure that any color coordinates with your garment colors. Avoid enormous or jangly earrings.

- ✔ **Necklaces can be of a precious metal, such as silver or gold, or of pearls:** Match your necklace shape to the collar shape of your blouse or other garment. A V-shaped necklace with a round collar doesn't cut it. Avoid fake pearls. Avoid pendulous necklaces that wouldn't be out of place on a witch doctor.

- ✔ **Watches can be either analog or digital:** All things considered, analog watches (those with faces and hands) are still better than digital watches, and a large digital watch that boasts an altimeter and a computer isn't appropriate, even if you did wear it on your last trip to Everest. Choose your watch band carefully: Make sure that it complements your other jewelry and garments. Either leather (black or brown) or matte metal bands are acceptable, with a slight edge going to black leather.

Avoid joke watches, cartoon watches, and watches that are hard to read or require a professional maintenance team.

Turn your alarm watch off during meetings!

- ✔ **Brooches and pins should be worn only when you don't wear a necklace:** Make sure that the brooch is large enough not to be lost but not so large as to draw attention to itself or look like a *Star Trek* "com" badge. Brooch shape is best coordinated with suit style: edgy with blunt cut jackets, V-necked and square-necked blouses, rounded with round necked blouses.

- ✔ **Rings should be simple and few:** Big sparklers are not appropriate at the office, unless they're part of your engagement ring. Your best bet is to limit rings to a wedding ring/engagement ring/anniversary ring set. If you must, you may add a small class ring or family heirloom on the ring finger of your right hand. Save the rest for your weekend job as a belly dancer.

Glasses

At one time large, brightly colored or metallic glasses were thought to bring authority to women in business. Those days are gone, and so too are all the tired facial muscles that went along with these glasses.

Today's look in glasses is small and stylish. Glasses are one of the few places in business dress where you're allowed to assert your individuality even in conservative environments. Like ties, glasses are a small enough part of the overall look to tolerate creativity without ruining the wardrobe. Of course, with this choice comes the responsibility to assert yourself with care. You can certainly wear your red glasses with the pineapple inlays on the temples, but you may also want to have a more subdued pair ready-to-hand if you're meeting with old Mr. Fuddyduddy to discuss his annuity portfolio.

Never wear tinted glasses in the office. They make you look shady! Lenses that change color with available light are, however, acceptable.

Casual Wear for Men

Remember that business casual and Friday casual are distinct from one another. Business casual generally means khaki pants, a plain polo shirt or a long-sleeved button-down shirt, a V-neck sweater, sometimes a sports coat or blazer, and brown leather shoes. Loafers are a good choice, and you should wear socks. Friday casual includes all of the above, adds jeans and tennis shoes, but does not include your pajamas or your favorite ratty cut-offs and prized Metallica T-shirt from high school.

Don't forget these general guidelines:

- ✔ A short sleeve shirt is, by definition, always a casual shirt.

- ✔ Khaki and flannel pants are casual for most businesses.

- ✔ Tank tops, shorts, and sandals are weekend wear.

- ✔ Advertising, artists, and fashion types can wear leather jackets

- ✔ Plain shirts are best, in general; shirts with ads on them are for fishing.

- ✔ Button-down Oxford shirts are casual; T-shirts are for musicians, computer types, and mowing the lawn.

- ✔ Loafers and dark walking shoes are casual; clean sneakers, running shoes, and hiking boots are for playing but can make occasional appearances on Fridays.

- ✔ Blazers and sports coats are casual for some businesses, dressy for others.

Formal Business Clothes for Men

Men don't have as many options as women. *Formal* means a suit of some sort, but dressing well means much more than slapping on a suit, as we explain in the following sections.

Creating a professional wardrobe is expensive. That's why you have credit cards. Buy the best quality you can afford. Your wardrobe is an investment in your profession. Treat it accordingly.

Suits

If you're a professional, you probably own at least a few suits: two or three made from wool for autumn and winter and one made from cotton or tropic weight wool for spring and summer. When choosing a suit, look first for fabric, fit, and comfort; look second for style.

Your suit fabric should never shine or change colors in different lighting.

Fabrics include wool, cotton, linen, and various microfibers. Wool is easily the most versatile of the three, coming in both summer or tropic weight and winter weight and in a variety of fabric styles. *Worsted wool* is composed of tightly twisted fibers — gabardine and crepe are worsted wools. Various woolen fabrics, such as tweed and flannel, are more loosely twisted. *Wool blends* are fabrics in which wool is woven with microfibers such as nylon, Lycra, or polyester. Although wool blend suits aren't as traditional as worsted wools or tweed, they are strong, durable, and feel good.

Cotton and linen suits are also available. One classic cotton suit is the seersucker, a vertically striped affair rarely found off the East Coast or out of the Deep South. Linen suits are popular in some quarters because they're comfortable in extreme heat and high humidity. But, be forewarned, linen wrinkles immediately. And, although these two fabrics have their adherents, tropic-weight wool is still by far the most popular choice for a summer suit.

As for color, navy blue, black, charcoal gray, and dark brown are the standard colors for business suits. Navy blue or charcoal wool are excellent choices for a first suit. Conservative pinstripe suits are acceptable in some businesses, as are some patterned suits. Khaki or tan make appearances in late spring and summer only. An exception: You can wear the camel hair sports coat year-round.

You can choose from three basic suit styles (and their multiple variations):

- **American cut:** These suits can have either two or three buttons and have center-vented jackets and natural shoulders and pants with a straight line.
- **Italian cut:** These suits have unvented jackets with padded shoulders and pants that are fuller than American cut suits.
- **British cut:** These suits have side-vented or unvented jackets with a square shoulder, tapered waist, and pants that are narrower than both American cut and Italian cut suits.

When standing or walking, button the top button of a two-button jacket; button the middle button of a three-buttoned jacket. Unbutton your jacket when sitting down. If you button all the buttons on a suit, you'll look like you did when you were a four year-old ring bearer at your Aunt Ellie's wedding.

Double-breasted suits rarely look as good as you think they will.

The only rule about fit is that you have the suit professionally tailored. Purchasing a $1,500 suit off the rack is absolutely pointless if it won't be tailored to fit you.

Brush your jackets and pants off at the end of each day and before you leave the house in the morning (if you don't have a clothing brush, you can use masking tape).

Shirts

Buy five long sleeve white shirts and five long sleeve light blue shirts (there's no such thing as a short sleeve dress shirt). If you work in a conservative environment, you've just finished your shirt shopping!

Collar styles come and go. Currently, spread collars, point collars of various extremes, and button-down collars all have their purpose. Spread collars are considered the dressiest because you can't wear them without a tie; point collars are the best compromise collar, because they look good with or without a tie; and hidden button-downs are increasingly popular. Button-down collars are still quite popular for certain professions (academia and publishing) and for casual wear days.

Socks

Socks are simple: Wear dark socks coordinated with the color of your suit. Wear khaki-colored or dark brown socks with khakis. Patterns are permissible so long as they're not ostentatious. Socks should be made of cotton, wool, or silk. Polyester socks will create problems we'd rather not discuss here. Socks should be mid-calf or full-calf in length, in order to prevent your untanned shins from blinding others.

White socks are unacceptable in business. And in case the thought crosses your mind, wearing no socks is equally unacceptable.

Shoes

As with socks, shoes are relatively simple: plain- and cap-toed Oxfords, wingtips, and plain or tasseled loafers are the extent of your choices for dress business shoes. Coordinate your shoe color with your suit color: black shoes with charcoal and black or navy blue suits; brown shoes with brown and tan suits. Keep them well-shined and use a shoe tree in your closet to retain shape. Don't let the heels get worn down.

Keep a black Sharpie marker with you to touch up scuffed shoes.

In some locations — from Texas west to Nevada and north to Montana — dress cowboy boots are acceptable with suits, as long as you are a rancher, a politician, or in the oil business. Most of the time, cowboy boots just make you look silly. So be careful!

Running shoes, hiking boots, or sandals with a suit are unacceptable.

Accessories

You're probably thinking "Real men don't accessorize!" Think again. It's the little things that matter most.

Ties

Ah, the tie! Do you use it to express your individuality or your bank balance? Or do you think that attempting to express your "inner soul" through your tie is lame? Either way, follow these simple rules with ties:

- Ties should be silk.
- Ties should be understated.
- Ties should be coordinated with the suit and shirt.
- Ties should end at the top of your belt.

Play it safe. Keep an extra clean white shirt and a couple of plain or understated ties in your office if you're partial to the unusual, just in case your conservative client Mrs. Fussbudget pays a surprise visit. Don't wear Mickey Mouse ties unless other people in your office wear Bugs Bunny or Dilbert.

The bow tie is a special case. If you work in a think tank or at an Ivy League university, bow ties are acceptable. But outside the tradition-obsessed halls of academia and jurisprudence, the bow tie is often (perhaps unfairly) treated with suspicion. So be careful: If you love yourself in a bow tie and think that there aren't enough bow-tied men in the world, go for it. However, recognize that your fastidious fashion statement will not go unremarked in Cheyenne, Wyoming.

Watches

If you go for status symbols, buy an expensive watch. Otherwise, a medium-range watch with a leather or a metal band is the way to go.

Hats

Forty years ago, fedoras were the hats of choice. Today, the only hat of choice it seems is the baseball cap. Think about baseball caps and let this suffice: Make sure that they're insignia-free and don't wear them indoors at any time. Other hats, especially winter hats of varying degrees of arctic protection, are acceptable in the elements but not in the building.

Briefcases

Briefcases are traditionally made from leather and either black or brown. Don't skimp on quality. If you choose a notebook computer bag instead, hold it to same high-quality standards you would a briefcase.

Sending All the Right Signals: Body Language and Comportment

Clothes may make the person, but body language may make or break the deal. How you carry yourself when engaged in conversation is often as important as what you say.

Body language is nonverbal, but it communicates volumes about you nonetheless. Paying attention to your body language communicates to others that you pay attention to detail.

Body language is an interpretive affair. Like most human behavior, your physical behavior is symbolic. Take some simple examples:

✔ **Cigar smoking is often thought to be expressive of financial and sexual prowess:** But, as Freud noted a hundred years ago, "Sometimes a cigar is just a cigar."

✔ **Failure to maintain eye contact during conversations is a sign of evasiveness and cowardice to some:** However, in some cultures, avoiding eye contact is polite behavior.

✔ **Stroking your chin while thinking is supposed by some to indicate reflection and deep thought:** But sometimes your chin just itches.

The truth is that practically *any* behavior you engage in can be freighted with significance. You may scratch your ear one evening in a bar and, unknown to you, signal the man with the newspaper that the diamonds are in the umbrella stand.

With almost infinite symbolic interpretations for body language, no wonder people are nervous about it! Your best bet is to know about some of the body language pits you can inadvertently fall into and how to avoid them.

Standing

When you stand, you want to stand with a straight back, middle section in alignment with your back, shoulders back, and head up. This posture connotes comfort with yourself and ease in the situation.

Slouching, sticking your belly out, stuffing your hands in your pockets, folding your arms defensively all suggest aggressive unease. Winding yourself up like a corkscrew, with your ankles crossed and your arms holding themselves, is the very picture of insecurity and nervousness.

Sitting

Take care in the way you sit, for no other position connotes so much on its own. Think of the diversity of sitting positions that you've seen in business meetings, from practically horizontal to alert and upright. Sit with a straight back and with your legs together in front of you or crossed, either at the knee or at the ankle.

(Given male and female physiology, the position of your legs while sitting can send some primeval signals to those around you. Take care that the signals you send are neither overtly nor covertly aggressive or sexual.)

- ✔ Jiggling your knee is a sign of nervousness.
- ✔ Leaning forward can, at times, suggest aggressiveness, so do so with care.
- ✔ Leaning back with your hands behind your head and your pelvis lifted is an unseemly display for a man: So is sitting with your legs open if no desk shields your conversation partner from you. Avoid sitting with one ankle over the other knee in all but the most casual of settings.
- ✔ Leaning back with your legs crossed and one side off the seat of the chair is an unseemly display for a woman: So is sitting like a sexy starlet on the *Tonight Show*.

Head movement

Head movements communicate important information. Nodding in agreement can be immensely helpful to others. Too much nodding makes you look like one of those bobbing dogs on the rear seat of a car. Shaking your head can signal disagreement or disapproval. But, again, avoid shaking your head too much.

Facial expression

Facial expressions are crucial in the repertoire of body language. No other aspect of your body carries the immense richness of nonverbal communication that your facial expressions do.

You already know that smiles are important signals of generosity and non-aggression. But forced smiles are neither: They're signals that you can barely tolerate the other person. And incessant smiles are signals of servility or foolishness.

Likewise, frowns signal disagreement, disapproval, and sometimes anger. But they can also suggest hard thinking and focused concentration.

Certainly, smiling while criticizing an employee, and frowning while closing a deal are both mistakes.

These are the most obvious facial expressions, but there are hundreds of others: an arched eyebrow, pursed lips, flared nostrils, squinting eyes, a wrinkled nose, a bitten lip, the tongue out of the mouth, a grimace, widely opened eyes, and on and on. Every one of them has a culturally agreed on set of meanings.

Take a day to monitor your most frequently used facial expressions and, once the inventory is complete, assess their appropriateness and their effectiveness. You'll probably be surprised at the kinds of things you weren't even aware you do!

Of course, you can learn to control all these motions and develop a poker face. Some people think that a poker face is a great thing to have in business.

Eyes

Maintain eye contact when talking with others. Do not study your hands or clean your fingernails while others are talking. When talking in a group, make eye contact with everyone and do not focus on only one person.

Hands

Some people talk with their hands, some stand there with their hands glued to their sides. Most people haven't the foggiest notion what their hands are doing when they talk.

Using your hands can sometimes be pretty effective, sometimes pretty aggressive, and most of the time totally irrelevant. Sometimes using your index finger can be effective in emphasizing a point. And plenty of chest-pointing bosses use their hands in a barely controlled way to assert their power over you.

Controlling your hands takes effort and willpower. Again, monitor your hand movements. Avoid sweeping, cappuccino-clearing gestures during meetings. If you have to, sit on them.

Personal Hygiene and Grooming

Wearing the right clothes and having perfect body language does no good if you haven't bathed or your nails are dirty. Bathe or shower every day and use a deodorant or antiperspirant. Body odor is a definite taboo.

Hands

Follow these guidelines for your hands:

- ✔ Keep your hands and fingernails scrupulously clean and well cared for.
- ✔ Don't bite your nails or cuticles.
- ✔ Keep your cuticles pushed back.
- ✔ Get an occasional professional manicure — both men and women benefit from this treatment.

Women

Women should follow these guidelines for their nails:

- ✔ **Clear nail polish is easy to maintain:** If you wear colored nail polish, stick to red or pink and get a professional manicure weekly.
- ✔ **Nails should be no longer than half an inch beyond the end of your fingers:** If you can't pick up a dime with your finger tips, your nails are too long.

Men

Nails should be clean, short, and filed. Axle grease under your finger nails does not make you look macho. You may buff your nails if you wish.

Hair

Hair should be clean, well-combed, and trimmed. Eliminate dandruff with a good shampoo. Other than that, almost anything goes. Of course, anyone looks bad in a "mullet."

Women

Keep your hair out of your eyes. If your hair is long, consider pulling it back, but avoid looking like a schoolgirl. Barrettes and other ornamentation should be simple. Mohawks, insignia, and Jell-O dyes are appropriate only for those businesses where multiple body piercings are also the norm.

Men

Keep your hair trimmed and orderly. Long hair is acceptable in some companies but not in others. If yours is too long for the company you've been hired at, you'll be told. If you aren't told, ask. If you hair is long, consider pulling it back in a ponytail. If you have a beard or other facial hair, keep it trimmed and free of crumbs. If necessary, shave your neck and upper chest to below your T-shirt line. Eyebrows, nostrils, and ears should be free of stragglers at all times.

Shave every day and before leaving the office, if necessary, if you have an evening appointment.

Face

Wash your face daily. If you have acne, consult a dermatologist; many excellent treatments are available.

Makeup

Makeup should enhance your natural features, not create new ones. A foundation that matches your skin tone, lipstick, mascara, and a light dusting of powder are often enough. Heavy eye liner, metallic or brightly colored eye shadow, and thick rouge are, well, only for the stage.

Teeth

Brush your teeth after every meal. Equip your office with a toothbrush, toothpaste, breath mints, and mouthwash.

Scents

Use perfume or aftershave/cologne sparingly so that it neither precedes you nor lingers after you.

Piercings and tattoos

As a general rule, tattoos shouldn't be visible during the business day. In more conservative business settings, remove your piercing ornaments during the day.

Part II
Opening Doors to Communication

In this part . . .

We help you get started by tackling one of your most frequently encountered challenges: meeting and greeting other people. Many of us get tripped up on introductions, so we set you on the right path of who to introduce to whom, how to use titles, and the all-important firm handshake. Then we give you tips on making sparkling business conversation that everyone will want to be a part of.

Speaking on the telephone is another time when manners seem to slide, so you'll discover how to speak and listen considerately on the phone. You'll explore new tactics for handling voice mail, call waiting, caller ID, speaker phones, cell phones, and beepers. We also look at the written word. We close with brand-new advice on navigating cyberspace.

Chapter 5

Meeting and Greeting

• •

In This Chapter

▶ Making introductions

▶ Remembering names

▶ Shaking hands

▶ Dealing with titles

• •

*I*n today's fast-paced, high-tech world, people tend to forget the importance of simple human contact and kindness — remembering peoples'
names, trying to make a good first impression and greeting people with a firm
handshake. We get asked many business etiquette questions, and invariably
we find that many of them center on introductions. And rightly so. Even
though people may have loosened up somewhat in their usage of titles, you
still find a very distinct pecking order to who is introduced to whom in the
business world.

Being able to introduce people and explain who they are makes everyone feel
comfortable in a new situation and is one of the most useful skills you can
acquire in the business world. The ability to confidently introduce yourself or
others demonstrates that you are at ease and in control — and by extension,
you set others at ease, too.

In this chapter, we introduce you to tricks of meeting and greeting people
that will make you look and be completely at ease in public.

Making Positive Introductions

Who goes first? Traditionally, in social situations a man is introduced to a
woman. In practical terms, this means that the man is mentioned last in the
introduction: "Stacey Jourdan, may I introduce Brad Johnston." Not so in the
business world! In business, introductions are based on a person's rank and

position in a company. Whether that person is a man or a woman, young or old, makes no difference. The highest-ranking person is mentioned first and then the person being introduced. Remember "Big, may I introduce Small."

Deciding who makes the introductions

In formal business situations, your host (generally, the most senior executive from the company that planned the event) meets, greets, and introduces you to other guests. In less formal situations, people frequently don the role of host for their immediate circle and facilitate introductions. And, if you enter into a group where introductions have already been made, introducing yourself is always appropriate. If your company is hosting the event, and you are the only or most senior representative of your company in a group, your job is to assume the role of host and make introductions.

Understanding the pecking order

You always introduce, or present, a "lesser" person to a more senior person. That means the senior person's name is first and the person who is being introduced, or presented, is named last, as in "Ms. CFO, I'd like to introduce Mr. Junior Executive."

So always introduce people as follows:

- ✔ "Executive, I'd like to introduce Assistant."
- ✔ "Client, I'd like to introduce My Company."
- ✔ "Governor, may I introduce Citizen."
- ✔ "Two-Year Employee, may I introduce New Employee."

A client is always the "more important person." You would introduce the president of your company (we'll call him John Cunningham), to the vice-president of your client's company (we'll call her Carol Miller), like this: "Ms. Miller, I'd like to introduce the president of Splash Graphics, John Cunningham."

When you're introducing two people who are of equal rank in the corporate hierarchy, introduce the one you know less well to the one you know better ("Mr. Longtime Coworker, I'd like to introduce Ms. New Acquaintance"). If you're in a group and making many introductions, it's helpful to give people a little information about each other to help them start a conversation.

You don't want to introduce two people and then walk away, leaving them with no information about each other's position and how they may relate to each other. You might say, "Mr. Shaffer, I'd like to introduce Mr. Raymond

Godfrey, president of Express Shipping. Mr. Godfrey, I think I mentioned once that Mr. Shaffer is the president of our company and used to serve on the International Shipping Council as well."

In a large group, introduce one person to a few people at a time. This way, you won't overwhelm anyone with too many new names and faces. If you get confused, that's okay: Just keep going and do your best. Everyone makes mistakes introducing others once in a while, and usually no one notices. Remember, in business introductions, follow the hierarchy: The "important" person's name is first; the person being introduced, or presented, is named last.

The proper way to make an introduction is to say, "Big, may I introduce Small." Many people say "I'd like you to meet . . . ," which has a completely different meaning. Meeting is accidental — introducing is, well, on purpose.

Introducing someone senior to someone junior

Always introduce junior executives to senior executives. For example, if you're introducing a junior account executive named Alex Goldberg to the vice president of your division named Joanne Michaels, the proper form would be, "Ms. Michaels, I'd like to introduce Alex Goldberg."

If someone uses her first and last name in introducing herself and that person is senior to you, you should still use a title and the last name. Don't use her first name unless she invites you to do so. If the person is of equal or lower rank, you can feel comfortable using the first name if that's how the person introduces him or herself.

Introducing your boss to a client

You introduce the president of your company, Chris Rosati, to the vice-president of your client's company, Myra Pay, as follows: "Ms. Pay, I'd like to introduce the president of Acme Graphics, Chris Rosati." You use "Ms. Pay" if you normally address her this way. If you normally address your client as "Myra", then the introduction should be "Myra Pay, I'd like to introduce the president of Acme Graphics, Chris Rosati." Ms. Pay will say, "How do you do, Mr. Rosati." Mr. Rosati will reply, "How do you do, Ms. Pay." They may both say, "Please call me Myra/Chris."

"How do you do" is not really a question. The correct response is "How do you do."

Introducing two people of equal rank

When you're introducing two people of equal rank in the corporate hierarchy, introduce the one you don't know as well to one you know better. If you and Mike Hirschman are both vice-presidents in your company's Chicago office and you see Valerie Martinez, a vice-president in the Los Angeles office, you say, "Mike Hirschman, I'd like to introduce Valerie Martinez. Valerie is vice-president of our Los Angeles office."

Here's my card

In Japan, businesspeople are introduced through their business card, which is a convenient and easy way to determine a person's place in the business hierarchy. In fact, the Japanese have five different forms of their language, and when each is used depends on a person's place in the hierarchy. For instance, you'd use a different form of the language with a waiter than with a CEO. That's why the Japanese pay so much attention to business cards: They use them to understand a person's place in the world and how to address them.

Introducing yourself

You often have to introduce yourself in business situations. If you're waiting in a conference room for a meeting to begin and someone new to you arrives, you stand, offer your hand, and introduce yourself and your role. For example, "Hi, I'm Mike Perez. I'm Chair of the Scottish Salmon Promotion Board." At that point, the other person can introduce herself to you: "How do you do, Mr. Perez. I'm Linda Pollack, and I'm going to be handling PR for the new lox campaign."

Never leave people guessing about your name. To save someone the possible embarrassment of forgetting your name, offer a handshake and give your name. "Hello, Allison Pay, glad to see you." Now the person can easily introduce you around. Even if the person remembers your name and says, "Of course, Allison, how could I forget you!" everyone will be comfortable and happy, and you'll have smoothed over a potential awkward moment simply by saying your name right away.

For information on making introductions at meetings, see Chapter 20, "Meeting Manners."

Remembering Names

Everyone has problems remembering names, at least now and then (and sometimes more). So what's the way to handle this embarrassment? Just laugh and make a joke out of it. I usually say, "Oops, I'm so sorry, I'm having a senior moment. Sometimes I can't even remember my own name!" When you couple a gentle joke with an apology, you're certain to be forgiven immediately.

Why do people have these memory problems and blocks anyway? Experts say they stem either from information overload, stress, not being a good listener, or all the above. Even the grand dame of etiquette, Letitia Baldridge, admits to introduction mistakes and forgetfulness. It's such a common problem, she calls us the "nation of name-mumblers."

If — horrors! — you forget someone's name when you're about to make an introduction, don't make a scene. It's not the end of the world. Simply say, "I've momentarily forgotten your name." The person should jump in and say, "It's Bill Clinton" (unless it's not Bill Clinton). You can say, "Of course, Bill, I'd like to introduce Linda Tripp." It's only a big deal if you make it into a big deal.

Tools of the trade: Tricks for remembering names

The ability to remember names and titles, especially in a large group, makes a lasting impression. If you can master this new form of professional polish, you will present yourself with confidence and authority — and outclass the competition. One of the greatest fears about introductions is forgetting a person's name or mispronouncing it. Don't panic! Remembering names is a skill, and one that you can acquire:

- ✔ **Repeat the person's name a few times to yourself after you're introduced.**

- ✔ **Use the person's name immediately in the conversation after an introduction.**

- ✔ **Immediately introduce that new person to someone else you know:** If you don't have an opportunity to speak up immediately, you may want to try finding a word association with the person's name, such as "Bob — B — Brown shoes."

- ✔ **Jot down the person's name if you happen to have a pad and pencil.**

- ✔ **Listen, listen, listen.**

Good listening skills and concentration are the real keys to recalling a name. If you heard the name but you didn't understand it, simply ask the person to repeat the name. And, if you happen to have a name that's easily mispronounced, you may jump in and help the person making the introduction. Many people find it helpful to find something your name rhymes with or something people can visualize. ("It's Sue Fox, like the animal.")

Should you mispronounce someone's name, simply apologize, ask for the correct pronunciation, repeat the name aloud, and continue with your introduction. You can also ask for a business card — just be sure to read it as soon as you receive it.

Many books have tips on how to improve your memory. Buy one. Put new skills to work right away. Research proves that the sooner you implement a new behavior, the better your chances of making it a permanent part of your behavior.

When people misintroduce you

If someone mispronounces your name or gets it completely wrong, just smile and say something like, "Thank you, but my name is Karen Miller, not Morton."

If you've been introduced to someone previously, allow yourself to be reintroduced if you're not recognized. Don't make it an issue.

Never walk up to someone and ask, "Remember me?" To do so is cruel! Always stop and reintroduce yourself politely. If you see someone you've met previously but can't remember the name, simply say something along the lines of, "I remember meeting you recently. Was it at the corporate headquarters?" Usually the other person is flattered that you remembered having met, even if you've forgotten the name.

Handling the Handshake

Does a handshake really matter? Think back to the last time you got a limp handshake or a bone crusher. What impression did it make on you? Was it distracting? disgusting? shocking? Whatever your reaction, you probably weren't feeling positive about the other person.

What a sloppy handshake says about the person behind the hand is that he or she just doesn't have things together. And if you're the sloppy shaker, that tells the client, boss, or interviewer that you have problems. That conclusion can lead him to make a subconscious decision that he doesn't want to do business with you — or that you won't make a good representative of his company.

The handshake is the physical greeting that accompanies a verbal greeting. Because the handshake is used universally in business, knowing when to shake hands and how to shake hands confidently is vital.

Getting the right form

What is a proper handshake? The act seems so simple, yet people get confused over how to do it.

Showing respect: Business card etiquette

The biggest mistake you can make when you receive someone's business card is to glance at it and slide it into a pocket. This treatment shows little respect for the other person's position and rank. When handed a business card, read it thoroughly. You may want to repeat the person's name for pronunciation and acknowledge the person's company as being well-respected, or ask about the duties of his or her position. Finally, express your gratitude for being given this information.

Not shaking hands is a very clear form of rejection and is extremely insulting to the other person.

In the United States, you're expected to offer a firm handshake and make eye contact at the same time. A firm handshake with good eye contact communicates self-confidence.

In U.S. etiquette, an appropriate handshake begins with the introduction:

1. **Extend your hand and grip the other person's hand so that the web of your thumbs meet.**

2. **Shake just a couple of times.**

   The motion is from the elbow, not the shoulder.

3. **End the handshake cleanly, before the introduction is over.**

   If you want to count, a good handshake is held for three or four seconds.

Understanding the protocol of handshaking

When someone makes an introduction, always remember to stand (if you're seated at the time) so that you can shake hands on an even level. That goes for women as well. However, if you happen to be seated at a table where reaching the other person is difficult or awkward, you don't have to stand.

If you're wearing a name tag, place it close to your right shoulder because that's where a person's eye naturally wanders when shaking hands.

Shaking hands can be awkward in some situations. Should you be introduced to someone when your hands are full, carrying files or other packages, don't try to rearrange everything. Simply nod your head as you respond to the introduction.

If you're having cocktails, hold your drink in your left hand while introductions are going around. Later on, you can switch to your right hand. You don't want to fumble with your drink or offer someone a wet or cold hand to shake. If you're wearing gloves as part of formal attire, always remove them before shaking hands (the same goes for wearing gloves outdoors — you should take them off, unless the temperature is bitterly cold).

By now, you understand — a hand that shakes properly shows a personality behind the hand worth knowing or hiring.

Knowing when to shake hands

The answer is, all the time. When in doubt, offer your hand. Shaking hands is appropriate when

- ✔ Renewing an acquaintance.
- ✔ Acknowledging someone who enters your office, cubicle, or home.
- ✔ Greeting a client, new coworker, host, or others you know or are meeting for the first time.
- ✔ Meeting someone you already know outside work or home.
- ✔ Concluding a transaction.
- ✔ Leaving a business or social event.

In fact, because you should shake hands more often than not, the real question is: When *don't* you shake hands? Mainly, you should avoid shaking hands when the other person has his or her hands full and putting everything down to shake your hand would be a big inconvenience. The final exception may be when the person you want to greet is someone much higher ranked than you and to whom you really have nothing to say. In this case, rushing up to shake his hand and introduce yourself would appear pushy.

Handling Titles and Forms of Address

What's in a title? A whole heck of a lot. In a business situation, titles are crucial when making introductions because they put the people being introduced into context for others. Is she or he a marketing person, a sales person, an engineer, an accountant? This information is critical to making

Avoiding the clammy hand dilemma

When at an event involving food and drink, you should hold your beverage in your left hand to avoid a cold and clammy handshake. If one hand is holding a drink, and the other an hors d'oeuvre, you should put the hors d'oeuvre down if possible. If doing so isn't possible, then simply nod your head in response to the introduction and apologize for having your hands full.

If you have a tendency to have cold hands, stick your right hand in your pocket to warm it up as you approach a situation in which you'll have to shake hands. And, if you have perennially clammy hands, try the high-school prom date approach and take a quick swipe of your right hand on your skirt or trousers, so that when you present it, it's dry. You can do so quickly and gracefully, and no one will be aware that you made the gesture.

We have one other suggestion. If you are prone to sweaty palms, try rubbing antiperspirant (unscented!) on your hand before meeting someone.

---

sure that everyone is comfortable with one another (and immediately opens the door to conversation that can ease initial awkwardness).

Even if you know someone well as "Bill Durkins," you should introduce him as "Dr. Bill Durkins." Your aunt may be "Sandra Andersen," but you should introduce her as "Judge Sandra Andersen." People want to know to whom they are speaking, so they can make appropriate comments.

Never assume that you can automatically can call someone by a first name. You should use a person's title until he or she invites you to use the first name. Stick with Mr., Ms., Doctor, General — whatever is right. In the case of a woman, if you're not sure which variation she prefers — Mrs., Miss, or Ms. — just ask her. However, if you know that the woman is a physician, a Ph.D., or a military officer, use the appropriate title.

Americans tend to jump to the first name very quickly as any recent phone solicitation will convince you. This trend is fine, but doesn't ease your obligation to wait until the person invites you to do so first. Let the host or your superior set the example, and then follow that lead.

When in doubt, err on the side of formality.

If someone has been an Ambassador, Governor, Senator, or Judge, she remains so all her life. Always use the title in front of the person's family name.

•

Chapter 6

Making Conversation

Few skills are more appreciated than the ability to make conversation. The person who is able to draw people into conversations, introduce interesting topics, and make everyone comfortable is valued in all situations, business and social. Conversation is an art as well as a skill.

In this chapter, you'll be introduced to some techniques for improving your conversational skills. In the first section, you'll discover that good speaking and listening skills require practice. In subsequent sections, we'll show you how to keep the channels of communication open in the office, how to mingle at social gatherings, and how to prevent some of the most common conversational mistakes.

Listening Well and Speaking Wisely

The wisest people seem to listen more than they speak. As a well-mannered person, you'll want to emulate that behavior. (By doing so, you not only you train yourself to listen better, but other people will also listen very carefully to the words you do speak.)

By listening well, you remember all of the conversation's major points, including any actions that are your responsibility. You can ask intelligent questions at the end of the conversation, and you may even learn something!

Listening well means more than just sitting quietly. Your body language shows that you're attentive:

- ✓ **Neither slump down in your chair nor sit rigidly without moving.**
- ✓ **Watch the speaker, and don't let your eyes wander all over the room.**
- ✓ **Sit comfortably without shifting every few minutes:** Crossing and uncrossing your legs signal boredom. For more on body language, see Chapter 4.

When receiving instructions from bosses or clients, repeat back what you think you hear them saying in order to clarify everyone's understanding of the issues at hand.

Making sparkling conversation

There's no one way to spark a conversation. The best conversationalists know that the topic depends on the group and the context of the event. One rule: Stay away from religion, politics, sex, and money. If you raise one of these topics, even in a joking manner, you're walking on thin ice as you never know whether you're offending other peoples' sensibilities.

If you're in a group of people and need to raise a topic of conversation, try one of the following topics:

- ✓ **Sports that are of national prominence:** Examples include the Super Bowl or the Olympics.
- ✓ **Current events:** Make sure to read the newspaper or a news magazine the day of the event. Appropriate current events include business news, personal interest stories, stories about nature, and stories about local civic accomplishments.
- ✓ **Positive items of interest to everyone in the company:** The new advertising campaign or the redesigned corporate cafeteria, for example.
- ✓ **Best-selling books.**
- ✓ **A compliment about the event, host, food, wine, or the venue.**

To stay out of hot water conversationally, avoid asking very personal questions (about someone's impending divorce or broken engagement, for example). Recognize when you've been speaking with someone for more than 10 or 15 minutes: This is your cue to move on to another conversation. Avoid using inappropriate language, such as slurs or curse words, and never tell a joke that you think may be even slightly off-color. (If you think the joke may be off-color, it probably is.)

How to be a good conversationalist

Good conversationalists all share these abilities:

1. **They know how to give and accept compliments gracefully.**

2. **They can talk about many different subjects and are able to maneuver through conversations pertaining to things they know little about without difficulty.**

3. **They can quickly discern potential topics of interest to any given group and steer the conversation in that direction.**

4. **They don't repeat gossip.**

5. **They never correct another person's vocabulary or grammar.**

6. **They know when to discuss business and when not to.**

7. **They involve everyone in the group in conversation, not just one person.**

8. **They know how to step in to fill in an embarrassing void in conversation.**

9. **They have a good sense of humor and are able to relate stories well.**

10. **They can sense when they are boring people.**

People appreciate the conversationalist who stays away from talking nitty-gritty business at a company event. No one wants to get into a long-winded discussion on the outcome of your latest personal injury case as you detail everything your client did to make life difficult for you. Save it for Monday morning in the office.

Try to include everyone in the group in the conversation by asking various people questions and drawing out their opinions. For example, "Saugatuck sounds like a lovely choice for a vacation home, Stan. Larry, didn't you tell me that you summered in Michigan as a child?" If you've met a person previously at another event, do bring up your memories of it. ("I remember meeting you at the summer retreat last year. Wasn't Key West just an ideal location?")

As you circulate, make sure to hold your drink in your left hand, so that if you are introduced to someone, you don't extend a cold, wet hand to shake. For more about introductions, see Chapter 5.

Using tact in any situation

A tactful person is also a diplomatic person, which means gently conveying difficult information so that it's acceptable to the receiving party. Flatly issuing commands or loudly mouthing opinions are great ways to show complete ignorance of the use of tact.

Suppose you and your coworker are meeting with a client from a cough syrup manufacturing company about an advertising campaign. Everything is going fantastically well on the project, and you're ready to take the next step forward with your proposed campaign, when the client announces that his boss really wants to bring back Croupy Clown as the brand's spokesperson. Croupy really doesn't cut it in your new campaign. The non-tactful thing to do would be to blurt out your first thought: "Are you out of your mind?!?" This reaction may not achieve your objective of steering the client from that horrifyingly bad idea. What may work better? "That's an interesting idea. Why don't we take it back to the team and review our research on consumer response to Croupy? I'll give you a call tomorrow morning to let you know what we find."

Handling Office Conversations

Part of the reason you were hired is because your boss liked your personality and thought you'd "fit in" and become a valuable addition to the team. Keeping cordial relations with your boss is important, as is conveying that you enjoy his or her company as a person as well as in the capacity of your superior, so stop by for some friendly small talk.

Friendly chit-chat is appropriate if your boss' office door is open and if another member of the team is already there, having a chat. On the other hand, if your boss' door is closed, or if he's working quietly in his office, typing intently on the computer, he's likely trying hard to get some serious work done and won't welcome a frivolous interruption. Likewise, if your boss is on the phone or has a scowl on her face, you should probably wait for another time.

Developing cubicle courtesy

The cubicle is a curious invention. It gives the illusion of privacy without actually providing privacy. Although you can't see your coworkers, you can certainly hear them. Engrain that fact in your mind. Loud telephone conversations, or group social chats centered in your cubicle, can annoy people working nearby. Although everyone expects and accepts the occasional social call, receiving multiple calls (don't fool yourself into thinking that your next-door neighbor won't be listening), and constant visits from coworkers who want to chat will annoy everyone around you. Keep chatting to a minimum, or, if possible, make your personal calls while the people around you are in meetings or at lunch.

Chatting politely with coworkers

Be careful in the language you use with coworkers. Although slang may be all right among your friends, your coworkers may have sensitivities you're not aware of. Too much slang or use of foul language can turn off coworkers.

You'll likely spend more time chatting with colleagues than with your boss. Keep in mind that you want to be friendly, but not monopolizing of others' time. Never bother someone by talking when that person is obviously trying to concentrate on making a deadline. Keep secrets. Any new information is your personal property and you shouldn't share it with others. Keep personal discussions of your love life and your spouse to a minimum.

Make sure that the tone of your conversations is positive. The person who goes from cubicle to cubicle complaining and putting down other people won't go far. Use your office conversations to keep everyone informed on the development of a project of mutual interest. Don't boast to other colleagues about achievements or things your boss has said to you.

When a colleague has had bad news, such as a sick child or a project that didn't go well, stopping by to show your concern is perfectly acceptable. By all means, express how sorry you are and offer your assistance. If a colleague is feeling discouraged, offering some words of encouragement is compassionate. Even if you're in the middle of making a tight deadline, take a few minutes to help the other person. Some day, you may be the person needing help.

Respecting ethnic and cultural differences

Inadvertently insulting someone with a racial or ethnic slur is one of the fastest ways to completely embarrass yourself and hurt others. As a well-mannered person, you should have no problem avoiding this pitfall, because you're alert to your coworkers' sensitivities and needs! As people from different ethnic, cultural, religious, and national backgrounds unite, you need a tolerant and inclusive attitude, which means watching your language and your actions.

Learn the accepted terms for the ethnic groups, religions, and nationalities of those with whom you work. Get rid of all those slang terms that you may have heard in the past. Don't identify or refer to others by race or ethnic identity. People are people. Use names and titles and avoid other labels. Sexist terms are strictly taboo. A person is a sales representative, not a salesman or saleslady. An administrative assistant is not a secretary, and an information systems specialist is not a computer jockey. Be alert to a person's special needs. If one of your colleagues must be absent for a religious observance, offer to cover his responsibilities for the day. If someone needs a lift to the auto repair shop, volunteer.

Always make a conscious effort to speak inclusively, without letting sexist terms creep into your vocabulary — and listen to the things that slip out of your mouth.

Offering your opinion

Never interrupt or correct someone while she's speaking. If you want to offer a different opinion, don't just say, "Linda, you're wrong. If you took time to read the report, you'd understand." Better to avoid a confrontation and harsh words by not using the accusatory "you" and gently pointing out another point-of-view. For example, you may say, "Linda's point about our on-time delivery record is interesting. I was reviewing last year's customer service survey yesterday, and it pointed out a different reason why our delivery record may not be up to par."

Meetings are the place to show that you're a team player. Use "we" when referring to work done by your team. Acknowledge your coworkers' contributions by using "we" instead of "I" and "our" instead of "my." Try to avoid "I launched the new fundraising campaign." Instead, say, "Our team worked closely to launch the new fundraising campaign."

Mingling Effectively

Nowhere is the art of mingling more important to your career than at a company party. You should be mixing with as many people as possible, not just those in your department whom you know well. Believe it or not, mingling is a vitally important business skill. Mingling well demonstrates that you're a friendly, open, and engaged person who is interested in other people. Mingling poorly shows others that you're either unsure of yourself or so egotistical that you can't listen to others.

Make the rounds of everyone at the party. Don't spend all of your time talking to one person — you want to circulate. Remember that many other people will be anxious about mingling and will welcome your efforts at making conversation.

Make good eye contact, give solid handshakes, and try to speak to people you haven't met before. You never know what doors may open for you simply because you made the effort to greet your colleagues in another department.

Mingling doesn't mean being mercenary. The worst thing you can do while making small talk with a new group of people is to keep glancing around you for someone "better" to engage in conversation. There's no faster way to make someone feel unimportant. When you're speaking with someone, he should receive your full attention — no wandering eyes!

Cocktail parties and other "mingling" events are usually noisy and punctuated with interruptions. They're not the ideal venue for a serious business conversation, and people will appreciate your keeping the conversation light. If you see the potential for a fruitful business discussion, hand the other person your business card and say you will call to make an appointment to continue the conversation.

Recognizing and Dealing with Common Conversational Faux Pas

Many people are scared to death of conversing with others, particularly groups of people, mostly out of fear of making mistakes. Never fear. Making mistakes happens to everyone and with a bit of practice and planning before your next event, you can converse confidently.

The worst thing you can do if you've made a social faux pas is to slink off into a corner and vow to move out of town, assume an alias, and never see that group of people again as long as you live. Yes, that is a normal human reaction to embarrassment. However, you should fight it. Taking a deep breath, staying put, and facing the consequences — with a little humor — is much better.

Humor is the best way to diffuse a tense situation. Being able to laugh at yourself is sure to lessen the embarrassment of any mistake. A classic faux pas is one of making an assumption that's just plain wrong. Suppose, for instance, that you just offered a long-winded opinion on your extreme dislike of Frank Lloyd Wright's architecture, never imagining that anyone you're speaking with has any connection with architecture. Your best friend's neighbor Chris, looking irritated, tells you that she is related to Frank Lloyd Wright. Now you're in an awkward situation, which requires humor — and backpedaling. You may try saying something like, "Even though Wright isn't my favorite, even I can appreciate the genius that went into his designs. And besides, my friends all know me as having extremely poor taste in architecture." Then you apologize, profusely, for any unintended hurt feelings caused by your remarks (and you make a solemn oath to yourself to never, ever offer your opinion in such a harsh manner before knowing whom you're speaking with).

Some things never change. When you were a kid, remember how much better you felt when you just confessed to your mother that you were the one who broke the cookie jar; finished off the milk and put the empty container back in the refrigerator; let the dog out last night and forgot to let her back in? The same goes with etiquette blunders. You're much better off taking responsibility for your blunder than blaming it on someone or something else. Keep that in mind as you read about some common conversation mistakes in the following sections.

Saying something awkward while making small talk

Relating your grandmother's mysterious bladder problem to your client in the hospital system marketing department may seem just fine to you, but it may well cause the vice-president of marketing to feel squeamish. If your conversation partner begins moving away from you for no apparent reason or looks disturbed, you know you've hit on an uncomfortable subject. Religion, politics, how much things cost, salaries, gossip, and office secrets are off limits as conversation topics. Turn the conversation to current events, food, positive news about colleagues, hobbies, industry talk, current trends, or sports — all of these topics make for good small talk.

Cutting in on the conversation

Wanting to add your two cents to a conversation is only natural. However, if you feel the urge to cut in on someone else's sentence with a fascinating tidbit of information that you think makes you look witty and erudite, sit back and wait a second. If there's a pause, use it as your cue to talk. If a pause doesn't occur, or the conversation changes course, be content with the thought that, although you may have missed a chance to contribute your wisdom about the latest theory regarding the affect of debt on earnings per share, you at least look composed and cool.

Talking too loudly in a restaurant

Speaking loudly in public, especially in restaurants, is common nowadays. It's not the loudest person who impresses his dinner companions; it's the person with quiet confidence and good manners. Always try to use low, intimate tones.

If you're speaking loudly in a restaurant because you're talking into a cellular phone, shame on you. Cellular phones should be turned off before entering a restaurant. Even if you don't mind interrupting a business dinner with a call, others in the restaurant may appreciate having their meal in peace.

Drawing a blank on what to say

If you come upon a pause in the conversation and have no idea what to say, get the other person to talk about himself. For instance, mention an article you read and ask the person's opinion: "I've been reading everything I can about the XYZ Company merger plans, but I still wonder if it makes sense. What do you think about their plans?" Or you may ask about the person's recent travels. If all else fails, you can always compliment the event you are attending — whether it's the food, interesting guests, or a table setting.

Chapter 7

Minding Your Telephone Manners

· ·

· ·

*Y*ou're one of the new breed — you go everywhere outfitted with a wireless phone, a beeper, and a Palm Pilot. At your office, your phone
system has more gizmos than a star ship — you have voice mail, call waiting,
call forwarding, caller ID, speakerphones, and a headset. You are always in
touch, whether you're at a business lunch, on your way to the dry cleaners,
or in the backyard with your kids.

Funny thing, even with all your technologies at hand, you're still not pleasing
everyone. People seem annoyed when you fiddle with your pager during a
meeting. Your kids groan every time your wireless phone rings. And other
drivers look daggers at you when they see you chatting away in the car as you
weave your way in and out of six lanes of traffic at 70 miles an hour.

The problem isn't the technologies — it's the way they're being used and
abused. One of the telling symptoms of the need for new etiquette rules is
when newspapers, magazines, and business conversations are liberally dosed
with the latest funny story or outrageous thing someone has done with their
new technology. Think over the last few months: How many times has someone told you about something hilarious someone else did with their wireless
phone or beeper? How many articles and letters to the editor have you read
describing the outrage someone feels when a wireless phone starts to ring at
the worst time or the impossibility of finding your way out of an automated
answering system?

Pretty clearly, a lot of us need some help with telephone etiquette, so this chapter gives you the scoop on how to talk and listen on the phone, how to use the various phone answering technologies, and how to use your wireless phone and beeper with a minimum of intrusion into others' space.

Speaking and Listening on the Phone: It's Not a No-Brainer

Some people just don't know how to speak on the phone — you can hear every breath they're taking and the crunch-crunch of their afternoon Fritos, or they have the receiver so far away that it sounds like they're talking to you from the slopes of Mount Kilimanjaro. And some people don't know how to listen on the phone — they "uh-uh" whatever you say while you can hear the clicking of their busy fingers on the keyboard in the background or they talk so much that you can't get a word in edgewise.

It shouldn't be that way!

Getting the basics down

Here are the basics about communicating with one another. First, there's a speaker and a listener. In most circumstances, the speaker's job is to be as clear as she can be and to speak in a polite, even tone. The listener's job is, well, to listen to what the speaker says and then to respond appropriately.

Sounds simple, doesn't it? But it's *amazing* how easy it is to mess this up. Usually, we just forget. As speakers, we mumble, shout, whisper, or speak with food in our mouths. As listeners, we do other things when we're supposed to be listening, listen without hearing anything someone says, and respond to another person's question from left field.

Everyone gets overworked and distracted, and you will no doubt have those moments when someone calls you at exactly the wrong time. But it's crucial that you pay attention to what you say, how you say it, and how you listen and respond to others on the phone. Studies have shown that the number one reason why customers do not become repeat customers is employee indifference and rudeness on the phone.

So speak clearly and pay attention to your conversational partner. Practice if you have to with someone you trust. Find the correct distance to hold the receiver from you so that your voice sounds neither like part of the ambient background nor like a hectoring protester speaking into a bullhorn.

Recognize that, as good as they are, telephone microphones are not as sophisticated as all that. They still tend to make you sound like a hissing snake if you hold the receiver too close.

And practice listening, too. Make a point of turning off other noise-making equipment when you get a phone call, even if "Wild Thing" (your favorite Troggs song of all time) is on the radio. Turn away from your computer if you have to in order to avoid the temptation to fiddle with the document on your screen. Excuse yourself from any conversations you are currently having so as to give your telephone conversational partner your undivided attention.

Just putting your hand over the telephone microphone does not guarantee that the person on the other end cannot hear you.

Some people think that having three conversations going at once makes them look busy and important. But it rarely does — it usually makes them look frazzled and vain. If you positively can't stop what you're currently doing when the phone rings, or you're in the middle of an important conversation with someone in person or on another line, don't pick up the phone! It's better to let the voice mail system take a message than to divide your attention like that. Unless the caller has pre-arranged to call you at this time or it's the President of the United States calling to tell you that there really are asteroids heading for Earth and you're the only person who can save the human race, the call can wait.

Calling on the phone

Now for some basic telephone manners: First of all, prepare for the phone call before you make it. Have some idea of what you're going to talk about. Make notes if necessary, especially if you're forgetful. It's better to plan ahead than make a second call.

When you call someone, introduce yourself the right way: first, say "Hello"; second, identify yourself and your affiliation; third, ask for the person to whom you would like to speak. For instance:

"Hello, this is Tom Terrific from Terrific Technologies calling for Ms. Highandmighty concerning next spring's conference. Is she available?"

If Ms. Highandmighty is available, you will be transferred to her. When she answers, repeat your name and affiliation, state your business, and give an estimate of the time you think the call will take. For example:

"Hello, Ms. Highandmighty, this is Tom Terrific from Terrific Technologies calling about next spring's conference in Pago Pago. Do you have ten minutes to talk about marketing strategy?"

That's all you need. You've said who you are and what you want to talk about. Now, you pass the ball into the other person's court and let her respond.

If the person you are calling is not available, give your name, your company's name, your telephone number, a time you can be reached, and a brief message. Refrain from leaving a monologue to replace the conversation you would have had.

When your conversation is finished, end it cordially if possible and quickly. A business call is not a social call and there is no need to drag the conversation out beyond the business at hand. However, if you know the person well, you may end the conversation with a few questions about something personal, such as, "I was glad to hear your mother is back from the hospital," or, "How did Sarah's soccer game go?"

Keep the following tips in mind:

- ✔ Exercise patience on the phone and let other people finish their sentences.
- ✔ Focus on listening.
- ✔ Speak so as not to be misunderstood.
- ✔ Listen to what the other person is saying.

Watch out for these mistakes:

- ✔ Never sneeze, belch, blow your nose, snort, or cough into a phone.
- ✔ Never use phone calls as an opportunity to get caught up with paper shuffling.
- ✔ Never eat, drink, or chew gum while on the phone.

Answering the phone

Companies have lots of protocols for answering the phones. Some companies take the responsibility away from real people altogether and deed it to answering machines with menus. If well constructed, these answering systems can be helpful and efficient. If poorly constructed, they can be like entering Dante's Inferno: You enter and wither away, never to be heard from again.

The first contact a potential client or customer typically has with your company is when someone answers your company's phone. Make sure it's done well! When you answer the line, speak clearly, identify your company and ask the caller how you may direct the call or how you may help. Answer the questions if you can. If you can't, direct the call to the appropriate person.

Many different greetings are acceptable, but they all contain the following information: your company name and your name. Here's a greeting that gets it right:

"Good morning, Telepathy Incorporated, James Moody speaking."

Simple, succinct, and informative. If you say it with the right inflection in your voice — that is, upbeat and engaged — you will set the right tone for the rest of the conversation immediately.

So when you pick up the phone, remember to

✔ Stop whatever else you are doing.

✔ Speak clearly into the receiver.

✔ Be upbeat.

Putting a caller on hold is frustrating to the caller, so refrain from doing it unless you absolutely have to. If you have to, remember that it is easier on the caller if you ask, "Will you please hold for a moment? I'll go get that information" than if you command the caller to "Hold!" and push the button. Try your hardest to remember that people are on hold when you put them there. Update the caller every half minute or so on the progress you're making in putting her call through.

If you need to connect a caller to someone else, tell her the name of the person you are directing the call to and provide that person's extension number. If the call then gets disconnected, the caller will appreciate having the name and the extension when she returns the call.

Screening calls for others is a delicate matter. Not only may the caller feel slighted when an administrative assistant tells him that Mr. Bigshot is not available, he may resent telling an administrative assistant about the call and having the assistant determine its importance. Tact is necessary. Good bosses will provide their receptionists and administrative assistants with the protocols they wish to use for screening and the language to be used with callers. If your boss doesn't set the criteria for screening or the language to be used, ask her to do so.

If you're a manager, let your receptionist or assistant know if you do not wish to be disturbed or if there's an "A" list for the afternoon. Be clear about how you would like other calls handled. Always offer a way for callers to leave messages.

Dealing with the angry caller

Of course, not everyone will be delighted to be put on hold or screened. And some callers are just plain angry. How do you deal with the hothead *who will not be ignored anymore?!*

The first thing to do is distance yourself from the caller. The caller may have a legitimate complaint against your company. Then again, he may not. But until he stops calling you and your company every name under the sun there's no way for you to know. So give him time to vent — unless he's a serious volcano, he'll find his composure again within three minutes. If you have to, hold the receiver away from your ear, far enough to dodge the venom, close enough to hear what he says and to remember it. Write the substance of his complaint down. Write the abusive language down too, in case you, your boss, or the caller decide to take further action.

When the caller has finished venting, acknowledge that the problem is important and assure him that you will personally do what you can to solve the problem. Provide the caller with your name and your title. If you can't solve the problem, ask the caller if he will hold while you brief the person who can solve it. Do so. Transfer the call. Go get a drink of water. And treat yourself to something nice at the end of the day.

The receptionist or administrative assistant is responsible for making screening calls as pleasant as it can be. This is an important job and one that requires skill and practice!

Speaking on a wireless phone

Some wireless phones have problems of their own. One of the annoying things about talking on wireless phones is their habit of clipping off the beginning of words and sentences. When you're talking to someone on a wireless phone, the give and take of in-person conversation can lead you into a black hole of clipped queries about what the *other* person has just said.

To get out of the black hole, we recommend that you treat wireless phone conversations with all of the courtesy that you treat line phone conversations with, plus some. Remind yourself never to talk over your telephone partner's voice and to wait patiently until they have finished talking.

Another quirk of wireless phones is their occasional tendency to go out of range during a conversation. There's not much you can do to avoid embarrassment and frustration when you realize that the last two minutes of the review of the Spielberg flick you've been dictating to your editor drifted off into cyberspace. Take a deep breath and try again.

Instruments of Torture: Voice Mail, Call Waiting, Caller ID, and Answering Machines

These communications technologies are much more prevalent now than they once were, and they are undeniably helpful. Still, they have to be used with care, lest you use them as an opportunity to exercise your frustrations or inadvertently make your caller mad.

Voice mail

Voice mail systems allow people to leave a message for you when you are either not in your office or when you are on another line.

When you record a greeting for your voice mail system, remember that you are at work and not at home. Messages such as, "Hello, I'm Johnny Cash, and I'm not here" aren't helpful and messages such as, "I'm chillin' — leave me your 411!" will be indecipherable to most business callers. It's preferable to say something like the following:

"This is Georgette Johnson in the Billing Department at Blinkety-Blonkety. Please leave me a message and I'll return your call as soon as possible. Thank you."

Some people record messages on a daily basis or direct callers to others in the office who may be able to assist the caller. Most people change their message when they are out of town on vacation or away on business for more than a day. It is appropriate to inform callers when you will be out of the office and tell them that you will return their call when you get back. You may also leave the name and number of someone else in the office who can help the caller if he cannot wait until you return.

When you leave a message on someone's voice mail system, the first thing to do — before leaving the message — is to give your name, your company affiliation, your telephone number, and the date and time of your call. The next thing to do is to leave a short message that is direct and to the point. Message machines are no substitute for talking one on one, so don't think the person listening to your message needs to hear all of the gory details. At the end of the message, repeat your name and your phone number.

When you get a message on your voice mail system, remember to return it the same day, if possible, or the next morning.

Call waiting

Call waiting is, thankfully, losing out in popularity to voice mail systems, especially in business. If you find yourself using a phone equipped with call waiting, the best thing to do is to ignore the clicks. Remember that your current conversation takes precedence unless special circumstances apply.

Caller ID

There are uses for Caller ID. There are times when it is a tremendous advantage to know who is on the other end of the phone. For example, the four or five extra seconds you have to concoct your latest "why I haven't completed the X files" story can, on occasion, save your hide.

There are things to avoid with caller ID. Just because you were "suddenly" out of the office when Mr. Spudpucker called doesn't mean you shouldn't return the message he leaves on your voice mail system. Having not elected to answer the phone doesn't relieve you of your obligation to return the call. And it's better to avoid saying, "Hello, Jim" when you recognize the number. It's a little unnerving to the caller, who may wonder whether you have ESP.

Answering machines

All of what has already been said in the section about voice mail applies here as well. But there is one little issue concerning answering machines that requires separate treatment: Never admit to using your answering machine as a screening device. If you want to take the call, pick up and say something like, "Hi. Sorry, I was in the other room." This technique keeps your paranoid callers from feeling screened: "Well, I made it this time, but what about *next* time?"

Wireless Phones, Beepers, and Speakerphones

Now we come to the section where new phone manners are needed the most.

We don't know about you, but in the last few years, we have been astounded at the places people think talking on their wireless phone is acceptable. Walking down a city street is okay, but during a movie? In class? In a public rest room?! And beepers are only slightly better — granted you don't get people's conversations interrupting your business lunch, but that insistent "beep-beep-beep" is still annoying.

During a meeting of engineers, a junior engineer's beeper started going off. Unfortunately, he couldn't remember where he had put it. He frantically looked through his pockets, then his jacket, then his coat. He still couldn't find it. All the while the machine is beeping and the meeting has ground to a halt. Finally, the chief engineer instructed him to gather together all of his belongings and remove himself and them from the room until he had shut the thing down. The chief engineer then instructed someone to lock him out for the rest of the meeting. The next day, a brusque memo on beeper etiquette was in each person's mailbox.

Take care with your mobile and public communications devices — they introduce a whole set of issues about the extent of private space in a public world, issues we are all still sorting through.

Wireless phones

The popularity of wireless phones has exploded since the early 1990s and shows no sign of leveling off. The day may soon come when wireless phones are in virtually every adult's pocket or handbag. And it won't be long after that when people will walk around with wireless headset phones, talking to anyone other than the people they are with.

There is a place for wireless phones in today's business world. But that place is when you are alone — walking, in a cab, sometimes in a train. If you're using your wireless phone anywhere in public, such as in a station or mall, find a secluded corner to converse, away from others. Respect their right not to hear your conversation.

Remember that public phones have been around for a long time, usually in phone booths that protect you from noise and others from the details of your call. Keep the same principle in mind when using your wireless phone — try to construct a virtual phone booth around you for the duration of the conversation.

That's not always possible, and where it isn't possible you should be exceedingly sparing in wireless phone usage. Wireless phones have no place in restaurants, at the theater, movies, or at the symphony, in church or classrooms, or in a meeting. You are there to do something other than talk on the phone. Whenever you go into one of these settings, have the courtesy to turn your wireless phone off.

If you have inadvertently forgotten to turn the thing off and it starts to ring, apologize to those around you and hasten to quiet it, even if that means turning it off without answering it.

Better still, purchase a phone with a vibrating ringer — then no one but you will know that the phone is ringing. Of course, you have to be careful not to jump like someone just poured iced tea in your lap when it starts to vibrate.

Using your wireless phone while driving is an obvious temptation. But it's a temptation best resisted. Recent studies show that the accident rate for those talking on a phone while driving is equal to the accident rate for those who are legally drunk while driving. It's a dangerous thing to do. If your business is the kind that keeps you on the road a lot and you must use the phone in the car, try getting a hands-free model.

Never answer a wireless phone or begin a wireless phone conversation while in a bathroom. The potential for embarrassment is high.

Beepers

There's something curious about beeper-holders looking down at their waists every time their beeper announces a call. But in modern life these little devices come permanently attached to people in certain professions — construction and medicine, for example — and the intrusions they introduce must somehow be tolerated. Luckily, many beepers now come equipped with a vibrating mode. We can only hope that, within a couple of years, this new technology will spell the end to "beeps" in the theater.

Beyond that, everything that applies to wireless phones applies also to beepers — turn them off in meetings, restaurants, churches, and classrooms.

Speakerphones

Speakerphones are appropriate to use when you wish to have a group meeting with someone on the phone, but rarely otherwise. If you put people on speakerphone, by all means tell them that you are doing it, and tell them who else is in the room. Don't make the mistake of thinking that the person on the other end of the phone can't tell when you put them on the speakerphone. The additional echo of a speakerphone is instantly identifiable.

Suppose your caller is conferencing with three people in your office. First, introduce your colleagues to the caller. Second, when talking, be especially careful to identify yourselves to the caller at the beginning of your input to the meeting. Having no visual means to connect voice to person, the caller may be at a complete loss who is talking without repeated identification.

Speakerphones are loud! If you're using one, close the door to your office.

Conducting Conference Calls and Videoconferences with Care

Conference calls are increasingly popular, largely because the technology for them has improved so much in the last ten years. In the not-too-distant future, real-time videoconferencing will be affordable for most businesses. It is already a reality in a number of businesses.

Perhaps surprisingly, the videoconference is helping to re-introduce people to meeting manners. The explanation is straightforward: the camera has the unfortunate ability to focus on one person at a time. Any flaws in a person's body language — slouching in the chair, for example — becomes glaringly obvious on camera. Being part of a videoconference is a little like seeing yourself on video for the first time. All of those tics and quirks you thought you had mastered years ago suddenly slap you in the face!

Conference calls

The simpler case of a conference call has already been partially discussed in the section on speakerphones. Whenever you are engaged in a conference call, try to identify yourself each time you speak. That way, you can compensate for the lack of visual clues. And remember to be especially considerate about other people's contributions to the conference — give each person enough time to finish what he or she is saying before replying.

Videoconferencing

Given the growing trends of outsourcing and teams working together, and the increasing cost of air travel, the need for conferences between groups of people at opposite ends of the country — or the world, for that matter — has never been greater.

Some people appear to think that, since they are not sharing the same physical space with their videoconferencing colleagues, they are free to do things they would never dream of doing were they in the same room. But this is, pretty obviously, an error in judgment. You may not be able to see everyone on their end, but that doesn't mean they can't see all of the people on your end, and it doesn't mean that the roving camera won't find you just as you're counting holes in the ceiling tiles. If anything, you need to be *more* careful during a videoconference than you would be in a meeting.

When you are scheduled for a videoconference, begin your preparation for it well in advance. Train those who are unfamiliar with the format by staging mock meetings and videotaping them. Show everyone the tapes and make suggestions if needed. Have an agreed-upon agenda for the meeting in place if you can. Make sure that everyone whose input is required during the video-conference can make it at the scheduled time.

During the actual meeting, take care to sit properly, listen attentively, speak clearly, and be patient. Long-distance audio can introduce slight delays in the conversation. Be aware of them and compensate for them.

You never know when you are going to be on camera. So avoid slouching, picking at your clothes or body parts, twiddling your thumbs, playing with your pencil, or making faces.

Using Technology with Sensitivity

Not everyone can use all of the latest technology the way most can. People who have hearing or visual disabilities may have some difficulty using telephones, caller ID, beepers with alphanumeric displays, and other technologies. If you are a person with a disability, ask your employer to provide you with what is necessary for you to do your job. If you are an employer of a person with a disability, you should ask your employee how you can assist.

One of the most frequently used devices for people with hearing disabilities is the telecommunication device for the deaf (TDD). TDDs are small keyboards that plug into conventional phone lines, permitting people to type conversations on the phone.

Offices that employ people with hearing disabilities will have TDDs. If your company doesn't have TDDs and you receive a call from someone with a hearing disability, chances are that she will use a relay service. Relay services employ a hearing non-disabled person to mediate conversation when one side is without a TDD. The mediator is just that — a go-between for the conversation participants. So the mediator is not really part of the conversation.

Keep these tips in mind:

- ✔ When talking to someone with a hearing disability through a relay service, address the person you are talking to, not the mediator.
- ✔ When using a TDD, allow the other person to type in complete answers to your queries.

There you have them — a set of simple and easy to follow phone etiquette rules that will help you be your best on the phone and over long distances. We haven't covered all of the electronic wonders of the 21st century, however, so in the next chapter we'll show you how to behave on the Internet and on e-mail.

Chapter 8

Having the "Write" Stuff

*W*ith all of the spell-check, grammar-check, and letter-writing programs on computers, you may think you no longer need to know how to write well. Think again. Writing is still an essential skill for the professional, as you may have discovered the day your boss returned one of your letters sprinkled with her red editing marks.

Think about how many letters, e-mails, memoranda, and reports you get every week. Even if you're not a grammar expert, you can tell that some of them are more effective than others. Some are so disorganized that you can't find the point. Others are so brusque as to be a little offensive. With others, you look in vain for a paragraph that doesn't have a misspelled word. And then there is the effective letter or report: it's grammatically correct; it contains no spelling errors; its tone is appropriate to its content; it is direct without being curt; and it gets to the point quickly and stays there.

In this chapter, we show you how to compose business correspondence. You'll also learn how to avoid some basic grammatical, stylistic, and spelling errors; how to avoid some common word misuses; how to write in a consistent and well-organized manner; what to have in your stationery drawer; and how to address different people by their correct titles. By the end of the chapter, you'll no longer be intimidated by business writing. You may even have enough knowledge to become the office expert!

Communicating with Clarity and Courtesy

Perhaps you don't have a strong background in grammar. Maybe you avoided every university class with a heavy writing component. You're now the best technician in your division, but you're expected to write memoranda and letters to all kinds of people, and you don't have an administrative assistant. Result? Your trash can is constantly full of rejected drafts and the temperature rises to the boiling point every time you have to write a memo!

Clear writing is a skill that, for all but the luckiest of us, must be learned. Sure, naturally great writers exist, but for the rest of us practice — and lots of it — is required. The trouble is that you don't have time to practice. So you do it on the fly, with each piece of correspondence that you write.

We have two suggestions for you. The first is to read this section carefully. The second is to buy a dictionary, a thesaurus, and a copy of Strunk and White's *Elements of Style*. This little book (91 pages long) is recognized as the best primer on writing ever composed. There are other good writing books out there (and plenty of business writing books) but Strunk and White provides more about writing in less space than any book ever written.

With that said, it's time for your crash course in business writing. We will assume that you learned elementary grammar, and so, know the difference between a noun and a verb, a subject and a predicate, a proper noun and a common noun. If you don't, consult your Strunk and White.

Writing well

Clear writing requires a good grasp of grammar and spelling, a good vocabulary, the desire to not be misunderstood, and ruthless self-editing.

You're probably starting out with a good grasp of basic grammar and spelling. A good vocabulary is acquired in only one way — reading. To paraphrase, "You are what you read." Business executives around the world recommend that you read a lot of difficult material in diverse fields. This recommendation is two-fold: First, you learn new perspectives and information; second, you learn new words. Both help your writing.

The will not to be misunderstood is a crucial component in good writing. It is not the same as curtness or rudeness. It is only the intention to be as clear as you can be and to avoid all avoidable ambiguity. Remember that writing requires an attention to detail that is not needed in conversation.

Editing is perhaps the most difficult thing to do with your own writing. After all, you wrote it, so you don't *want* to change it. But you should, since, even for the trained writer, there are always changes to make.

Edit, edit, edit! Literally, at least three times. Before anyone else gets the chance to hack away at your work, be your own worst critic. Eliminate the grammatical mistakes, spelling errors, and poor style. Read the letter: Can that sentence there be clearer? Make it so. Reread the letter out loud: Perhaps that word there is too aggressive. Change it. Reread the letter: This paragraph isn't as clear as it should be. Rework it. Reread the letter: looks good? Give it to someone else; have them read it. When they can find no fault, reread it once more. Then print it, sign it, and send it!

Once you've got the kinks out of your correspondence and it's as clear as you can make it, you can add grace to it. Even the most damning letter of complaint can be polite. People often make the mistake of thinking that their expressed outrage is compelling to others. It usually isn't — the modulated, but clear, letter of complaint is more effective than the ranting letter.

You don't have to go so far as to call everyone "gentle reader" or "gracious madam." But by all means keep the name calling out of your business writing. Business writing, like all professional writing, is bound by the code that performance — not the person — is the subject of criticism. Focus on the topic at hand rather than the person who is talking about it, even if the person is a rude so-and-so.

- ✔ Never swear in business correspondence.
- ✔ Never call people names in business correspondence.
- ✔ Never make off-color remarks in business correspondence.

Courteous writing requires that your tone be moderate. Tone is a function of word choice and sentence style. Choosing your words carefully demands a vocabulary rich enough to have words from which to choose.

A letter composed of nothing but short sentences and commands is strident. Even if you are reminding a supplier of material three months overdue, you are better off composing a polite letter with a realistic threat attached than an impolitic letter with a vicious threat attached.

Speak softly, whether in person or in writing, even to your enemies. Your lawyers are carrying the big sticks.

Avoiding writing errors

Writing clearly requires that you eliminate the mistakes that threaten clarity. The first mistake is thinking that writing is no more than transcribed speech. It isn't. When we are talking in person or on the telephone, we rely on the context of conversation to fill in gaps and to compensate for being ungrammatical. That context is absent when writing, so the good writer makes sure that her writing is clear, grammatically correct, and to the point.

Once you acknowledge that writing is different than talking, it is important to eliminate the errors to which every writer is prone. Here they are:

- ✔ Spelling errors
- ✔ Grammatical errors
- ✔ Punctuation errors
- ✔ Disorganization
- ✔ Passive voice
- ✔ Overstatement
- ✔ Excess verbiage

If you recognize these sins, good. If not, take the time to learn about them.

Spelling errors

Believe it or not, spelling errors can doom business relations. It may be hard to believe, but clients notice when your letters aren't proofread.

A vice president of sales for an agricultural products company promoted a salesperson who handled regional accounts, mostly face to face, to the national division. Suddenly, her division started losing clients. He inquired after the matter with one of those clients, who told him that his new salesperson's letters and contracts contained numerous spelling and grammar errors. The client noted that running the letter through a spell check program was quick and easy, and that, surely, there were others who could proofread her work. If this attention to detail was unimportant to the salesperson, other details may be equally unimportant but much more damaging to his company. The vice president spoke to the salesperson, who explained that she had not done much writing in her former position. The company paid for her to take a business writing course. She is again a top salesperson.

Many spelling errors are easily remedied by running your document through your computer's spell check. But beware! Spell checkers don't catch all of the spelling errors that can creep into a document. The following poem goes through the spell check program on my computer (We won't say which word processor this is!) without setting off any alarms:

Eye halve a spelling chequer

It came with my pea sea

It plainly marks four my revue

Miss steaks eye kin knot sea.

Eye strike a key and type a word

And weight it four it two say

Whether eye am wrong oar write

It shows me strait a weigh.

Eye have run this poem threw it

I am shore your pleased two no

Its letter perfect awl the weigh

My chequer tolled me sew.

A trained eye is still better than the spell checker program.

Grammatical errors

Most people are bored to tears with grammar, and with good reason — it *is* boring! However, knowing your grammar is a necessary skill for composing effective business letters, e-mail, and memoranda. Repeatedly making grammatical errors instantly brands you as poorly educated and careless.

An attorney received a letter from an opposing lawyer. In two pages, the letter contained more than half a dozen grammatical errors. She didn't know the attorney in question, but she immediately concluded that he would not be an impressive opponent. Why? Since he hadn't corrected the grammatical errors in his letter, he probably wouldn't care enough to scrupulously review the particulars of the case. She was right — the lawyer in question failed to investigate the case fully and lost the case on the basis of that failure!

Of course, not everyone knows enough about grammar to make that kind of snap judgment. But *some* people do, and you never know ahead of time whether the person you're writing to is a grammar freak or a grammar know-nothing.

Bad grammar leaves a bad impression.

So you slept through your grade school grammar and your major in college required that you only take multiple choice exams, and in graduate school everyone was wowed by your fabulous technical expertise. Now you sweat bullets every time you have to compose a letter. Not to worry! Here are some of the most common grammatical errors and how to correct them:

Frequently misused words

The things people say by using the wrong word is a constant source of amusement. We've all seen David Letterman and Jay Leno parody advertisements that inadvertently say hilariously wrong things. Some words, though not all that funny, are frequently misused. Here are some of them:

- *Its, it's.* 'Its' is a possessive — 'The knife lost its edge.' 'It's' is the contraction for 'it is' — 'It's no surprise that Jim lost his job.'

- *There, they're,* and *their.* 'There' is variously an adverb, a noun, and an adjective — 'Stand over there' (adverb); 'You can take it from there' (noun); 'That woman there is the culprit' (adjective)

  'They're' is the contraction of 'they are' — 'They're at lunch.'

  'Their' is a possessive — 'Their jobs are on the line.'

- *Regardless, irregardless.* 'Regardless' is a word; 'irregardless' is not.

- *That, which.* 'Which' is often incorrectly used. Practice 'which' hunting. 'Which' introduces a parenthetical phrase within a sentence that can be removed without affecting the sentence's meaning — 'The

job, *which* we advertised in last week's paper, is in public relations.' If you can't remove the phrase without losing the meaning of the sentence, then use 'that' — 'The job *that* we advertised in last week's paper is in public relations.' In the first sentence, the main point is that the job is in public relations; the information about the paper is simply additional. The second sentence means the job we advertised in last week's paper was in public relations. All of the information is important.

- *Your, you're.* 'Your' is a possessive — 'Your clothes are ready.' 'You're' is the contraction of 'you are' — 'You're late.'

- *Are, our.* 'Are' is a verb — 'You are good.' 'Our' is a possessive — 'Our game has been called off.'

- *Can, may.* 'Can' expresses ability — 'I can do that.' 'May' expresses permission — 'You may leave early this afternoon.'

- *Less, fewer.* 'Less' is used to modify nouns that cannot be counted — 'There is less water in this glass.' 'Fewer' is used for things that can be counted — 'There are fewer jelly beans now.'

Subject/verb agreement

If the subject of the sentence is singular, then so is the verb; if the subject is plural, so is the verb. This is true even if there are intervening words between the subject and the verb.

Mistake: The job description — a full-time shipper in a variety of small business settings — are not detailed enough.

Better: The job description — a full-time shipper in a variety of small business settings — is not detailed enough.

The subject is the job description, not the business settings.

Subjects such as *everyone, everybody, neither, nobody, someone,* each take a singular verb.

Mistake: Everyone has their own idea.

Better: Everyone has his or her own idea. *or* Everyone has an idea. *or* We all have our own ideas.

Mistake: Neither Tom nor Judy are here.

Better: Neither Tom nor Judy is here.

Verb tense agreement

The tense of the verb (present, past, future) should remain constant in a paragraph unless it is clear why it isn't.

Mistake: In your letter of complaint, you *mention* three instances of poor service. These were (1) that our receptionist *is* rude to you; (2) that our shipping department *failed* to notify you that your order had not gone out as promised; and (3) that our customer service representative *had never* returned your calls.

Better: In your letter of complaint, you *mentioned* three instances of poor service. These were (1) that our receptionist *was* rude to you; (2) that our shipping department *failed* to notify you about your order; and (3) that our customer service representative *failed* to return your calls.

Sentence fragments

A sentence is a complete thought that must have a subject and a predicate phrase including a verb. Sentences that lack either subjects or predicates are sentence fragments.

Mistake: We are unwilling to take subsequent action. While we acknowledge your concerns.

Better: We are unwilling to take subsequent action, even though we acknowledge your concerns.

Run-on sentences

Run-on sentences include too much for a single sentence:

Mistake: Mr. Weaver informed us that his Tonka truck was irreparable but that he didn't want to trade it for a similar toy, instead he wanted to get a cash refund so that he could buy his son a different toy which we disagreed with and so refused his suggestion.

Better: Mr. Weaver informed us that his Tonka truck was irreparable. However, he didn't want to trade it for a similar toy, preferring instead to get a cash refund so that he could buy his son a different toy. We disagreed with Mr. Weaver and refused to accede to his demand.

Dangling modifiers

Modifiers are sentence clauses that modify or affect the subject of the sentence. Modifiers dangle when what they modify is unclear. The results are often quite funny. The following was written by a man in a description of an ad campaign being considered by his company:

Mistake: Numerous times, I sat in my living room and watched June Cleaver vacuum and dust while wearing a dress, high heels, and pearls.

The clause "while wearing a dress, high heels, and pearls" is meant to modify "June Cleaver." However, it actually modifies the author!

Better: Numerous times, I sat in my living room and watched June Cleaver vacuum and dust while she wore a dress, high heels, and pearls.

Punctuation errors

Punctuation errors are among the most common writing errors. They make your correspondence look unprofessional.

Here, then, is a brief refresher course on punctuation.

The *comma* marks a pause, sets off parenthetical material, separates main clauses in a compound sentence, or follows introductory expressions.

Mistake: If you're going to buy a camera you should get a flash.

Better: If you are going to buy a camera, you should get a flash.

Mistake: If you're going to buy this camera which is not good in low-light situations you might also consider a flash.

Better: If you're going to buy this camera, which is not good in low-light situations, you might also consider a flash.

Mistake: You are going to buy this camera although I think you should also buy the flash.

Better: You are going to buy this camera, although I think you should also buy the flash.

Mistake: For heaven's sake; if you are going to buy this camera you must buy the flash.

Better: For heavens sake, if you are going to buy this camera, you must buy the flash.

Of course, good writers can correctly use commas in an intimidating fashion. I recall a sentence in an article written by a professor that contained nine words and seven commas, all of them correctly used!

The *period* ends a sentence.

Mistake: Please consider our proposal, we think you will agree that our service has overwhelming advantages.

Better: Please consider our proposal. We think you will agree that our service has overwhelming advantages.

The *semicolon* marks the end of a thought to which the next thought is intimately linked, or punctuates lists that are longer than three items.

Mistake: When using our product, care is required, without proper care, all warranties are null and void.

Better: When using our product, care is required; without proper care, all warranties are null and void.

Mistake: When using our product, care is required, first, open the cap carefully, Second, avoid all skin contact, Third, use in well-ventilated room, Fourth; throw rags or brushes contaminated by our product away.

Better: When using our product, care is required: first, open the cap carefully; second, avoid all skin contact; third, use in well-ventilated room; fourth, throw rags or brushes contaminated by our product away.

The *colon* marks the break between a sentence and a list that follows. Look at the last example for an example of a properly used colon. The colon is not used in lieu of a period, a comma, or a semicolon.

The *dash* takes the place of commas (when offsetting a parenthetical remark), periods (when the succeeding sentence has the same subject), and colons (when the material following the dash expands on something before the dash). The dash is more informal than any of the punctuation marks it replaces. When used sparingly, it can be an effective tool.

Mistake: Tom who never said a mean thing about anyone admitted to thinking that Terry was vicious.

Better: Tom — who never said a mean thing about anyone — admitted to thinking that Terry was vicious.

Mistake: The term is two years, it can be longer if requested.

Better: The term is two years — it can be longer, if requested.

Mistake: We are proud to introduce new products, a golf ball cleaner, two new styles of spikes, the Big Ben at a new, low, price, and titanium drivers specially designed for left-handed players.

Better: We are proud to introduce new products — a golf ball cleaner; two new styles of spikes; the Big Ben at a new, low price; and titanium drivers specially designed for left-handed players.

The *apostrophe* forms a possessive or a contraction, not plurals.

Mistake: Toms shoe's are brand new.

Better: Tom's shoes are brand new.

Mistake: Your too much!

Better: You're too much!

Except in rare instances ("Jesus" and other names, "conscience" and a few other words), even words that end in -s have apostrophes added.

Mistake: Is that Charles' report?

Better: Is that Charles's report?

What do you do with plural words that you want to form a possessive for? You add an apostrophe but no additional *s*.

Mistake: The teams's managers met in Boston last week

Example: The teams' managers met in Boston last week

Disorganization

Since words are organized into sentences, and sentences into paragraphs, and paragraphs into the finished product, start with your sentences. Make sure that they are grammatically correct and that they say what you want them to say — and don't say anything that you don't want them to say.

Paragraphs composed of nothing but grammatically correct sentences are a good start. But your paragraphs need also to be organized. Typically, the most important sentence is the *topic sentence,* in which you identify what will be discussed in that paragraph. The balance of the paragraph is devoted to articulating, defending, explaining, or describing what you announce in your topic sentence.

Mistake: There is a golf course nearby and the pumps were plugged in at the time of the house inspection. Mr. Oily informs me that he did not mislead you about the need for sump pumps on the property. We are not really sure what this litigation is about. Mr. Oily put the pumps in after spring rains one year and did not conceal this fact during the inspection.

Better: We are not sure what this litigation concerns. First, Mr. Oily did not mislead you about the need for sump pumps on the property. Mr. Oily put the pumps in and disclosed this at the time of the house inspection. Moreover, they were running at the time of the inspection. Furthermore, the golf course is clearly visible from the property.

The first paragraph meanders through events not obviously connected. The second paragraph starts with a topic sentence that tells you exactly what will happen. The other sentences defend the claim made in the topic sentence.

Passive voice

Passive voice is diagnosed easily: When the subject of the sentence is no longer the actor who does things, you have passive voice. Look at the difference between these two sentences, which "say" the same thing:

Mistake: We were told by the director that our scene would not be shot because we were likely to be hit with rain before the afternoon was through.

Better: The director told us that the forecast for rain would probably scuttle our shoot.

The first sentence is in passive voice, the second is in active voice. The first sentence implies that no one is responsible — things just happen.

Excess verbiage

Bad writers use more words than are needed. Good writers don't — they know what words will convey their message efficiently. You improve your writing immediately by eliminating verbiage.

Verbiage is like a jungle: too much lushness and you can't see the sky.

Mistake: Due to the fact that any and all persons who had relations in connection with the re-organization of the hospital have experienced the move that human resources has had to make to the west wing owing to their downsizing, it is perhaps to be expected that some procedures have suffered.

Better: Human Resources' move to the west wing has caused some procedural problems.

Chop! Chop! Chop! Out of the suffocating verbal vines emerges one clear sentence.

Writing Business Correspondence

A letter is still the single most important form of communication in business. It is less ambiguous than a meeting simply because no one has to rely on memory to fix what occurred — there, in black and white, is what you said. That's why important business decisions are formalized in a letter.

Since correspondence is so crucial, it is in your self-interest to make a good impression with it. Whether it's a job offer letter, a job rejection letter, a daily memorandum, or a stock offering, make sure that your prose is clean and direct, that your points are clearly made, that you have a coherent structure, and that you use good paper and a high-quality printer.

Business letters

A business letter is planned, composed, revised, edited, edited again, and, finally, typed. Your letters should be flawless all of the time. That means that you don't simply dash them off. No, you plan the letter, making an outline of the points it is to contain. You compose the letter carefully, making sure that your grammar and style are consistent throughout. You revise and edit until it shines. And *then* you sign it.

Most business letters are written with the intention to get the reader to respond in some way. Given that goal, your writing should be efficient, clear, error-free, friendly, and pertinent.

When composing business letters, keep the following in mind:

- ✔ Use high-quality paper with at least 25% cotton rag content.
- ✔ Never send a letter written in anger unless you've waited 24 hours to review it.

- ✔ Plan your correspondence before writing it — know what you want to say and in what order you want to say it.

- ✔ Compose your correspondence after planning it — use direct, active language, vary your sentence structure, adopt a moderate, friendly, tone, and give clear directions.

- ✔ Revise the letter after it has been written to take account of any new information.

- ✔ Edit the letter for spelling, grammar, style, tone, and content.

- ✔ Edit again.

The form of a business letter is standardized. All business letters have:

- ✔ Dateline — three to six lines beneath the letterhead, flush left or hard right. The dateline contains the month, fully spelled out, the day, and the year.

- ✔ Reference line — one or two lines beneath the dateline, flush left, and repeated on each additional page. The reference line contains case or file numbers or policy numbers.

- ✔ Recipient address — three to six lines beneath the dateline, flush left. The recipient address is composed of:

  - • Addressee's courtesy title and full name. Courtesy titles in business are *Mr., Ms.,* and *Dr.* See next section for table of proper use of titles. Spell names out completely.

  - • Addressee's business title. This appears on the next line beneath name.

  - • Business name. This appears on the next line beneath business title. Spell it *exactly* as it is on *their* letterhead. If they abbreviate "Company" to "Co.", then you do, too.

  - • Street address. This appears on the next line beneath business name. Spelling numbers out is no longer necessary, unless confusion results — "1745 26th Street" is just fine.

- ✔ Greeting or Salutation — one or two lines beneath the last line of recipient's address. Usually, it is "Dear Ms. (Mr., Dr.) followed by a colon:

  Dear Dr. Jones:

  Dear Ms. Smith:

If you use first names in person, then you may do so in your salutation.

A comma is used in the greeting in personal letters; a colon is used in business letters.

✔ The body of the letter — one line beneath the greeting. The body of the letter contains whatever you have to say in the letter. Be polite and courteous, but don't be a windbag. Pay attention to the tips already provided.

✔ Complimentary close and signature — two lines beneath the last line of the body of the letter, flush left or centered. All of the following are appropriate in business letters where the addressee is unknown to you:

> Yours truly, Very truly yours, Yours very truly
> Sincerely, Yours sincerely, Sincerely yours

If you know the addressee by first name, the following can be used:

> All the best, Best wishes, All best wishes, Regards, Kind regards, Kindest regards

Immediately below your complimentary close you hand-write your signature, full name if the addressee is unknown to you, first name only if you're on a first name basis.

Immediately below your signature you type your signature, with whatever complimentary and academic/professional degrees and ratings you like to see following your name.

✔ Final notations — two lines beneath your typed signature appear any final notations. If, for example, the letter is typed by someone other than yourself, that person's initials appear here. If you are enclosing something with the letter, you may type the notation "enclosure" or "encl." If you are sending copies of the letter to someone else you may type "cc:" and the alphabetically listed names of those receiving the letter.

Memoranda

"Memorandum" is singular; "memoranda" is plural. If your Latin is weak, try "memo" or "memos". Memos are written communications within companies or within units within companies. Memos typically make announcements, discuss procedures, report on company activities, and disseminate employee information. They're informal and public. If you have something confidential to communicate, don't do it in a memo.

An employee in a start-up Internet company was experiencing frustration with her boss's erratic schedule. Rather than discuss it privately, she wrote a nasty memo to the CEO. The CEO posted the memo in the coffee room, alienated the new employee from her co-workers, who supported the company's founder despite her unconventional working hours.

The tone of memos is usually informal and friendly. Although there is no need to be curt, officious, or patronizing, a certain succinctness is acceptable. Structure the memo so that the most important information comes in the first paragraph and that subsequent paragraphs spell out what is discussed in the first paragraph.

All memos are structured similarly. They have:

- ✔ An addressee — flush left, in capital letters, near the top of the page
- ✔ The sender — flush left, in caps, immediately below the addressee
- ✔ Date — flush left, in caps, immediately below the sender
- ✔ Subject — flush left, in caps, immediately below the date

Some people appear to think that the world can never have enough memos and stuff others' mailboxes to overflowing with them. Remember that everyone is busy and has a job to do. Other people appear to think that memos, since they are public, are effective management tools. While memos are effective for direction and suggestion, criticism and praise are best given in person. If you must use a memo to criticize, make sure that the criticism is not of the person but of the performance.

Handling Formal Correspondence and Forms of Address

You will at some point have the opportunity to host social business events, to respond to an invitation, or to announce something for the business.

Invitations

Include every bit of information that is required for the invitee to decide whether to accept or decline the invitation. Make sure that everyone who should be invited is invited. That means, among other things, consulting with all of the department heads and other relevant people about their guest lists.

Although casual invitations are often extended by telephone, more formal or larger events call for written invitations. Whether in person or in writing, here's a checklist to guarantee that you include what you need to on the invitation:

- ✔ **Who is the function's host?** Having an executive name him or herself as host gives the invitee a person to contact and thank.
- ✔ **What is the function?** The nature of the event should be explicit.

✔ **Where is the function?** The place where the function will be held and the phone number of the host is listed near the bottom of the invitation.

✔ **When is the function?** The time that the function will begin is listed. If it's a cocktail party, the time that the party will end is also listed.

✔ **Will there be food?** If there will be a sit-down dinner, the invitation should say "Dinner." "Cocktails" on an invitation means that there will be hors d'ouevres but no more. "Buffet Supper" means that there will be something more substantial than hors d'ouevres but less substantial than dinner. "Cocktail Buffet" means that there will be something more substantial than hors d'ouevres but less substantial than a buffet supper.

✔ **Will there be dancing?** If there will be dancing, say so.

✔ **Are sports involved?** If there will be volleyball, basketball, swimming, hang-gliding, or golf, say so.

✔ **What is the expected dress?** The style of dress for the event should be specified. "Formal" or "Black Tie" means tuxedos; "Business Dress" means suit and tie; "Informal" and "Casual Dress" both mean business casual.

✔ **How should invitees reply?** If a reply is requested, the letters "RSVP" usually occur near the bottom of the invitation. If you see "Regrets Only," that means that you do not have to respond if you *are* going, but do have to respond if you are *not* going.

"RSVP" and "Regrets Only" are not the same thing! "RSVP" means *respondez-vous, s'il vous plait* — please respond. Whether you are going or not going, you respond. This is considerate to the host, who will incur expenses securing food and drink for the number of people they expect.

Thank you notes

Thank you notes are sent to the host of a function within a day or two after the function. They are short, gracious, and on point. They're not for discussing business or bringing the host up to speed about your family life.

Thanking people for something usually follows the form in which the invitation was extended. If you receive a telephone invitation, a telephone thank you is appropriate, although a thank you note is a nice touch. If you receive a written invitation, then you should write a thank you note.

Thank you notes are not reserved for parties and dinners. The general rule is this: if someone goes the extra mile for you, then a thank you note is appropriate; if it is just day-to-day business, a verbal "thank you" is good enough. Thank you notes are always appropriate for gifts you've received.

When you write a thank-you note, remember to do the following:

- Thank the person for the gift.
- Recognize the effort that went into giving the gift.
- Tell the person how the gift will be used.

Announcements

Businesses on occasion make public announcements of important events, such as a move, a significant new hire or promotion, a meeting, or a significant death. If you are asked to compose such an announcement, there are three things to keep in mind.

- First, keep it simple.
- Second, get to the point immediately.
- Third, print announcements on correspondence cards, not letterhead.

Corporate and executive stationery

Every corporate and executive office has a variety of stationery in its drawers. Each has its function. But all of it shares some characteristics. First, the paper should be of high quality. Paper for business letters should contain some rag cotton content, typically about 25%. When you're at the paper store, you can determine the rag content by looking at the box the paper comes from. You will also want paper that is watermarked, and you can determine whether the paper has a watermark by holding a piece of it up to the light — you will be able to see the watermark embossed on the paper.

Second, the stationery should be uniform in color, weight, and letterhead across sizes. Your company needs an identity, and one of the ways that you establish your identity is through your stationery. Having one type font for your letterhead and another for your monarch sheets makes your corporate identity look uncertain.

Here are a few more guidelines:

- Don't skimp! Stationery is an essential part of your corporate identity.
- Quality usually trumps gimmicky color, shape, and design.

Here's what goes in the stationery drawer:

Corporate letterhead

8½" x 11", high rag content, with the following relevant information printed on it:

- ✔ Business name
- ✔ Business address
- ✔ Business telephone number
- ✔ Business fax number
- ✔ Business e-mail or Web-page, if appropriate

Businesses that are partnerships, such as law firms and group medical practices, typically list all of the partners or members on the letterhead.

Envelopes are printed with the company name and address.

Plain sheets of paper

8½" x 11", same quality as corporate letterhead. This paper is for letters longer than a page (second and subsequent pages are not presented on letterhead).

Monarch paper

7¼" x 10½", high rag content. Used for personal business letters. They are printed with the following information on the letterhead:

- ✔ Person's name, but not the company's name
- ✔ Business address

If monarch sheets are used as corporate letterhead (as is sometimes done by consultants, physicians, and attorneys), include business name.

Envelopes are printed with the person's name and business address.

Correspondence cards

Small, typically 4½" x 6½", nonfoldable cards for personal messages, announcements, and thank you notes. They have the following information only:

- ✔ Person's name, not business name
- ✔ Business address

Envelopes are printed with the person's name and business address.

You may also use a fold-over card of the same size. These are sometimes called an "informal" and may have a logo on the front.

Business cards

Generally 3½" x 2", although other sizes are increasingly seen in certain businesses. The business card is presented to others at business functions. The card should contain the following information:

- ✔ Person's name and title
- ✔ Business name
- ✔ Business address
- ✔ Business telephone number
- ✔ Business e-mail address
- ✔ Business fax number
- ✔ Business Web page address

Your company logo may be incorporated into the design of the business card. You may also include a brief description or motto of your business.

While some prefer to leave the back of the card blank, you may print additional information about your company on the reverse of the card.

Chapter 9

Navigating the New Cyber-Rules

• •

In This Chapter

▶ Traveling with electronic tools

▶ Communicating around the clock

▶ Having great etiquette on the Internet

▶ Understanding the rules for pagers, laptops, and palm organizers

▶ Using fax machines

▶ Guarding information

• •

*N*ew technology has turned business on its ear — and created a whole new set of etiquette conundrums. Pagers, cell phones, e-mail, and countless other time-saving devices save us time, but they also contribute to the ever more hectic pace of life and work. In this new environment, where everyone is trying to fit more activity into less time, misunderstandings about etiquette are bound to arise. But though Emily Post didn't know anything about e-mail, she did know that the essence of etiquette is to put others at ease. That's at the basis of the rules you'll read about in this section. Also be sure to review Chapter 7, "Minding Your Telephone Manners."

Traveling Gracefully with Your Electronic Tools

If you're like many professionals today, you own several beeping, blinking, plastic-encased gadgets that keep you connected to work, home, and all the information you need while you're on the road. It's not uncommon these days for busy people to carry a phone, pager, laptop, and handheld computer all at one time. While these tools may be useful, they can also contribute to a cluttered, disorganized — and therefore unprofessional — look. Women usually stuff their numerous devices into a purse or tote that, when slung over one shoulder, ruins their posture and causes back and neck problems. Men, on the other hand, tend to clip these black plastic boxes on their belts, resulting in unsightly bulges under a suit jacket, not to mention a certain nerdiness.

How to survive without these tools? One option is to consolidate gadgetry. Many cell phone/pager combinations are now available, and more are sure to come. Most cell phones also store at least a few key phone numbers so that you can leave your calendar/e-mail/memos gadget behind in many situations. And new combo phone-organizers are on the way.

As long as you're leaving things behind, go all out. Do you really need your cell phone at every meeting or meal? You shouldn't be accepting calls at these times, anyway, and you can surely excuse yourself and find a land line if you really need to make a call. Your laptop probably isn't necessary in most situations, either. Leave it in the car or back at the office, and you'll project a more polished appearance. As an added bonus, you won't have to worry about leaving it at the restaurant or in a taxi.

If you must carry everything with you, try to keep it all in one place. A briefcase in leather (or nylon for more casual environments) works nicely. For women, a purse will do, as long as it is reasonably sized and isn't so heavy it makes you stand or walk with a slouch.

When traveling:

- If you're carrying a laptop computer, try placing your bag on a wheeled carrier to get through the airport instead of carrying it in hand or over your shoulder. Specially designed laptop bags also work well, and some of them can be converted to a regular briefcase for tomorrow's meeting.

- Airport security officials may ask you to turn off your laptop, pager, or other device. Comply pleasantly with their requests. After all, they're just doing their job, which is to keep YOU safe!

- When the flight attendant tells you to turn off all electronic devices, do it. Your electronics could interfere with the plane's communications, jeopardizing a safe takeoff or landing. How will you explain to CNN that checking your voice mail was more important than the lives of your fellow travelers?

- Never talk on a cell phone while the flight attendant reviews safety information. In fact, you shouldn't talk at all during this presentation. While you may be a seasoned traveler, other passengers may need to hear this potentially life-saving information.

- If you're using your laptop on the plane, watch your elbows, especially if you're in the dreaded middle seat. If your typing causes you to intrude on other passengers' precious personal space, don't type. You won't be able to get much done while they're glaring at you, anyway.

'Round-the-Clock Communications

In the old days, workers in the vast majority of professions had very predictable work hours. Most professionals worked from 8 or 9 o'clock in the morning until 5 or 6 p.m., and any incomplete work waited until the next day. People took lunch breaks every day. When Mr. Threemartini was out for the afternoon, there was generally no reaching him unless the situation was urgent. He would return calls the next morning when he arrived at the office to find a stack of pink phone messages.

How things have changed! Many people check messages or e-mail before leaving home in the morning. To save time, people often eat lunch at their desks, or even in the car as they run noontime errands.

In some offices where non-stop work is valued, late-night e-mails are a badge of honor. Colleagues who send e-mails at 2:00, 3:00, 4:00 a.m. may be insomniacs or new parents, but they are obviously more dedicated than you are. In the old days, your boss might have a great idea in the middle of the night, but she would have to wait until you arrived in the office the next morning to tell you about it. Today, she can e-mail you her great idea and several associated assignments while you sleep. As a result, you may leave the office one evening feeling caught up and competent, only to face a barrage of new e-mails at 8:00 a.m. the next morning.

A senior executive at a large corporation, someone who relished having the last word, was infamous for his middle-of-the-night e-mails. Any work that was finished by the evening on one day would be greeted the next day with responses like, "I've come up with another angle that you forgot," resulting in that never-quite-caught-up feeling among employees. At first, his colleagues were concerned about his obvious trouble sleeping. Soon, however, they were too busy with job interviews at other companies to pay much attention.

In such an environment, it's important for all of us to be a bit flexible in understanding the needs and priorities of our colleagues. If you're the boss, don't expect your 3 a.m. e-mail to have been read by the 8 a.m. staff meetings. If you're the employee, be aware of your boss's idiosyncrasies and learn to anticipate them, even if you'll never love them. If you're in either position, don't page someone after hours unless it's an absolute emergency or you have discussed it in advance. ("Page me when you get those numbers, Smithee, and I'll call you from the Prime Minister's dinner party.")

🖌 If you're seized by a fit of creativity in the middle of the night, read your e-mails again the next morning before sending them. Your idea (not to mention your level of coherence) may look different in the light of day.

✔ Don't practice voice mail avoidance by returning all your calls at odd hours. If someone has left a message for you requesting specific information, it's fine to leave a specific answer late at night. If someone needs to talk to you, however, don't return the call at 10 p.m. and then insist smugly that you have done your part. You're not fooling anyone.

✔ If you send an e-mail that needs an immediate response, call to warn the recipient. Better yet, plan ahead to avoid the rush altogether.

Civility with the Internet

Some observers of the "new economy" believe that the Internet has been a great democratizer, because it has made great volumes of information available to everyone with a computer and a modem. It's true enough that people who have never left Flapjack, Idaho can now take virtual tours of the Louvre. It's also true that the world is made up of two kinds of people: those who know how to use the Internet with élan, and those who don't.

First and foremost, keep in mind that a business Internet account is for business. Even if it seems that "everyone's doing it," resist the temptation to shop for shoes online during that interminable conference call. Some employers may allow you to use your Internet account for personal use during breaks or lunch hours, but ask first.

Even if you don't find the ethics compelling, be aware that many employers monitor employee Internet use. Find out if your company has an official policy on Internet use, and be sure to follow it carefully. After all, wouldn't it be embarrassing to explain that you were fired because of "hampsterdance.com"?

Of course, it goes without saying that there is NO excuse for viewing — ahem — "adult" Web sites while at the office, even if it's after hours and you're the only one there! Despite the uproar about children discovering inappropriate Web content, it's not easy to happen upon hours of dirty pictures by accident. And with the current legal climate around sexual harassment in the workplace, most employers have a "zero tolerance" policy for this kind of behavior.

A LAN administrator at a large company came into the office one weekend to install some software on his department's computers. While sitting at the desk of an attractive female coworker, he took a detour into the seamy side of the Web. Unbeknownst to him, a security camera was taking it all in (don't ask us for the details). When his colleague arrived at work on Monday to several messages encouraging her to submit erotic photos of herself, it didn't take long to figure out what had happened. Sadly, this man lost his job — and what would have been a good recommendation for another job — over a stupid mistake.

As you are navigating Internet or Intranet sites at work, you are bound to run into a problem here or there with obsolete links, error messages, or outdated information. Some sites overtly solicit your information with "Contact Us" or "Feedback" links on a page. Your feedback is important, but remember that a real person will be reading your e-mail. That means saying something like, "As a frequent user of your site, I find this problem frustrating"; rather than the slacker-like "Your site is lame and your company blows!" The ruder and less rational your feedback, the more likely that the webmaster will dismiss it as the ravings of a lunatic shut-in.

The same courtesy applies if you are in charge of a site's content or design. Out of respect for your users, you should make sure content is accurate, timely, and updated whenever necessary. The site's design should make it easy for users to find what they need. And don't forget that not every surfer has your state-of-the-art setup — if you must use intensive graphics and animation, also offer a low-graphics version for the technology have-nots.

E-Mail Etiquette

A couple of years ago, e-mail surpassed postal mail as the highest-volume carrier of messages. Its popularity has been booming ever since, and it shows no signs of stopping. Though volumes have been written about the etiquette of communicating through this new medium, many of the worst offenders don't seem to be listening. Are you one of them? This section outlines some of the pitfalls of instantaneous communication.

The best feature of e-mail is also the worst — communication with one or many people, across the hall or across the world, can happen immediately. That can be a tremendous asset when you need that kind of power. It can also be a real problem when it is used as a substitute for thoughtful, meaningful communications.

One problem with over-using e-mail is that tone can easily be misunderstood. In person or on the phone, listeners can easily get visual or verbal clues emotion and nuances, particularly sarcasm. Even in the age of irony, and even if you use the ubiquitous "smiley face," readers may miss your point entirely. For example, "I heard Thursday's staff meeting went really well!" has a completely different meaning spoken in a sarcastic tone (the meeting didn't go well at all) than it does spoken in a happy, direct tone. Chances are good that your readers will misunderstand this statement in an e-mail.

In a conversation, people often ask clarifying questions. For example:

"Did you send that report to Steve?"

"Steve Ferrill?"

"No, Steve Peterson. He wanted me to add some information about SLAs."

"Well, I sent it to Steve Ferrill. What's an LSA?"

It's easy to see how, in an e-mail about "Steve" and "SLAs," both parties could easily end up confused. That's why it's best to re-read your e-mail for clarity and maybe follow up with a phone call if you don't get a prompt response.

Here are a few stylistic mistakes that people make when using e-mail:

- Forgetting the rules of spelling and grammar. Perhaps because of the sheer volume of e-mails we send, they tend to be a very informal medium. Informality, however, does not mean sloppiness. Watch for:

  - Sentence fragments. Bullet points are acceptable, even encouraged, to make a message easy to read. Sentence fragments — sentences that do not contain both a subject and a verb — are not.

  - Spelling errors. If you're not a good speller, use the spell checker that comes with your e-mail package.

  - If you're not sure about the rules of grammar, read Chapter 8, and purchase a style manual, such as *The Elements of Style*.

- Omitting a greeting and/or closing. Is it really that hard to type, "Hi Charlene" or "Best wishes, Biff"?

- Using ALL CAPITALS. For one, capitals are harder to read than regular text. In addition, many people view their use as the e-mail equivalent of yelling — so if you wouldn't scream it in the conference room, don't write it in all capitals. Yes, it may be easier to type this way, but you're not afraid of a little hard work, are you?

- Using all lowercase letters. Are you e.e. cummings? If not, proper nouns, names, and the first letter of each sentence should be capitalized.

- Cursing. Though you should watch your language at work in general, spoken expletives immediately float away into the air. Written ones sit there on the computer screen, maybe for longer than you want them to.

- Sending a message to too many people. Does everyone on your project team need to see the details of setting up a conference room for next Thursday? No. Once you have completed the legwork with the person or people who are really affected, you can notify others with a single message.

✔ Using "Reply All" or a similar function instead of "Reply to Sender." If your manager sends out a message thanking everyone on the team for great work on the project, don't respond to the entire group telling her that it was your pleasure and that she's a great leader. Your colleagues will savagely delete your irrelevant e-mail, and your reputation as an obsequious twit will be confirmed.

✔ Also double-check the list of recipients for your e-mail — especially if it says something potentially negative. A PR executive once received a particularly irritating e-mail from a despised colleague. The executive forwarded the note with her sarcastic commentary to a friend, or so she thought. In fact, she had hit the "reply" button and sent the e-mail right back to her nemesis. Imagine the humiliation when she had to apologize!

Some other e-mail annoyances are simply the result of taking too little time to think. They include

✔ Forwarding a long chain of e-mails around and around. If the information in past messages isn't really necessary, delete it. If it could be useful, keep it in, but provide a brief summary at the beginning of your message filling readers in on the highlights.

✔ Forwarding a long chain of e-mails without changing the original subject line. This results in subjects like "FW: FW: RE: FW: RE: Our Meeting". No wonder people aren't reading your messages; if they can't figure out right away what the message is about, they may set it aside "for later" when they have more time to decipher it. "Later" is often "never." Instead, come up with a specific title, like "Response Needed — Scheduling Questions for June 15 Meeting." If people still don't respond, at least you'll have the satisfaction of knowing that they realize exactly what they're missing

✔ E-mailing someone who sits across the aisle from you. If you're recapping a meeting, it's fine. But if you have a question for discussion, try the old-fashioned approach of speaking to each other.

✔ Sending and receiving personal e-mail from work. First, the equipment and Internet time belong to your company, so it's probably a violation of your company's policy. And, while we know you would never send anything potentially offensive or harassing, it could be equally damaging to receive such material from a friend.

There are a number options for setting up a free, Web-based e-mail box, such as `www.hotmail.com`, `www.yahoo.com`, and many others. These mailboxes allow you to retrieve e-mail from any pc — whether at work, at home, or on the road. While we still don't advocate that you retrieve personal e-mail at work, this is the cleanest option for doing so.

Still other e-mail faux pas are a result of, well, — we hate to say dim-wittedness, so let's call it a misplaced sense of camaraderie.

✔ While everyone loves a good joke, the novelty has worn off of Internet "humor." Long lists of "You Must Be a Texan If," "Why I'm Glad I'm Not a Woman," "You Were a Child of the 80s If . . .", and so on, are strictly off limits at work. Your friends probably don't want to see them again, either.

✔ The same goes for exhortations to save the rainforest, warnings about new kinds of cancer, and pleas to send greeting cards to 10-year-old cancer victims. While virus warnings can sometimes be helpful, the vast majority of them turn out to be scams. Delete those e-mails and check a reputable virus information Web site for the real scoop.

✔ Don't even get us started on chain letters. Suffice it to say that

- You will not win a million dollars if you forward a chain letter.

- You will not be mired in bad luck if you don't forward a chain letter.

- Your friends — and especially your colleagues — will not think better of you just because you forward an e-mail about love and friendship to everyone you know.

- Bill Gates will not send $500 to everyone who forwards this e-mail.

Phew! Is there anything else that can go wrong with e-mail?

Well, yes.

E-mail is a great tool for venting your spleen. Unfortunately, you shouldn't do it at work.

✔ Don't use e-mail to lambaste a colleague, and especially don't copy others on the message. That's tantamount to chewing someone out in front of a room full of his peers. Disagreements or discipline are best handled in person, or at least over the phone.

✔ If you receive a scathing e-mail, resist the urge to write a similarly scathing message in return. Take the high road. Offer the olive branch. Or, at the very least, distract the other person by making him wonder why you haven't responded.

✔ Never, ever write something in an e-mail that you wouldn't want published in the newspaper. Even if you send them to someone you trust, e-mails with sensitive, mean, or potentially embarrassing information have a way of being forwarded beyond your original audience.

E-mail is a great solution for:

- ✔ Preparing a group of people for a meeting. "Thank you for making time to attend Wednesday's board meeting. Before we meet, please review the attached articles about Attention Deficit Disorder in adults and be ready to discuss them."

- ✔ Setting up meetings. "Possible dates for our retreat include July 10, July 11, and July 15. Please let me know which dates work for you."

- ✔ Recapping spoken conversations. "As we discussed this morning, Miss Amplebum, Big-N-Wide Corporation will supply 75 seat cushions for the football game next Saturday."

- ✔ Transmitting regularly scheduled news feeds, reports, and so on.

- ✔ Distributing exactly the same information to multiple recipients.

E-mail can be helpful for many other kinds of communications needs, as well. The important point is that it should not be a substitute for other types of communications — such as face-to-face discussions and telephone time — and it should not go on for too long. After two back-and-forth e-mail exchanges on the same issue, it's time to pick up the phone.

Finally, be aware that managers in e-mail-intensive companies may get 200 or more messages PER DAY! Take pity on them; be brief, and if you don't get a response when you need one, follow up by phone.

And, of course, you should return your e-mail messages promptly — even if it's only to say, "I received your message but won't be able to give it my full attention until next week." If your e-mail package will support this feature, it's also a good idea to set a "vacation autoreply" when you will be out of touch for more than a day or two. It will respond automatically to correspondents (usually only once to each individual) to let them know you're away and not reading e-mail.

What about Internet chat?

Internet chat services, such as AOL Instant Messenger, are increasing in popularity. To use them wisely:

- ✔ Follow the standard rules — ugly language, vicious gossip, and confidential information are still taboo.

- ✔ Use chat judiciously — while it can be handy, it can also be distracting for the person you are chatting with.

- ✔ Is someone distracting you? Politely tell them you can't chat now and will get back with them later. Better yet, shut down your chat application.

Discreet Pager Use

Some people feel they're constantly on a short leash, and hearing the pager go off is like being jerked by a choke chain. Others enjoy the knowledge that they are constantly in touch, and that their input is valuable in the event of a problem. Love 'em or hate 'em, pagers are around to stay.

In the early days of pagers, all beeps were pretty much the same. Today, users can choose to disturb a quiet room in a variety of ways — with *the William Tell Overture,* Beethoven's *Für Elise,* and so on. Fortunately, almost all pagers now have a vibrate mode. This is the preferred mode for your pager at all times!

- If you're a man, you can clip the pager to your belt, and leave it on vibrate all the time. Problem solved!

- If you're a woman, you may not always be able to have your pager clipped on, so carrying one requires a little planning. If you're driving around town or are in some other location where it won't disturb anyone, you can leave the tone on. *As soon* as you arrive at a meeting, theater, turn the pager to vibrate and either put it on the table in front of you (good) or in your purse (better, you can check it at the end of the meeting and no one will hear it). A vibrating pager on a desktop can be startling, but is not as obnoxious as a beeper tone.

- If you must have your beeper tone on, make sure you know exactly where the pager is so you can shut it off immediately. Every second you spend fumbling through your jacket pockets while the pager plays "God Bless America" is more bad business karma piling up.

- If you're talking to someone, don't look at your pager for a message while they are speaking. If absolutely necessary, wait until it is your turn to speak, then excuse yourself for a moment. Even better, wait until your meeting is over to check the message.

- If you must return a page immediately, step out of the room. Do *not* carry on a phone conversation while others are trying to pay attention to the meeting!

Remember, *always* set your pager to vibrate mode in theaters (including movie theaters) and at houses of worship. Getting beeped during a funeral is funny on *Saturday Night Live,* but terribly embarrassing in real life.

During a management meeting at a large communications company, the CEO requested that everyone in attendance turn off their pagers and phones. He told them that the decisions being made during that meeting were more important than *any* other issue that day. About 15 minutes into the meeting, one of the managers received a loudly audible page and jumped up from his seat to find a phone. The CEO locked the door behind him. No more beeps were heard that day!

Laptop Computers

What possible etiquette pitfalls could surround laptop computers, you ask? There are a few:

- ✔ Some keyboards are quieter than others, but loud typing during a meeting can be very distracting to your colleagues. If you're getting the look of death from the person sitting next to you, switch to a pen and paper.

- ✔ Ditto for conference calls, where ambient noise can literally drown out speakers. Set your phone on "mute" unless you're speaking so others won't hear your typing.

- ✔ If you're at a large meeting and there are limited telephones, don't hog one of the lines by downloading your e-mail. Chances are you're only receiving chain letters and stupid jokes, anyway.

Handheld Organizers

You won't believe this, but there's not much to say.

- ✔ Keep your organizer (by this we mean a Palm Pilot or similar device) neatly tucked away at mealtime, not sitting on the table.

- ✔ Don't use the "reminder alarm" function — you may hear beeps when you least expect them.

- ✔ Don't "beam" your business card to anyone at a state dinner unless the President or another head of state starts the ball rolling.

- ✔ Don't swear or cry when your device crashes.

- ✔ Finally, don't sneer at those of us who still use pencil and paper.

Fax Machines and Other Office Equipment

Remember that Golden Rule we talked about a few chapters back? It still applies. The key to using and sharing office equipment is to remember that it belongs to everyone.

- ✔ If you notice that the fax machine or copier is out of paper, put in more paper.

✔ If the fax machine or copier is broken, either fix it (if you know how to do so without making the problem worse) or call someone who can fix it. Then, put a sign on the equipment letter other users know the problem has been called in.

✔ If you need to make lots of copies, and someone else only needs to make a few, let her go first.

✔ Similarly, if you drink the last cup of coffee, start a new pot. Don't slink out of the break room hoping no one will notice.

✔ And while we're at it, don't make a big mess. Clean up your spills. Throw away your trash. And for heaven's sake, don't leave food in the sink! Have some sympathy for the person who has to clean the office after you leave.

✔ Have respect for the people who fix your office equipment, maintain computers, replace light bulbs, and vacuum up your crumbs. Think of how much more pleasant your job is because of them!

Information Security

Technology has made communication easier for you and me. At the same time, it has made communication easier for the bad guys — those who want to steal your company's proprietary technology, employee social security numbers, or other confidential information. Yes, it all sounds a little like the X-Files, but information security is part of business etiquette. After all, what could be more impolite than letting your company's secrets fall into the wrong hands?

Many companies will ask employees to sign a confidentiality agreement when they are hired. This agreement states something to the effect that the employee will not share any information learned at the company to help another company succeed. These agreements aren't just a formality; they're important legally binding contracts for how you should conduct yourself. If you sign one, get a copy of it and understand what it says.

Many larger companies have very specific guidelines about information storage and security, document retention, and so on. If you're not sure about your company's guidelines, ask. And don't leave any hard-drives behind the copier or coffee machine!

✔ If you work with vendors, don't reveal more about internal projects than they need to know in order to complete the job. Don't share lists of employee names and phone numbers.

✔ When you leave your desk for more than a minute, turn on your screen saver and set a password to lock it. If you're not sure how to do this, check with the person who set up your computer.

✔ When you leave at night, lock up disks and documents. If you're the type who has piles everywhere, make sure the piles of confidential information are inside your locking cabinet and the piles on the floor are magazines and unopened mail.

✔ Be careful about whom you give your social security number to, and never reveal someone else's social security number (if you know it) to a third party. At the same time, however, be aware that larger companies use SSNs more frequently than small ones to keep track of employee information.

✔ If you travel with a laptop computer, don't leave it in an unlocked conference room or sitting in plain sight in your hotel room.

✔ Back up your work frequently.

Those are some rules for cyber-etiquette — for today! As technology continues to evolve, so will our ways of dealing gracefully within it. The most important thing to think about is other people's needs and comfort — and with those in mind, you will rarely make a mistake.

Part III

Overcoming the Big Etiquette Challenges at Work

The 5th Wave   By Rich Tennant

"The next part of your employment test is designed to determine your sense of humor."

In this part . . .

We present tips and strategies to help keep you sane. We also cover office conflicts and help you decide when and how to get involved. Then, we tackle the subject of stress and how to keep your cool under pressure. We discuss some ethical dilemmas that occur at work and use real-life scenarios to illustrate the right and wrong ways to handle them. We close with a discussion of office romance and sexual harassment — and how to draw the line between the two.

Chapter 10

Dealing with Difficult People

· ·

· ·

*Y*ou know who these people are — the manager who can't control his temper, the assistant who spreads malicious rumors about others, the shipping clerk with the social skills of a mollusk, the colleague who stabs you behind your back to get ahead, the leering network-technology specialist. They're in every business and at every level, and they can make your life miserable.

Some people are difficult because of their personalities; others are difficult because of their position in the company. In this chapter, you'll learn some helpful techniques for coping with both kinds of difficulties. By the end, you still won't be a qualified therapist, but you'll know enough to help yourself and others through a wide range of challenging situations.

Dealing with Teams and Rivals

Most businesses have a defined hierarchy; even businesses that don't appear to have much of a defined hierarchy normally do. With a hierarchy comes competition for the top spots, and with competition comes rivalries and the need to cope with them. Some companies reward intra-office competition; others work to defuse it by team-building and training on how to have fun at work. You'll soon know which kind of structure your company has.

Teams

Many companies organize teams of people to work together and to defuse competition among employees. While this might help the company in some ways, productive individual initiative is always valued. Everyone knows this, so everyone tries to find a way to both be a good team player *and* stand out from the group. Sort of like being the Michael Jordan of the office.

Some people get recognized by engaging in outrageous stunts and by practicing crude self-promotion. Sometimes these tactics work, but, for the most part, they don't. The trick is to get yourself recognized while not losing your status as a team player. That takes tact and respect for others. It takes good manners.

Good manners are particularly important for your rise to the top. You will get noticed simply by respecting other team members and by being gracious. Your fair-mindedness and graciousness, *all by themselves,* set you apart from most of your colleagues. They show others — managers in particular — that when you're a member of a team, you aren't a credit hog or a thief. You share credit where credit is due.

Of course, you want to ensure that your contribution to the team is recognized and not stolen by another. You can do this while maintaining your manners by speaking well at team meetings and by writing memos that give your contribution its proper emphasis. Sometimes, if you offer your contribution in a team meeting, it becomes team property. You are then faced with a choice: Either allow it to become team property or wait until your initiative can be recognized outside of the team, say, in a meeting with the superior to which the team reports.

Rivals

Most people aren't interested in your interests or in hindering your progress. But some people have the same goals that you have. If you're at roughly the same level of the hierarchy, these folks are, in some sense, your rivals. Your respect for others and good manners are again among your best allies when handling them. You can even use manners to defeat the bad apples who play dirty.

Some rivals play rough — they blast away at you in meetings, they go behind your back to superiors, they spread rumors about you. Rough players will scope you out to see whether you're willing to play their game. If you're not well versed in their techniques, you'll lose, for they rely on their knowledge of you and their ability to bait you into doing something you'll regret.

You don't want to play this game for three very good reasons. First, rivals who play rough have probably been doing it since childhood. They're good at it. Second, good managers recognize rough players for what they are and don't tolerate them for long. Third, the most effective counter to rough rivals is demonstrating that, even though you recognize them for what they are, you won't be ruffled and cannot be bothered to lower yourself to their level.

Your best bet is to expose the rough players for the bitter so-and-so's they are by killing them with good manners. When they arrive at the office every day before you do, compliment them on their initiative. When they criticize you in a meeting, thank them for their views and politely point out that there are other pertinent facts, which, were they to have known them, may have changed their mind. When they maneuver to oust you from the A-team, counter with your credentials and your track record of teamwork.

Luckily, most rivals are not that rough — almost everyone is interested in getting promoted, but most people rely on their good work and their good reputation to get the promotion. Again, good manners are an integral part of your good reputation, so use them to your advantage.

If — just out of obtuseness — someone picks on your work and your input in meetings, stand up to them politely and firmly. The workplace is governed by professional civility — you are under no obligation to be the butt of someone else's meanness. If you have to, go to the offender's superior and ask that the offender be notified that you have had enough. If the carping is persistent, write it down and submit the concerns to a superior. If it is the superior who is picking on you, go to his or her superior.

Sometimes your closest rival is also a friend. And it may happen that you are promoted over your friend. So long as the friendship is firm, your promotion will be recognized by your friend as a reward for work well done. If the friendship doesn't survive the promotion, it probably wasn't that firm to begin with, and you're lucky to learn that sooner rather than later.

Problem Personalities

Your best behavior will be taken by a few as a weakness to be exploited. Show them otherwise. There is no better gauge of your strength of character than your unfailing politeness. It's the hothead, the rumormonger, the credit hog and thief, the manipulator, the malcontent, and the bully who show that they're weak. By acting in the way they do, they betray their own belief that they can only succeed, if they succeed at all, by abandoning their control.

The person who treats others with respect is a walking refutation of social cheaters.

We know what you're saying to yourself: "That all sounds fine, but you have no idea how the jerks I have to put up with treat me. Having good manners sounds fine in theory, but, when the chips are down, I'm gonna have to fight back, aren't I?"

True enough, you need to know how to handle colleagues and superiors who are problems. But there are lots of ways of defeating these problematic people other than fighting back on their terms.

The hothead

Hotheads have a hard time controlling their tempers. Most hotheads are embarrassed by their bad tempers and, after flailing away for five minutes, apologize profusely.

The way to deal with a hothead is to let him blow his stack . . . privately, if at all possible. Suggest that he vent in his office. This will not go down well with the hothead, since he probably requires an audience. If you're well suited to it — that is, if you have a hide as thick as an elephant's — offer to listen to him. If not, tell him that you're sorry, but you'd prefer that he not let off steam in your presence. This won't always work, but at least you'll have said what you need to if, when it happens again, you leave the room.

If you have to put up with a hothead in a group meeting, the advice above may not work. In such a situation, you may have no alternative but to listen to him rant for a couple of minutes. Most hotheads are finished quickly, but while they are ranting they may turn vicious. Pretend you're listening to a play and are not involved directly. This is difficult, especially if you're the object of the rant. Just remember enough of the diatribe to write it down. You'll have witnesses from the meeting. When you go to the hothead's supervisor to complain, you'll have the necessary information for a peaceful resolution of the problem.

The rumormonger

Gossip is unavoidable and, for the most part, benign; it's just everyone's way of showing that they're interested in other people. You do yourself no favors standing proudly aloof from all the tidbits that fly around an office. On the other hand, you don't want to be labeled a gossip either. So, while you can be receptive to it, it's not in your best interest to spread negative or potentially damaging information about other people. Instead, focus on positive gossip!

The rumormonger is a different story. He lives on gossip and uses it to skewer others and to advance his own career. He's trouble for you because you may become the subject of some juicy bit of his gossip.

There's only one way to deal with the rumormonger when his attention turns to some salacious tidbit mentioning you: Confront him. You're under no obligation to confront him if the gossip is about someone else, although you may wish to come to the defense of a friend or a colleague. But if it's about you or yours, confront the rumormonger politely and publicly, politely because you do not wish to embarrass him, publicly because you want to ensure that others hear him recant. Even if the gossip is true, you want to make sure that it comes from the proper source, not the rumor mill. True gossip is still gossip and needs to be handled the same way.

Keep the following in mind.

- ✔ Malicious gossips rely on the shadows to flourish. Confronting them publicly forces them out of the shadows. Most will wilt on the spot.
- ✔ Ask the gossip where he heard the rumor. When you get the name, talk to that person, too. Repeat as necessary.

The credit hog and thief

The credit *hog* tries to take all of the credit when some is due to others. The credit *thief* takes any credit she can find, even when it belongs to someone else. Dealing with either the hog or the thief requires the same skill: Ensure that you get the credit you deserve. This is easier said than done sometimes, but it can be done. A private chat, in which you point out that other people helped on the project and deserve credit, can sometimes work. When it doesn't, offer to write the update memos so that the credit hog doesn't have the opportunity to monopolize reporting on the project. If that doesn't work either, talk to a superior. Point out the problem and ask what to do.

The bully

The bully tries to threaten you into doing things you'd rather not do and aren't required to do. There's no way to deal with a bully other than to stand up to her on the first occasion and to continue standing up to her. The problem is usually that you are so astonished by what she's doing that you can't think of a snappy comeback.

Luckily, you need no more of a snappy comeback than your good manners. When your supervisor tells you on Friday to get those reports ready by the end of the weekend or you're toast — and you know that they don't need to be ready until the following Friday — reply that, sadly, you have firm plans for the weekend. But couple that politely phrased refusal with the offer to take the reports with you and to do whatever is necessary to have the reports by, say, Wednesday.

Our advice:

- Never allow yourself to get flustered by a bully. They rely on your discomfort to get their way. Always be ready with a calm and polite retort that offers some compromise between what they want and what you're willing to do.

- If you're unlucky enough to work for an unrepentant bully, look for another job. It will never get better.

The manipulator

Manipulators tell half-truths; they lie; they reveal only what they think is in their interest to reveal; they routinely conceal information from you. They're a royal pain-in-the-you-know-what. You get to the point where you're convinced that, in order to counter them, you must anticipate what they will do the next time it's in their self-interest to massage things to get their way.

Don't bother: Manipulators are masters at their craft and you're not going to outdo them. Have your ducks in order so that, when they start their little game, you can counter with the facts.

Some manipulators sugarcoat their machinations with offers of generosity. You'll soon learn that to their generosity a tit-for-tat is always attached. Learn quickly and be safe: Refuse their offers!

Here are some more ideas for dealing with the manipulator:

- If the manipulator tries to get you to do something that you think is against policy, put him off long enough to check on the policy yourself.

- If the manipulator tries to slide something unwanted past your team, challenge him in public to defend his suggestion.

- If the manipulator succeeds in getting you to do something you know is a mistake or is against your interests, it's never too late to put the facts in writing and submit it to the proper manager

The malcontent

These are the kind of people who, when you say "Good Morning," will accuse you of being friendly because you secretly hate them. Their responses are so far from the norm that you can't anticipate them — and don't even think of protecting yourself from them. Malcontents are impossible.

Happily, most malcontents are not a threat and do not require that you do anything other than continue to be your usual friendly and polite self. They can stew in their unhappiness if they wish. If they slide into manipulation or bullying to feed their perverse happiness of resentment, action is probably required. But, again, the best action against manipulation and bullying is blithe disregard of the attempts to goad you into something you'll regret. Let them try to irritate you — Mom was right — just ignore them!

The Machiavelli

The Machiavelli is your worst enemy, for she wants power and nothing but power. Worse, she's smart, calculating, and tenacious. She will adopt whatever pose she needs to in order to get more power.

Our advice — stay away, far away. Most Machiavellis self-destruct and those who don't are poison to you. The truth is that most Machiavellis are pretenders — they're crude and, sooner or later, they'll make a fatal miscalculation. Once they do, you can watch them free-fall out of the company without going along for the ride. Those who are successful rise only to a certain level, beyond which their naked lust for power is harmful to the company. There they will fester, becoming malcontents. And you already know how to deal with malcontents!

Of course, you can't always stay away. Some people have power junkies for their boss and some people have no choice but to work with one. These are among the most difficult environments you can work in. If the Machiavelli is your boss, know ahead of time that power, for him, is something that only one person can have, and that person is him. There is no extra power to share with you. Our advice for those who find this kind of working relationship intolerable is to look for another job.

If you can't avoid working with a Machiavelli, you'll have a struggle on your hands. You rightfully don't want to acquiesce to his every demand, but you know that fighting him will, in all likelihood, be a losing battle. Our advice for those who find themselves in this unenviable position is simple: Do what you can to protect yourself within the confines of civility. If the Machiavelli starts picking fights, you can fight back more effectively with politeness than you can by playing his dirty games.

Count to Ten and . . . Relax

No, you didn't really deserve that dressing down from your boss. And you certainly didn't deserve being called an "incompetent moron" or any of the other names she saw fit to utter. But she's your boss and, except for these tirades, she's a pretty good one. Besides, it's probably just the stress she's under from the new Bigsley contract.

There are hundreds of irritants in a workday — the person who smacks her lips eating breakfast at her desk; the person who's a drummer for Nine Inch Nails during all of your phone calls; the person who puts his dirty running shoes up on your desk when he talks to you; the boss who yells too much; the colleague whose cologne permeates your cubicle like smoke; and all of the problem personalities we write about earlier in this chapter.

What are you supposed to do?

Petty annoyances are an inevitable consequence of being with other people in confined spaces.

The first thing to do is to count to ten and relax. Others *will* irritate you. You just have to be ready for it. If you're constantly surprised at the strange things people say, eat, or smell like, your first change should be of your expectations. People are different, often irritatingly so — deal with it! After all, remember the morning affirmation of Marcus Aurelius, an Emperor of Rome: "Today, I will be surrounded by people who irritate me. I will not demonstrate my irritation."

The next thing to do is to figure out the most helpful strategies for cooling your temper when the temperature starts to climb. We'll talk about this matter in more detail in Chapter 12, but here we present some simple suggestions for those first few minutes when you're worried you're going to explode.

When someone does something that really bugs you:

- ✔ Look away and count to ten . . . repeat as necessary until you calm down!
- ✔ Excuse yourself from the situation to get a drink of water.
- ✔ Imagine that you're doing your favorite activity in your favorite place.
- ✔ Remind yourself that, in a certain number of hours, you'll be on your way home.
- ✔ Return to your desk or office, sit quietly for a few minutes, and plan your response.

If you're in a situation where you have to make an instant response to an incredibly annoying comment, swallow hard and be polite, but remember to stick up for yourself and your ideas.

Do No Harm

The first rule of good manners is to respect other people and be attentive to their needs. If you're a vegetarian and you have a meat-eating colleague, you can expect that she'll bring some lunches that won't look appetizing to you. If your boss can't get through the day without swearing at least once, accept the inevitable, count to ten, and move on.

Of course, these simple tactics don't always work. When they don't work, keep in mind that, whatever you do in response, you should try not to exacerbate the situation. You do harm when you take an already bad situation and make it worse by your own actions. If you respond to someone else's dirty dealing by returning the favor in kind, you only jack the stakes up for the dirty dealer to retaliate. Now you're in trouble — this is a never-ending cycle.

Some people take the maximum-explosive-outburst approach to difficult situations — just out-shout and out-bully everyone right at the beginning and everyone will toe the line. Sometimes, these people are effective . . . in the short-run. But they're never effective in the long run — those who work for them become sullen, diffident, and unproductive, constantly afraid that the other shoe is going to drop.

You don't want to be that person. And here your civility is a real boon. If you've habituated yourself to replying in a polite, well-modulated manner, and always taking other people's concerns into consideration, you're likely to be the peacemaker and the person of good will your colleagues can't manage to be. And, by being the peacemaker and mediator, you will never do more harm than has already been done.

Keep the following tips in mind:

- ✔ When the temperature goes up, actively look for ways to cool it down.

- ✔ Acknowledge that what the upset person has to say and how they say it are different; focus on what is being said, not on the ugly manner in which it is being said.

- ✔ Never join in the fracas between two people. Suggest that the warring parties back away long enough to compose themselves.

- ✔ Listen to each side of the dispute.

- ✔ Find merit in what each party says and look for a compromise solution.

Helpful hints for dealing with an invasive question

Some people just don't know any better than to ask questions you have no interest in answering or to engage you in conversation on topics that you would rather not discuss. Sometimes, these people are just trying to be friendly. Unfortunately, they just don't know that their excessive inquisitiveness is unacceptably invasive.

Suppose your colleague Raul asks you about the story he saw in the paper about your dad's recent arrest for gardening in the nude. You're embarrassed by the question (and by your father!), and had hoped that the matter would never come up. Do you:

a) Say that it's a long family tradition to garden in the nude, and wink.

b) Give Raul a withering glare.

c) Apologize, but reply firmly that you will not answer the question.

d) Ask Raul why he's asking.

Not surprisingly, any of (a) through (d) is fine. Each has its advantages, and each has its disadvantages.

Generally, the best approach to responding to impertinent questions is politely asking the questioner why he's asking. Smile. This usually embarrasses the other person enough to withdraw the question.

Chapter 11

Managing Office Conflict

. . . .

. . . .

For many people, conflict — at work or at home — is difficult. You probably know people who would rather move than confront a neighbor about his barking dog or the annual Summer Picnic and Bagpiping Competition. Believe it or not, some conflict is actually helpful.

In this chapter, you'll learn why. You'll also be introduced to some effective conflict-management tools. You and your colleagues can get along better by knowing them. More importantly, you and your boss can get along better, too!

Realizing That Conflict Can Be Good

Though it takes guts, conflict can be useful, even energizing. At work, it can help bring up issues that need attention, such as processes that don't make sense anymore but are "the way it's always been done." Conflict can also give birth to excellent ideas. If everyone agrees with the first idea the boss tosses out, that may be the only idea that ever comes up — even though it may not be a very good one. When the team debates an issue, however, many more thoughts and opinions emerge, and they often produce a superior result.

Debate can be productive, but once a decision is made, it's time to get in line. Don't undermine the team by saying things like, "Well, it wasn't my idea, but I guess we're going to go with that stupid ad campaign anyway."

Brainstorming

Brainstorming is a term that's bandied about in companies everywhere, but it's rarely understood. In true brainstorming, all ideas are thrown on the table (or on the whiteboard) without any comment from anyone about which ideas are good or bad. Once all ideas are out, a facilitator guides a (respectful) discussion about all the ideas, and the best ones float to the top. It's a great way to get input from both those creative-but-timid employees and the mouthy, confident ones.

R-E-S-P-E-C-T. Aretha demands it, and your colleagues deserve it, too. In fact, perhaps the single most important key to effective conflict is to respect others' opinions and their right to speak up. If someone works in the same place you do, chances are she's done something right to get there. Even if you totally disagree with a colleague's opinion, you can still respect her intelligence and integrity. If you're sure that she's a moron, keep it to yourself — even when you chat with your office buddies.

Showing respect for others' opinions is more than biting your tongue on witty putdowns. It also includes controlling:

- ✔ Facial expressions. Even when your mouth is closed, rolling your eyes and smirking show a lack of respect.

- ✔ Body language. Refrain from shaking your head or looking around the room as though you can't wait for the other person to finish.

- ✔ Kicking other colleagues under the table and giving them significant looks. You're not fooling anyone.

When the conflict involves people and their behavior, however, it usually becomes significantly more challenging, and it's often a serious drain on energy and resources. It's in these cases that conflict turns from productive to destructive, for, in many cases, people with personality conflicts simply *don't* have much respect for one another, and that can make for a difficult situation.

Managing Conflict with Your Peers

You've been working for months to get promoted, and you've finally made it to that corner cubicle that's near the snack room, the restroom, *and* the parking lot. Life is good for the first few days as you work on the great new strategy you'll present at Friday's meeting.

You make your presentation, and you feel great. Until a voice pipes up from the back of the room: "We tried that last year, and it didn't work." Maybe it's the person who was passed over for the promotion you got. Maybe it's the person who takes a pessimistic view of everything. Maybe it's that woman you stood up on prom in high school, who, 15 years later, has returned to haunt you. Whoever it is, your shiny new idea has been scratched and dented.

There are lots of ways to manage office conflict *ineffectively* — locking your door and blasting your radio is one; taking aim with coffee is another. Try a more productive solution. It's okay to think some evil thoughts at this point, as long as they stay inside your head and don't appear on your face or fly out your mouth. It's also okay to go home tonight and complain to your long-suffering spouse, friends, or dog. Pretty soon, however, you're going to have to discuss the issue in a mature and professional manner with your detractor.

Vent if you must, but not at work

It may help you to complain about this person to someone else, if you can find someone who's willing to listen. Avoid venting to other people at the office or other people who know the person. Even if you trust the person you're venting to, your comments may eventually get back to their target, causing an even bigger problem.

The privacy of your car is a great place to vent your frustrations, as long as you *don't* vent them on other drivers by driving aggressively. Use your commute time to say all those things you would never say at the office. Once you get them out, you'll probably feel better. Just ignore those people in the next car who are pointing and gaping; you're emotionally healthy.

Put yourself in the other person's shoes

Try to understand where the other person is coming from. Are you new to the department, newly promoted, much younger or older, or much more beautiful than your peers? Consider the fact that some people may be intimidated by you, and be professional and respectful until they get to know you better.

Has the other person in this conflict been in his or her job for a long time?

If so, a certain weariness may have set in after years of the daily grind.

That's a problem you can't fix. You can, however, be willing to listen and compromise while not letting that person affect your own attitude.

Practice active listening

Most of us spend plenty of time talking, but not much time hearing what other people have to say. Here's how to become an active listener:

- ✔ **Set the stage** by setting your phone to "do not disturb," turning away from the computer or other distractions, and facing the person you're talking to. If people have a habit of barging into your office, close the door or find a conference room or a quiet corner of the cafeteria to have important discussions.

- ✔ **Sit in a neutral position.** Sitting on opposite sides of a conference table puts you on equal footing; sitting behind your desk while the other person sits in front of your desk gives you more perceived power. That's just what you *don't* want in this situation, because it immediately puts the other person on the defensive.

- ✔ **Clear your mind of your own point of view.** Your goal is to listen and understand your partner's point of view without considering how it stacks up with yours. During a discussion, we often miss someone else's point because we're busy thinking about what we want to say next. If you're concerned about being able to respond to everything later, take notes. (If you take notes, you may want to explain that you're doing it in order to really concentrate and remember. Otherwise, your partner may think he's undergoing a psychological profile.)

- ✔ **Encourage the other person to keep talking** by nodding your head or asking him to continue, but don't interrupt. Wait until the other person has said everything he wants to say. At that point, you should understand his point of view, even if you still don't agree with it. That's your basis for negotiation and compromise.

Ask clarifying questions

So some strategy was tried before and it didn't work. Ask your partner to explain more about how or why it didn't work. Were the circumstances the same? Was the project funded and supported by upper management last time? Was it given enough time to work? You should be open to accepting that your plan really won't work and that you need to start over. On the other hand, you may be able to identify problems that could be fixed this time around.

Be willing to compromise your ideas

Somehow, *compromise* has turned into a bad word in our culture. There's no reason for that. While you may not want to compromise your *ethics,* most work situations don't require you to. But you can almost always find some areas where you're willing to give up an *idea* in order to gain something else. Another term for this: consensus building.

On the other hand, don't compromise your ethics

If a peer suggests you cheat a supplier, for example, let her know you're not comfortable doing it. If she insists, you may need to involve your manager. If the manager also insists, it's time either to use your company's open-door policy to go over your manager's head. It might also be time to buy *Job Searching For Dummies.*

Always try to manage peer conflict by yourself first. Involve your manager only if it's really necessary. It's a good experience for your next move up the organizational ladder.

Look at the big picture

Perspective is important. Yes, work is a big part of your life, but it's not your whole life. Keep in mind that this challenging person is only one person and that, in today's job-switching environment, you probably won't be working with her forever.

Restrict your comments to behavior, not personality

Never say something like, "you're a loudmouthed jerk, and I can't understand how someone like you ever got into management." Instead, say, "When you interrupt me during meetings, I feel like I can never finish what I have to say. I think that's one of the reasons we can't seem to get past this conflict." The next time the person interrupts you, call him on it. Some people — especially those from families of ten children, who are accustomed to fighting for every shred of attention — aren't even aware that they're cutting other people off.

Watch your language

If you're in the habit of swearing at work, stop. Even if you only do it when you're angry, many people will be so shocked by your inventive variations on the "F" word that they'll be unable to concentrate on what you're trying to say. Swearing does not make you appear more intelligent.

Resolving a Conflict with Your Boss

Again, it comes down to respect — on your part, on your boss's part, or both. She may see you as a threat, a loudmouth, unintelligent, or just plain obnoxious. You may view her as incompetent, unfeeling, or a young whippersnapper with nothing to teach you. However, she has a direct effect on your future, even if you think of her as Machiavelli on acid.

What to do? Remember: Show some respect. Look for her good points — she does have at least one, and probably more. Try to understand her point of view and the pressure she's under as a manager. Concentrate on her behavior and treatment of you, not her annoying laugh or unsettling physical attributes. Most of all, remember that she's the boss, and that's not likely to change.

If you feel you're being treated unfairly, address it with her directly and politely. As a manager, she should be open to constructive criticism. If she refuses to acknowledge your concerns, weigh your options. You could put up with your current situation. You could look for another job. You could talk to Human Resources for advice — and if they have had numerous complaints about her in the past, one more complaint could be what they need to take action. Finally, you could approach *her* boss, which may help significantly, but which puts you at risk of alienating her. Unfortunately, there's no single right answer here. Use your best judgment.

Managing Conflict If You're the Boss

Managing people isn't always easy, especially when you have to handle disputes and conflict within the office. That's why you're getting the big bucks. One of the reasons you're a manager in the first place is that you get along well with others and you've demonstrated your coolness under fire in the past. So, get ready . . . the qualities that got you the promotion will now be put to the test on a regular basis in keeping those two brilliant hotheads you hired from ripping each other to pieces. And while you're keeping them from engaging in their favorite pastime, you'll also have to protect yourself from becoming their next victim.

A manager at a large tech company had been dealing with two employees, Sally and Phil, who were constantly at each other's throats — arguing loudly in staff meetings, spreading vicious gossip, even threatening each other with bodily harm. He was tired of these disruptions, but so far his reprimands had not worked. Finally, he blew up in a staff meeting, called them both idiots, and suggested they go back to the sandbox where they belonged. Phil immediately made a call to Human Resources, and the manager ended up with a reprimand. Don't let it happen to you!

What did this manager do wrong? He violated one of the cardinal rules of employee relations — don't ever ridicule an employee, and don't discipline an employee in front of other people.

Address small problems before they become big ones

If a new employee is listening to loud music at his desk, don't wait for another employee to complain. Instead, you could say something like, "I'm not sure if you've had a chance to read the employee handbook yet, but we suggest that people listen to music with headphones." Chances are he'll be happy to comply, and you will have nipped a problem in the bud. Good for you!

As a good supervisor or manager, you're proactive and polite about small problems so that you don't have to be reactive and rude when they fester into big problems.

Try a one-on-one

If the problem seems to be primarily one employee, meet with him alone. Find out what the problem is without being accusatory. For example, instead of saying, "Everyone here knows that you and Sally can't seem to get along, and it's damaging our productivity," say, "It seems to me that there's something going on between you and Sally. Is that true?" If so, ask the employee to tell his side of the story. If he insists there's no problem, talk to Sally.

Try sitting the two of them down

Again, your approach should be exploratory, not accusatory. If they try to interrupt each other, say, "Sally, I promise to listen to everything you have to say, but at the moment Phil has the floor." Make sure you've scheduled plenty of time to hear them both out. If one or both of them want to meet with you alone, make time for that, too. No, it's probably not how you want to spend your time — but that's management.

Don't play favorites

You may like Phil better because he has a better sense of humor or he brings in bagels every Friday. Put that aside and focus on behavior only in this particular conflict. If Phil is the one acting inappropriately, you need the maturity as a manager to let him know, even if it affects your friendship.

Appeal to their sense of teamwork and fair play

Let both employees know that you have faith in their intelligence, ethics, and ability to work things out. Ask each of them to identify an area or two where they could compromise to make things work, and ask them to commit to changing that behavior.

Let them know you're serious

Be sure they know that maintaining the status quo is not acceptable. You'll be watching, and if they don't follow through on their mutual commitment to change behavior, they'll be hearing from you again.

Don't be afraid to ask for help

Your manager relies on you to handle what you can, but he's also there to help you when you need it. After the current crisis has cooled down — or before it happens — ask about management training that will help you deal with these situations. If your company doesn't have a formal training program, there are plenty of training outfits that would love to help you. Check your local yellow pages or the Internet.

Employees in a professional environment very rarely resort to physical attacks, but it has been known to happen. Be ready to cut the discussion short and call Human Resources or Security if things get really out of hand. (If you suspect in advance that there may be a problem, consider informing Security in advance.) Whatever you do, don't participate in the violence yourself.

If, in the end, the warriors just can't get along, a manager is going to have to make a painful decision to split them up, either by reassigning one or both of them or by firing one or both of them. A good manager knows when to bring the ax down when, despite her best efforts and the best efforts of the warriors, things just don't get better.

Managing Conflict If You're a Spectator

Whether you're a manager or not, don't allow yourself to be sucked into conflicts that don't concern you. Many people who have good conflict resolution skills themselves — and many who don't! — can't resist the temptation to "help" others with their problems. Don't do it! At least one of the parties will probably resent your intrusion, and other people will perceive you as a meddling busybody without enough work to do. People who try to solve other people's problems at work often find conflict oddly titillating and like to gossip. Even if you don't deserve that reputation, you may get it if you're not careful.

Maria, a computer programmer, had always prided herself on the good advice she gave her friends about their relationships at work. In fact, many of her friends came to her seeking advice. Maria knew she would make a great manager, but so far she hadn't had that opportunity. So when she saw two people at work continually angry at each other, she wanted to help. She talked with Venkat and Bill separately to find out their respective sides of the story, then served as a go-between.

Unfortunately, her good intentions backfired. Both Bill and Venkat thought she was taking the other person's side, and they both stopped talking to her. Her manager got wind of the situation and asked Maria to please concentrate on her own work. Maria was crushed because she was only trying to help. That fall, however, she started back to school and is now a licensed corporate conflict manager. She has gained the authority and expertise to do what she loves — helping people work out their differences in the office.

If your peers come to you for advice at work, resist the temptation to get involved. It may be okay to suggest strategies that have worked for you in the past, such as, "When I had a problem with one of my colleagues last year, I just sat down and had an honest discussion with her, and it was really helpful. She just didn't realize that she was bothering me, and I learned some things I did that bothered her." But never get involved in the current situation or make comments like, "I've heard that Ronnie's a total nightmare to work with. I feel sorry for you." That only further polarizes the situation. Don't take on other people's problems — instead, give yourself a pat on the back for having learned how to resolve your *own* conflicts!

Chapter 12

Grace under Pressure: Handling Stress

*M*ost people lose their temper at some point in their professional lives. Some lose it so quietly you wouldn't know they're mad if it weren't for the steam coming out of their ears; others blow their stacks in great displays; still others go after anyone within earshot. And then there are those amazing few who seem never to lose it — either they wait until they're in their office to wig or they're one of those rare few who are *always* in control.

If you're one of that rare breed, there's no need to read further in this chapter. (You can, however, help the rest of us by telling us how you do it!) If you're not one of them — if you're like the vast majority of us — you'll benefit from what we have to say here.

We don't suggest that you become so detached from your job that you never feel the urge to blow up, or that you become so hyperstoic that you're like Spock or Data. We do suggest a few techniques for learning how to control the urge to vent or fume. These techniques can, if practiced, curb the urge to yell and carry on. They can even help minimize the thoughts that prompt the urge to yell and carry on.

Count to Ten

Having good professional manners requires that you consider the desires and needs of others when you act. But you don't have to stop thinking or feeling. No one can stop you from thinking that the shipping department let you down by sitting on your order for the E-Riches account for a week just to prove their power. No one can stop you from feeling betrayed when the person you thought was your best friend turns around and stabs you in the back.

Thoughts like these typically happen without you wanting them to — they just occur as a response to certain situations. But there are two things you can do to control what happens with them once they've occurred:

- ✔ Insert a checking mechanism before you act on enraging thoughts or before you say anything to others.
- ✔ Develop a different attitude that can help to defuse enraging thoughts from bubbling up in the first place.

Of course, implementing these two techniques is easier described than accomplished. The second technique is, after all, no less than changing your habituated ways of reacting to others' behavior; it takes an *enormous* amount of effort. The first technique is easier to implement. So let's turn to that.

Check Yourself before Responding

So the boss decides that you're going to be the fall guy for losing the Hong Kong real-estate deal. Never mind that he insulted the representative by stuffing her business card in his pocket without looking at it; never mind that he called her at 3 a.m. to talk business; never mind that you're the one who mollified her when your boss made promises that he couldn't keep. Never mind all that. Your boss blames you for blowing the deal.

Life stinks sometimes. Now, you're mad, really mad. You want to walk right into your boss's office and read him the riot act. You want to walk into *his* boss's office and tell *her* exactly what you think. And if none of that works, you'll settle for strangling him!

But you can't. You can't because he's your boss and, if you throttle him, you'll be in jail. You can't because you'll lose a job which, except for this event, you really like. You can't because there are the kids to think about. And, when it comes right down to it, you can't because you have too much self-respect and respect for everyone else.

That's the key — self-respect and respect for others. Self-respect because you don't want to be the kind of person your boss is. Respect for others because, even though your boss is a manipulator, he isn't the only person in the office and no one else deserves your rage.

Paul has a terrible stress response. When the work starts to pile up, he becomes virtually paralyzed with stress. He can't set priorities — *everything* becomes equally important. As a result, he convinces himself that he doesn't have enough time to do even the most urgent things, let alone anything else. Worse than that, he doesn't know how to deactivate his stress without lashing out at other people, usually his colleagues. Consequently, the other members of the department fear him and rearrange their own work to minimize the chances of his stressing out. His supervisor is going to send Paul to a therapist, who will teach him some stress management tools.

So what do you do when you've been treated badly or you're under so much stress that you don't know whether you can stand another day?

Respect yourself and those around you, even when stress levels hit critical . . . *especially* when stress levels hit critical!

Fine, you say, but how do I carry that out?

Respect for yourself means that you will try to do and say only what the best version of you would do or say. The best version of you thinks things through carefully, doesn't fly off the handle, and responds appropriately to stressful situations. That's your best you, and trying always to be that person is how you practice self-respect.

Respect for others means that you will try to do and say only what the best versions of others would respond well to. Appeal to their thoughtfulness, to their sense of fair-mindedness, to their ability to stay cool under fire.

Other people can't be used to get what you want because they too have feelings and thoughts. They too are hurt by many of the things that hurt you, and are pleased by many of the things that please you. Trying to always remember this and to guide yourself accordingly is how you practice respect for others.

If you're a manager, practicing respect for your subordinates is especially important. As a manager, you have opportunities to abuse others. Given your position of authority, you are, for example, *expected* to assess your subordinates' performance. Try to ensure that exercising this duty doesn't become the opportunity to relieve your stress by treating them disrespectfully.

Still, you may have trouble implementing what, in your mind, you know is appropriate. You may know that respecting others is good in theory, but how do you stop yourself from getting involved in a yelling match?

There are lots of ways to try to curb your impulse to respond. Here are some:

- Look away and count to ten . . . repeat as necessary until you calm down.
- Excuse yourself from the situation to get a drink of water.
- Imagine that you're doing your favorite activity in your favorite place.
- If your tormenter won't let you leave, imagine him wearing clown make-up or being doused in noodles (there are many variants of this technique).
- Remind yourself that, in four hours, you'll be on your way home.
- Return to your desk or office, sit quietly for a few minutes, and plan your response.
- Return to your office and do 25 jumping jacks.
- Promise yourself that, when you get a minute, you will write everything that happens down and file it for use at the right time.

Check Your Attitude

Now comes the hard part — trying to rearrange your beliefs, hopes, expectations, and desires to curb your emotional response to stress.

This is hard because you've had a lifetime of accumulating habitual responses to stress. You've become accustomed to responding to stress in a particular way, even if that way is hard on yourself and everyone around you. In some ways, even a poor stress response can help. The problem is that you feel guilty about the verbal assault you inflicted on your assistant, or you're still hurting from the bruise on your forehead you got from banging your head against the wall.

A lot of people have unpleasant stress responses. That's hardly a surprise — stress is an automatic response that brings out the worst in most people. But you can, with practice, *control* that response by disentangling the *need* for reducing stress from the *techniques* you have for doing it. You can think about your stress response, identify its irritating or damaging qualities, and reorganize your response to stress so that those qualities are jettisoned.

Give yourself daily reminders

The first thing to do is to remember Marcus Aurelius' daily meditation, also mentioned in Chapter 10: "Today, I will be surrounded by people who irritate me. I will not demonstrate my irritation." Of course, it's not only people that cause stress, so perhaps a slight reworking of Aurelius is in order:

Today, you will be surrounded by people who irritate you and situations that stress you out. You will not demonstrate your irritation or stress without first thinking about if and how you want to express it.

Reminding yourself of this — every day — helps prepare you for the stress that inevitably accompanies people in professional life. When the stressful situation arises, you can say to yourself, "Well, I expected this. Now, what can I do about it to solve the problem?"

Reorganize your stress response

While reminding yourself that you will be irritated and you will be stressed might help you be prepared for stress when it does occur, a daily reminder isn't the only thing you need to do to defuse or reorganize your stress response. In order to successfully reorganize your stress response, you do two other things:

- ✔ **Exercise.** Exercise either in the morning or at lunch if you tend to stress out at work, or, if you keep it all bottled up until you get home, between work and home.

- ✔ **Focus on solutions.** Tell yourself that you will not do what you normally do when you stress out, that you will focus on the problem and solutions to it rather than on its role in causing you stress.

Thinking about solutions takes lots of practice. You won't always succeed. That's okay — that you think about solutions at all puts you ahead of the curve and doing so will work at least some of the time. Keep practicing. It will work with increasing frequency.

Once you've successfully deactivated your habituated stress response, it's time to inaugurate a new one, one that lacks the bad, old qualities and replaces them with constructive, new ones. Here, again, focus as much as you can on responding politely and with moderation. Try to think the situation through until you've found a solution that respects yourself and others, one that doesn't focus on who is to blame for what, but on who can do what to solve the problem.

Six steps to stress reduction

1. Analyze your stress response and identify its annoying and damaging aspects.

2. Expect stress and irritation every day.

3. When stress or irritation happen, immediately tell yourself that you will not respond in an annoying or damaging manner.

4. Calm down enough to think.

5. Think about what you want to say or do in response.

6. Respond in a moderate and constructive tone.

Now, it's time to put the six-point program to the test. It takes time, self-awareness, and lots of practice to cultivate new habits. Luckily, humans are remarkably creative and malleable. You, too, can manage stress with grace!

Chapter 13

Following Your Conscience: Ethical Dilemmas at Work

*N*o one is immune from ethical dilemmas at work. If the company you work for is well organized and has a clear set of policies, ethical dilemmas can be minimized. But they can no more be eliminated than can the pleasure you get from doing a good job. Ethical dilemmas are part of life, so they are part of your professional life as well.

Some ethical dilemmas are unique to professional life, some are never found in professional life at all, and some are found both in and out of professional life. Rearranging the truth on your taxes is something you may be tempted to do in your private life, but being asked to cover up an accident for the company is unique to your job.

Some ethical dilemmas are trivial, some devastating. If you work at a camera store and steal a roll of film, that's a small, but actionable, transgression. If you steal a $5,000 video camera, that's another may — not only will you be fired if caught, you're likely to be prosecuted. And if you catch another employee stealing the $5,000 video camera, you're in another kind of dilemma.

Ethics is a complex subject, where intuitions are often in conflict with each other. No single chapter in any book can hope to capture every nuance of the ethical issues that emerge in the workplace. But we do offer some suggestions about some of the most common ethical issues arising at work.

In this chapter, you're introduced to some of the ethical issues that come from your role as an employee. Guidelines for spending company money and for guarding proprietary company information are typical examples. Some of the most troubling issues emerge from the interaction of your professional life and your private life, so you'll also get some advice on these matters. Finally, there are some ethical issues that arise because someone else asks you to do something that you know is wrong.

Preparing Expense Reports and Spending Company Money for Entertainment

Pretty obviously, when you work for a company, you are employed to *work* for them. In return, you receive a salary and the opportunity to learn a great deal. While you're at work, your time should be spent doing what you are expected to do. You're not expected to straighten out your private life or to browse the Web for hours on end looking for interesting facts about Tahiti.

That principle applies in general. When you're doing the company's work and spending money as an employee, you may ask the company to reimburse you, and when you are not doing the company's work or do not spend money as an employee, then you may not ask to be reimbursed.

Your company may ask you to travel. While you're business traveling, you are expected to remain focused on your job. Of course, you will incur expenses while doing the company's work on your travels. And you may ask the company to compensate you for those expenses.

It's your responsibility as manager to be educated about expense report policies. If your company doesn't allow any gifts or alcohol charges as expenses, inform your employees of that before they travel. If there are exceptions, employees need to know what they are. Suppose, for example, that one of your sales representatives stays at a friend's apartment when she travels to New York for a convention, saving the company $280 a night for five nights. Can she claim the $20 bottle of wine she gave to her hosts as an expense? How about the taxi ride to and from her friend's apartment and the convention? How about the taxi ride back from the Broadway play to which she took a client? How about the ticket for the play? Make it clear.

Keep these tips in mind:

- ✔ When you fill out your expense report, be sure to have all of the receipts for money spent while you were on company time.

- ✔ Keep an envelope with an elastic closure for expense report receipts.

- ✔ Clarify what is and what is not an acceptable expense *before* going on your trip.

If you host a business dinner while traveling, that can usually be included in your expense report. However, if you work for a company that will not compensate for alcohol, not even wine at dinner, try to separate the alcohol portion of the bill from the meal portion. If you can't do that, compute the amount spent for the meal and the proportion of the tip that went to the waiter for the meal and submit only that.

A sales representative at a major pharmaceutical company attended a professional convention in Las Vegas. While he was there, he hosted a client dinner at a casino restaurant. Things went very well at dinner. One of the male clients recommended that they go to a strip club. Not wanting to offend the client, the sales representative agreed. Some of the other clients decided against the excursion and left the group. The remaining four ended up spending about $250 of the sales representative's money for drinks. He submitted the expenses to his company. The company refused to compensate him, despite the fact that a large order was a direct consequence of the evening's excursion. They refused on the grounds that it was company policy not to pay for drinks, much less drinks at a strip club. The sales representative never recouped the $250.

This is a case of poor judgment — the sales representative knew the policy and should have suggested some other venue for doing business. But there are other cases in which employees add to expense reports claims that are not business-related expenses at all. This is padding an expense report, and it is grounds for dismissal in some companies. Surprisingly, it is encouraged in other companies. It is the manager's job to make clear to all concerned what policies your company has.

Our advice is simple — don't pad your expense reports unless instructed to do so. If you rent a car for a business trip and add three days to the trip for a little sightseeing, you are not entitled to charge the company for those three days. If you buy your daughter a gift at the airport gift shop, you are not entitled to charge the company for it. Smart accountants have seen most of it before and you're unlikely to get away with it. But that's not going to the heart of the matter. You don't want to pad the expense report because it's unfair to the company. Even if the company isn't always fair to you, that's no reason to be unfair to them.

Understanding Loyalty, Confidentiality, and Security

Typically, you work for someone else who pays you a salary. That relationship establishes the expectation that you owe the company or the person you work for your professional loyalty. And it almost certainly means that you will learn things that, if disclosed, would damage others or the company. But what are you supposed to do when, in the name of loyalty, you're asked to do something wrong? And how far are you obliged to respect confidentiality?

Loyalty

You are loyal to your friends, family members, colleagues, or bosses when you direct them to things that will benefit them, keep them safe from things that will harm them, and defend them against attack. You can also be loyal to a thing, a concept, or spiritual beliefs. You can be loyal to your car by getting it repaired rather than selling it, you can be loyal to your country by promoting it to others and by defending it, and you can be loyal to a religion.

Loyalty is a valued commodity in the business world. Many employers list it as the single most important virtue that an employee can have. It's not surprising that loyalty is so valued — employees who look to promote the business's interests and defend it against competition are essential for a successful company.

When the company's values overlap with your own, loyalty to the company is easy. Trouble arises when either a colleague or a boss asks you to do something you know is wrong and invokes your loyalty in making the request. This kind of request or demand can come camouflaged in many ways and may never be explicit. But the implication is always clear — you are expected to do something you know is wrong in order to demonstrate your loyalty either to your colleague, your boss, or that amorphous entity, the company.

Cindy, the Chief Financial Officer of Wingding International, was on the road frequently and was sometimes burned out. She occasionally took a day off to recharge. Her long-time assistant, Tom, covered for her by telling investors and others that she would return to the office the following day. One day, Cindy asked Tom to tell the owner of the company that she was in Denver. She was, as she told Tom, at Pebble Beach. Tom agreed and, when the owner called, he dutifully informed him that Cindy was at a meeting in Denver. Unfortunately, the owner was calling from the golf course, where he had just seen her. Tom was fired over the phone. Cindy was fired at the third tee.

Loyalty gone too far? You bet! People in positions of authority shouldn't ask their subordinates to lie for them. If you're a manager and you're doing something on company time that you shouldn't be doing, just tell your assistant that you're unavailable. Don't try to take advantage of someone else's loyalty, to you or to the company.

Likewise, subordinates shouldn't agree to lie for their bosses. Loyalty is one thing, lying in the name of loyalty is something else entirely. If your boss asks you to lie for her, politely give her an opportunity to back away from the request. Tom could, for example, have asked: "You want me to tell the owner you're in Denver arranging financing when in fact you're at Pebble Beach?"

If your boss doesn't back down from the request that you lie, ask an even more pointed question, such as: "You want me to lie?" If your boss doesn't get the hint that you're unwilling to comply by now, tell her politely that, as much as you respect her and enjoy working with her, you won't lie for her.

Be prepared for the worst. Some bosses will take your refusal in stride, and some won't. For those who do, you've established a ground floor and your boss will respect you for it. For the boss who is angered by your refusal, you can expect anything from a grunt of disapproval to a campaign of discrimination.

Confidentiality

As an employee, you know things that, were they to be disclosed, might hurt you, your colleagues, your bosses, or your company. Many companies have nondisclosure and confidentiality agreements written into employment contracts. Many others discuss confidentiality in their employee guidelines. Take confidentiality seriously!

Generally speaking, two kinds of confidential information exist — the first is proprietary company information; the second is information about people.

When you refuse to do your boss's bidding

When your boss goes after you because you won't do something wrong, the following tips may help:

- Keep a record of all incidents when your boss asks you to do something unethical and your responses to those requests.

- Keep your records at home. Do not keep them at work, where they could be stolen.

- Follow the instructions for combating unethical behavior found in the company's policies and procedures documents, if your company has them.

- Direct your concerns to the Human Resources department, if your company has one.

- Look for a new job.

Company information

Every business has proprietary information — information about jobs, lay-offs, performance reviews; information about patents and contracts; information about sales and earnings; information about product developments. The list goes on and on. What should you do as an employee to avoid disclosing confidential business information?

Your boss will, if he's on the ball, inform you about confidential information. He'll give you answers to the following questions:

- ✔ Which documents are confidential? Are there degrees of confidentiality? If so, what are they?

- ✔ Are you and your boss the only people who can look at these documents? If not, who else can look at them?

- ✔ Are you given the authority to open packages that say "Personal" or "Confidential" on them? If not, does anyone other than the addressee have that authority?

- ✔ Should you clear all requests for confidential materials with your boss? If not, under what conditions can you exercise your own judgment? If so, what should you do if your boss is unavailable?

- ✔ Does anyone have permission to remove things from your boss's office? If so, who? If not, how should you handle such requests?

Having this kind of blunt discussion with your boss will show your boss that you care about confidentiality issues and are willing to work to protect it.

If you're privy to confidential proprietary information, you bear a duty not to disclose it. This duty requires, among other things, that you learn how to live with secrets. Learning to live with secrets, in turn, requires that you be alert to what you say in the company of others and that you be alert to others' attempts to get information from you. Don't take these duties lightly! Your job depends on doing them well.

These guidelines can help you:

- ✔ Know who's authorized to discuss confidential matters and discuss confidential matters only with them.

- ✔ Practice self-control by being the model of discretion in all situations.

- ✔ When in public, speak softly so that others do not overhear you.

- ✔ When asked for confidential information, reply that, because it's confidential, you can't divulge it. If someone persists, politely point out that he or she is out of line. If that doesn't work, try a blank stare.

✔ Do not allow others to read your computer screen or peruse your desk top — put confidential documents face down or in a locked drawer when you're not looking at them.

✔ Do not tell your spouse or life-partner all the details, even if you're tempted to do so!

Personal information

The other kind of confidential information that you can gain is personal information of an embarrassing sort. Everyone knows that administrative assistants sometimes learn things they would really rather not know about their bosses and that bosses sometimes ask employees to report things about colleagues that are really none of the boss's business.

This kind of knowledge can put you into a real bind. If you find your boss *in flagrante delicto* one Saturday morning, you've seen something that will forever affect your working relationship. And if it wasn't his spouse, so much the worse! Not only will both of you be embarrassed, but you'll probably be put in the compromising position of being asked to lie about it if you're ever asked.

Likewise, if you're at a restaurant and overhear a conversation at the next table about a psychiatric patient who you just happen to know socially, your relationship to him will be different thanks to the psychiatrist's indiscretion.

These kinds of breaches are entirely avoidable, but only by those responsible for committing them. Whenever someone else, either through what he says or does, discloses something that you would rather not know, you're placed into a coercive position — either keep the secret or snitch. Both options are unpleasant.

To keep this kind of thing from happening to you, the first line of defense is always to stop someone from saying something before he says more than you want to know. There are two ways to do this. First, distinguish between friendly exchanges of benign information and malignant exchanges of harmful information. Second, ask whether, given your professional relationship, he really wants to do so. Most of the time, this will prevent the situation from going somewhere both of you will regret. Having avoided the issue, make sure that it never comes up again.

Sometimes, of course, preventive measures don't work. Either a colleague just blurts something out, or you stumble on to something you shouldn't see, or you find yourself overhearing something you shouldn't hear. In these kinds of cases, you're stuck. Through no fault of your own, you know something about someone that you shouldn't know. The best general advice is then to act as if you never had that bit of knowledge in the first place. This is not always easy, and you won't always succeed. But at least you will have tried to not act on something you shouldn't know.

Here's more advice that can help:

✔ Think to yourself: Do I want what I'm about to do on videotape? If the answer is "no," don't do it.

✔ If someone discloses confidential information about clients or patients to you, your best recourse is to keep quiet. If it continues, you could consider approaching his or her supervisor or boss with the breach of confidentiality. It is the supervisor's or the boss's responsibility to correct the problem, not yours.

Security

If you've read everything so far about loyalty and confidentiality, you'll know most of what needs to be done to ensure that confidential information isn't leaked. But there are a few loose ends still to tie up.

Stealing from your company — whether it is a product or some office supplies — is wrong.

Another serious issue is maintaining the security of hard copy and electronic documents. Luckily, there are some straightforward steps you can take.

✔ Don't leave confidential documents unattended on your desk. At a minimum, turn them face down when you leave. Better still, put them in a locked drawer.

✔ If you have confidential documents at a meeting, keep them under wraps until needed. Return them to your briefcase or portfolio as soon as they are no longer needed.

✔ When transporting confidential documents anywhere, put them in an envelope or folder. If you leave the office with them, put them in a locked briefcase.

✔ When mailing confidential documents, place them in an envelope marked "confidential" and then place that sealed envelope in another envelope also marked "confidential." That way, no one can pretend they didn't see the warning.

✔ Never throw confidential documents away. Shred them.

Your computer support team will no doubt develop security measures to protect sensitive electronic documents. Various encryption codes, password procedures, and clearance procedures may already be in place. Follow those procedures and use those codes consistently.

You can also take or recommend additional measures, if you think that electronic security is lax. Ask your manager for suggestions. Information security is, after all, her responsibility. Talk to the resident Information Technology officer about what she does to protect documents, then recommend that everyone follow her example. Here are some ways to protect confidentiality while using computers:

- ✔ Remove printouts from shared printers as soon as possible.
- ✔ Store document- and program-disks in a locked drawer.
- ✔ Turn your computer off at night.
- ✔ Don't share disks.
- ✔ Don't send confidential documents by e-mail, unless you are certain that your system is secure.

Mixing Personal Business and Work

In many businesses, the workday is much less structured than it used to be. Flex time, personal days, home offices, and the conveniences of electronic devices have worked together to make the 9 to 5 workday a thing of the past in some companies. Even in companies with rigid structures, there's much more flexibility than before.

Additional flexibility to the workday is a huge change, and a real boon. However, some new problems have been introduced into the business environment — and some already-existing problems have been exacerbated — by the flexible workday.

If you are a manager, try to make things easy for your employees. Give them standing permission to pick up their dry cleaning or to get a haircut. Be accommodating when someone's day care arrangements fall apart and a child ends up in the office unannounced. Your courtesy will be repaid with loyalty and hard work.

For employees, the line between work time and private time has blurred recently, and the desire and the need to take care of personal business during the workday has in some cases become acute. If you have a lot of autonomy in structuring your day, and if you act in a professional manner, mixing private and professional activities is not likely to cause problems. If you don't have much autonomy or if you allow your personal business to interfere with your real business, you'll end up in a bad situation.

Doing your personal business on company time

Many employers understand, even encourage, employees taking enough time to do short personal errands during the day, so long as the work is completed. Again, if you're the manager, it's your responsibility to make company policy clear. Some companies offer *electronic concierge* services that perform personal errands for their employees or arrange for dry cleaning to be picked up at the office or home. These are a real boon to employees.

The difficulties introduced by kids are another arena where sympathetic managers and understanding colleagues are a necessity. If your colleague leaves work early every Wednesday to take his son to violin practice, that doesn't mean he's getting a perk that you're not. He may have to compensate by working on the Saturday that you spend ballooning in New Mexico. This kind of rearranged workweek is a common feature of the contemporary economic landscape.

(Boondoggle) personal calls

Abusing phone privileges is a recurring employer complaint. Spending two minutes talking to your daughter about her pet mouse is fine; spending half an hour talking to your best friend about your latest round of golf while there's a deadline looming isn't. Keep it short and to the point, especially if you're in a cubicle. Avoid screaming arguments with your spouse.

E-mails

Your work e-mail account is for work-related e-mails. If you want to join chat rooms or dating services, do so from some other computer (like the one you have at home). And refrain from sending racy e-mails or highly critical (or *flaming*) e-mails. We cover this topic in more detail in the chapter on cyber-etiquette.

Your e-mail is company property and may be monitored. If your boss finds questionable e-mail, she may have grounds for discipline or dismissal.

Computer games

Some people are addicted to computer games. But some professional adults are a little too fond of computer games, too, and this fondness can impinge on work. Don't let this happen to you — you get bug-eyed and pretty irritable when you realize that you've just been playing for two hours and that the Webding report is due this afternoon. If you have to, remove the games from your work computer and put them where they belong — at home.

Web browsing

Yes, well, we all know what I'm talking about, don't we? Employers in the last ten years have lost untold work hours to employees' Web browsing. No doubt looking at the Himalayan Adventure Outfitters Web site will get you stoked for your next climb in Nepal, but, really, it can probably wait until you get to some other computer — like the one at home. And browsing for just the right coffee mug for your new office can take hours. Believe me, we know!

At work, your Web browsing should be confined to the personal time that you are given. Managers bear the responsibility of letting employees know the expectations, here as elsewhere. If it's okay with you for an employee to watch the Sam Donaldson Web cast on his break, by all means say so. But also say that, when break time is over, it's time to get back to work.

Finally, we have to say it again — stay away from porn sites while you're at work. If you get caught looking at them, you'll be in *big* trouble. And chances are increasingly good that you will be caught. Employers everywhere are installing software that tracks the Web sites visited by employees. Is getting a cheap thrill really worth a dressing down from your boss? Is it worth your job? Probably not.

Separating personal space and business space

One of the consequences of the additional flexibility in the workday is that the line between personal space and professional space is fuzzier now than it has ever been. There's no doubt about it — the new casualness has caused more than a few privacy problems.

Keeping your personal life personal

Taking care of too much personal business on company time is a bad idea. You also have to be careful about involving your business colleagues in your personal life.

There is no specific rule governing how much of your personal life to reveal to your colleagues and your employer. You can divulge it all if you're comfortable doing so. But remember that some people would rather not know about your latest Atlantic City escapade. Most people are better off not knowing how much you hate your ex-husband or ex-wife.

> ✔ Not everyone in your workplace wants to know everything about your life.
>
> ✔ What you divulge today could come back to haunt you tomorrow.

Take a moment to assess your colleagues and yourself before shooting from the hip about your private life. Do your colleagues regularly share their private lives in any detail? If not, that's a sign that you should think twice about sharing yours. Do your supervisors manipulate the information others have divulged? If so, that's a sign, too. Do you really want anyone other than your family and closest friends to know what you're tempted to report to your colleagues? These are difficult issues, but the wise thing to do is to err on the side of discretion. If you confide to a coworker that your parents are driving you insane and he repeats that to your supervisor, your supervisor might see fit to be hyper vigilant when assessing your performance. If you tell your boss that you'd like to bring your girlfriend *and* your new wife to the company's family day and he gets a sick look on his face, you've badly miscalculated.

Until you can accurately gauge your colleagues and supervisors, it's better to keep some things close to the vest.

Remember that people can say one thing and then do another. Here's an anecdote that perfectly illustrates how a private matter can be manipulated.

A Chief Operations Officer of a medical analysis company claimed he wanted his company to be like a family. He encouraged employees to say what they wished without fear of recrimination or retribution. A doctor confided to him that, despite her objections, a former lab assistant was falsely spreading a rumor that they had an affair. Expecting the COO to offer some sympathy, or perhaps even talk to the former assistant, the doctor was shocked when the COO instead inserted a report on the matter in her file that suggested that she was responsible for fostering the relationship. Only repeating the entire embarrassing episode to the CEO got the report removed from her file. She never confided in her COO again.

Keep in mind that your lifestyle can become relevant to your employer if that lifestyle has a negative impact on your performance. If you publicize your long tradition of leaving work and getting drunk every Friday while still in uniform, you could be called into your boss's office to hear a lecture on the virtues of sobriety and the importance of being a good company representative at all times.

There are some personal issues that are probably best kept from colleagues and supervisors. Your family's health history is nobody's business at the office. If you are rash enough to tell someone that the men in your family have a history of prostate cancer, you shouldn't be surprised when the Human Resources person asks you about it one day while he's filling out an insurance questionnaire. And if you're vain enough to tell your supervisor that your uncle is Bill Gates, you shouldn't be shocked when she tells you that she has a great idea for Microsoft. She just needs your help setting up a quick interview with your uncle.

Keeping your professional life professional

Just as it's probably wise to keep some of your private life away from the office, it's also wise to keep some of your professional life away from your private life.

Your romantic partner doesn't need to know everything about the petty office politics to know that you're stressed at your job. And if there is business information that you can tell your friends or your romantic partner only by violating client confidentiality or company policy, then you are obligated not to tell them.

Not telling your closest friends or your romantic partner something can be very hard. Psychiatrists, medical doctors, and lawyers face this dilemma on a regular basis. The sympathetic friend or romantic partner acknowledges the difficulties entailed by professional codes of conduct and will not pry.

Violating client confidentiality is grounds for dismissal in some professions and expulsion from some professional organizations.

Pressing for personal information from someone bound to professional confidentiality may cause the end of the relationship.

Drawing the line between the private and the professional

Not only are there things about you that your colleagues don't need to know, there are some things about you that no one at your workplace has any right to know. For example, your political views are irrelevant in the vast majority of business situations. So, too, are your religious beliefs, your ethnic background, your family's lifestyle, your sexual orientation, and your hobbies. And while your moral values may be pertinent, try always to keep the dogmatic elements out of your workday environment. These are private matters that you should not impose on others and that others — including your employers — may neither impose on you nor base employment decisions on.

Of course, that these are private matters doesn't prevent bad employers from trying to make them relevant for your job. Although many companies are much more progressive now than they were even ten years ago, it's a cruel truth that gays, lesbians, and transgendered individuals, as well as those who have nontraditional families and unusual hobbies, have to be more careful than others when discussing these matters with colleagues. The situation is improving — slowly — but unless you work for an enlightened employer and with enlightened colleagues, you should be very careful about disclosing any details about your personal life that could alienate some of your coworkers.

For example, we know someone who collects totemic fertility symbols from around the world and who belongs to an international society of like-minded collectors. You can guess what happened when she revealed this to a coworker. She quickly learned how prurient the imaginations of some people are! And she quickly learned how popular her collection made her with both men and women!

Here's some advice to keep in mind:

- No one at work is entitled to know everything about you. If someone's asking you to reveal a private matter, just say, "I prefer to keep my private life private, thank you."

- If someone persists in asking impertinent questions despite your repeated refusal to answer them, report the matter to a supervisor.

- If it's your supervisor who won't let up on the impertinent questions, report the matter to his or her supervisor.

How to Say "No" and Maybe, Just Maybe, Keep Your Job

Some ethical dilemmas come not from you taking advantage of your employer, but from your employer taking advantage of you. These problems are tough because you're no longer in control. If you routinely browse the Web while at work, you can change that. But if you're asked by the owner of a company to falsify employee records to avoid paying Social Security taxes, you are no longer in control. For not only is the request unethical, it's combined with the implicit threat that if you won't do it, you won't have a job.

This is a classic professional dilemma. Variations on it are faced by millions of workers every year. Your success or failure to deal with situations like this depends more on your tact, diplomacy, and good manners than on anything else.

As always, the first thing to do is to try to defuse the situation by giving the other person the option of retracting the request or demand. Try one of the following:

- Repeat the request — say, "Let me make sure that I heard you correctly. You would like me to misreport our earnings this quarter. Is that correct?"

- A blank stare.

- Silence.

✔ Say, "I'm not sure I heard that."

✔ Say, "I'm sorry, let's look for another solution."

✔ Say, "Excuse me a minute, I'm going to go for a drink and when I get back, we can start over."

The hope with all of these maneuvers is that the person making the improper request will think twice and retract the request.

These techniques won't always work. You may be faced with a choice — go along with the unethical request and compromise yourself in the process, or refuse to go along with it and face the consequences.

It's almost always in your self-interest and in the interest of your company to refuse an unethical request from another employee.

If you stand by your refusal, you will no doubt face some criticism and some discrimination from the person making the request or demand. She may brand you as disloyal or as not being a team player. Let her do so. Others will notice when you're persecuted for no apparent reason and will, more often than not, guess what happened.

You may lose your job. That's unlikely, but it does happen. Most of the time, your refusal probably will only result in her trying to get someone else to go along. Maybe she'll find a co-conspirator. Maybe she won't. But you won't be going along for the long tumble out of the company that she's likely to take when her shenanigans are discovered. And they usually are.

There are exceptions to this. Sometimes you run across a powerful, protected, and truly malicious Machiavelli who makes you an unethical offer you can't refuse if you hope to keep your job. Faced with this kind of monstrous choice, you can either accept the offer and keep your job or you can quit. Our advice is to quit on the spot — unless you're in the mafia. Remember that there are other jobs out there.

Of course, there are lots of other ethical dilemmas you could face at your job that aren't covered here. Some excellent resources exist for understanding the difficulties you face in your job. We recommend:

✔ www.bullybusters.org. Bullybusters is a nonprofit organization devoted to preventing bullies from ruining your career.

✔ Gary and Ruth Namie, *The Bully at Work* (Sourcebooks, 2000).

✔ Rushworth Kidder, *When Good People Make Tough Choices: Resolving the Dilemmas Of Ethical Living* (Fireside, 1996).

✔ Joseph L. Badaracco, Jr., *Defining Moments: When Managers Must Choose Between Right and Right* (Harvard Business School, 1997).

Chapter 14

Handling Sexuality at the Workplace

Romantic attraction is a fact of life — so it's a fact of professional life. Sometimes it's one-way rather than mutual, and romantic attention is sometimes forced instead of consenting. In the workplace, this can come coupled with unequal power, leading to sexual harassment. Although never condoned by company policy, sexual harassment occurs with frightening regularity in the workplace.

Most of the time, however, romantic attraction is mutual, or at least consenting. But there are plenty of reasons not to let others know about a romance, not the least of which is that you may not know if it's going to work out. Unfortunately, no secret is more likely to be exposed and become the subject of gossip than a romance. Few office romances remain under wraps for long, and when they're exposed, trouble sometimes follows.

In this chapter, we cover what sexual harassment is, how to avoid it, and what to do if you encounter it. You will also get a few pointers for handling office flirtations and romances.

Avoiding Sexual Harassment

A difference exists between office flirting and romance, on the one hand, and sexual harassment, on the other. Flirting is sometimes annoying, romances are sometimes forbidden by company policy, but sexual harassment is illegal.

Even today, after sexual harassment laws have been on the books for more than thirty years, there is uncertainty and confusion about what sexual harassment actually is. Many companies have mandatory sexual harassment seminars for all employees. If you're not in such a company, or if you haven't yet attended one of these seminars, here is the definition of *sexual harassment,* derived from Title VII of the Civil Rights Act of 1964.

Sexual harassment occurs whenever:

- An insinuated promise of a job or a promotion is made in return for sexual favors, or demotion or firing occurs for refusing to comply with a request for sex.
- Or, a hostile work environment is created.
- Or, an explicit requirement exists that you engage in certain behavior in order to keep or get a job; or employment decisions are premised on your response to another's behavior; or someone else's behavior creates a hostile or abusive work environment that changes the conditions of your job.

The first kind of harassment is by far the easiest to understand. It's the *quid pro quo* (this for that) form of harassment, in which one person, usually a woman in a subordinate position, is asked by another person, usually a man in some position of authority, to provide sexual favors in return for a job or a promotion. Although male-to-female harassment is the most common form of *quid pro quo* harassment, it's not the only kind. Gays, lesbians, and transgendered individuals increasingly face sexual harassment as well, and more and more men are facing sexual harassment from women as women climb to positions of power.

Quid pro quo harassment has a long history. It has long been a favorite practice of people in positions of authority. But it's wrong and you don't have to comply. Period. The category of harassment that is the most difficult to pin down is that in which there is a hostile work environment. Recent legal cases have found that unwanted touching, unwanted flirting, nude pictures of men or women, lewd body gestures and comments, and some comments about appearance and dress all rise to the level of a hostile work environment, and therefore qualify as instances of sexual harassment.

A female employee of a municipal utility company told a dirty joke to a male coworker. The male coworker was not offended, but another coworker passing them in the hallway overheard the joke and was offended. She claimed that the two people in question had a practice of exchanging dirty jokes in earshot of her and others. Despite her protests to them, she claimed that they continued the practice. Management sided with the offended employee and placed formal reprimands in both of the other employees' files. Subsequently, both were denied promotions.

The ribald camaraderie that used to exist between many men in male-dominated workplaces is a thing of the past. The old-boy practices of telling dirty jokes and pinching secretaries are, like racist comments, strictly out of place in today's workplace. The employee who fails to take this to heart is in for some very rough sailing.

The third kind of sexual harassment rises above the other two in severity. One might get a hint from a supervisor that sexual favors will be rewarded with a job promotion. But if the *quid pro quo* is made explicit, the matter rises to the third level of harassment and it needs to be turned over to another supervisor or the Human Resources department immediately.

Likewise, if you're a woman working in a mechanic's shop and a fellow mechanic has a couple of pin-ups on the wall next to his workstation, that probably rises only to the level of a hostile work environment. However, if you walk into work one day and find the walls of your workstation liberally plastered with offensive pictures, the conditions of your job have materially changed. That qualifies as harassment rising to the actionable level.

Pretty clearly, you don't want to work in a hostile environment or in an office where the management team thinks it is a perk of the job to have their pick of the latest recruits. How, then, do you avoid harassment?

The first responsibility is the supervisor's or the manager's. Supervisors and managers set the tone for the office. If he makes it clear that sexual harassment will not be tolerated, you're lucky. He may allow some frivolity, but he should be explicit that predatory behavior will not be tolerated. If he doesn't, you may have no choice but to go over his head.

✔ Conduct yourself professionally at all times. If you treat others courteously and professionally and make no sly allusions to sexual matters, chances are pretty good that you will be treated the same way.

✔ Take care with your wardrobe, especially if you're a woman. Revise it to avoid clothes that send an unwanted sexual message to others. Remove the heavy mascara, plunging necklines, supershort skirts, and nosebleed high heels. Men should avoid tight pants and muscle shirts at work.

✔ Remember that some people's personalities change when they travel. When on business trips, avoid meeting others in hotel rooms and leave bars and restaurants when it becomes clear that your colleagues are more interested in getting drunk than in relaxing after a hard day.

✔ Keep your ears open to rumors about sexual harassers. Rumors are often unreliable, but if you keep hearing the same thing about the same supervisor, it is wise to verify the rumor and, if verified, stay away from private encounters with that supervisor.

✔ Don't discuss your sex life at work. "Don't ask, don't tell" applies to everyone.

Confronting Sexual Harassment

Your attempts to avoid sexual harassment won't always work. If you're being harassed, you're entitled to protection. Unfortunately, taking that protection before you give the harasser an opportunity to change his or her behavior will instantly brand you as a troublemaker. So, the first thing to do if you're being harassed is to confront the harasser as politely as you can. Tell him or her that the behavior is unwanted, unappreciated, and that you want it to stop.

If it's a simple misunderstanding, telling the harasser to stop ought to do the trick. But there are plenty of cases in which this won't work. Suppose you're in the boss's office with no witnesses. Telling him that his advances are unwelcome may not deter him. In such a case, you have no alternative but to leave his office as soon as you can, with as much dignity as possible. As soon as you get back to your desk, write down the date of the harassment and what happened. Take it home. Keep it there. He may never harass you again, but if he does, you'll be keeping a record of it.

✔ Keep at home a record of all incidents of harassment. Do not keep them at work, where they might be stolen.

✔ Follow the instructions for combating harassment found in the company's policies- and procedures-documents, if your company has them.

✔ Direct your concerns to the Human Resources department, if your company has one.

✔ Do not ignore harassment, hoping it will go away. It won't.

In some cases, formal charges may be your only option. In such a case, contact the Equal Employment Opportunity Office or the National Organization of Women. Both organizations can help you determine whether your case is strong enough to pursue and, if so, how you should pursue it.

If you love your job and you love working for the company and you want to stay there, don't let yourself be intimidated by the prospects of filing a harassment charge. Sexual harassment charges are, of course, not to be undertaken frivolously or under false pretenses, but they are not to be avoided from fear, either, if they are well founded.

In filing a harassment charge, you will have to rely on your supervisor to set the tone. Your supervisor's responsibilities are two-fold: first, ensure that the person bringing the charge is treated fairly and neutrally; second, ensure that the person charged is treated fairly and neutrally. Fulfilling this dual duty is one of the hardest things a supervisor has to do, but it's essential if the individuals involved are to avoid premature vilification. If your supervisor is the one doing the harassing, you really have no choice: You will be reporting him to his supervisor.

Having said all that, charges levied against others can have a negative impact on the person bringing the charges. Not only do you have the burden of proof in any legal proceedings, but you must also bear the burden of being thought a disloyal rabble-rouser by some of your coworkers.

The legal burden is hard to bear — you must prove that you were treated worse than others, that the harassment was intentional, and that there was no other reason for the employment decision about you than your refusal to accept the *quid pro quo.* That's a lot to prove.

The social burden is worse: You will be ostracized by some of your colleagues. So, remember:

- ✔ Bringing a sexual harassment suit against a coworker or a superior might result in your being fired on trumped-up charges. It probably will result in your being made to feel very uncomfortable at the workplace by some of your colleagues.

- ✔ As hard as it is to bring to light, sexual harassment cannot be tolerated. If you file a sexual harassment charge, tough it out. You're doing the right thing!

Dating Someone from Work

Romances happen in the workplace on a regular basis. Statistics show that almost half of all marriages are the result of meeting at work. Usually, everything works out — lovebirds work comfortably with each other and they live happily ever after. Occasionally, things don't work out — the dating couple is embarrassingly gushy at work, they sneak off for *long* lunches, they bring their personal troubles to work, or one of them promotes the other unfairly.

Flirting

Flirting with someone is harmless unless the person you are flirting with doesn't want to be the recipient. But, as you know by the time you're old enough to work, you don't begin a work relationship by flirting. You begin a relationship at work professionally, getting to know the person on a professional basis first. If he's single and you're single and you think that your interest in him will not be immediately rebuffed, it's perfectly all right to ask him out for a drink after work.

If he says "no" and is not obviously disappointed that he can't make it, let the matter go. Your persistence is a pestilence. If, on the other hand, he seems disappointed that he can't accept, suggest that you reschedule for some other time. When he jumps at the opportunity, you will know that your attraction to him is reciprocated.

If you're not interested in someone else's flirtations, there are a number of ways of informing the flirter of that fact. You can try simply ignoring the suggestive remarks or you can tell the truth — you're not interested in having any relationship other than a professional one.

Each strategy has its risks — if you try ignoring flirtation, the other person may think only that you're obtuse and may increase the voltage; if you tell the truth, feelings may get hurt. Such is the stuff of adult life. The best advice we have is simple — try always to take the other person's feelings into account when you deliberate about what to do with an unwanted flirtation, and if you end up hurting someone's feelings despite your best efforts otherwise, accept it and move on.

Dating

When dating someone in the office, remember two things: First, check the company's dating policy, and, second, keep your public displays of affection out of the office.

And keep this advice in mind:

- ✔ If your company permits dating among coworkers and doesn't require disclosure, you are under no obligation to disclose an office romance. If it looks like it's going to last, it is polite to inform your supervisor.

- ✔ If your company does not permit dating, then you either keep your job or keep the romance or try to keep both by keeping the romance a secret. Know ahead of time that the last strategy will probably fail.

- ✔ If your company permits dating but only on the condition that it's disclosed to the appropriate person (a supervisor or someone in Human Resources), comply with the policy as soon as you can.

Some people prefer to keep their private lives completely separate from their professional lives. If your company does not require disclosure and you don't want to say anything, then, by all means, don't.

Having an office romance is thrilling. Anticipating the evening during the day can, however, lead some people to distraction, and distraction can, if not curbed, result in embarrassment and the loss of one's job. Beware! Your excitement, while contagious to your loved one, is best ignored during the workday. Otherwise, after sending your lover a saucy memo, you may find yourself out on the street. Remember:

✔ Closet and office trysts are mighty risky and will get you fired if discovered.

✔ Racy e-mails are, like all e-mails, property of the company.

Problematic romances

Many companies discourage romances between people of unequal rank. The reasons are obvious. People will suspect (and may be correct to suspect) that any promotion or special treatment of the person of lower rank is a result of the romantic relationship with the person of higher rank. And, if the romance goes sour, there is simply too much risk that the person of higher rank will make life miserable for the person of lower rank. No company wants to put itself at risk of a sexual harassment suit that might result from a failed romance.

Most companies therefore require that relationships between superiors and subordinates be disclosed immediately, usually by the person in position of power. In most cases, that disclosure immediately results in the superior being taken out of the evaluation loop of the subordinate. Another common consequence is that one of the two, usually the subordinate one, is transferred to a different job.

One other problematic romance is that between a company representative and a client or customer. Take care that your romantic involvement with a client or customer does not entangle you in a conflict of interest in which you give the client preferential treatment because there is a personal relationship between the two of you. In cases like this, it is preferable to ask that you be reassigned rather than risk embarrassment and possible legal action.

Romance in the contemporary office is not easy. But, following these tips and avoiding the obvious faux pas, you can still find the love of your life at work . . . if you're lucky!

Part IV

Entertaining for Business

The 5th Wave   By Rich Tennant

"Oh, will you take that thing off before you embarrass someone!"

In this part . . .

We put you through a real etiquette workout, reviewing everything from table settings and wine choices to buffet lines and company retreats. Then, we figure out the office party minefield. Should you give a gift? And if so, what? We close with a reminder about combining alcohol and work functions, and we give you some tips for handling them both gracefully.

Chapter 15

Business Meals, Dinner Parties, Juggling Food and Drink

*W*hy combine food and business? At first the answer may seem simple: time. While it's true that there often aren't enough hours in the day to complete business unless you schedule some meetings during mealtime, remember that sharing a meal is also a time-honored way of cultivating trust.

In a business meal, the devil and the deal are in the details. In this chapter, we show you some clever ways to stay organized, save time, and build relationships. And we'll provide suggestions for entertaining at home without anxiety. In the next chapter, we introduce you to the nitty-gritty of polite dining.

Organizing a Business Meal at a Restaurant

The most typical times for business meals are breakfast and lunch. Dinner is usually reserved for special occasions or out-of-town guests. Breakfast meetings are good if your time is limited and your agenda is short, but keep in mind that not everyone is an early bird. Lunch is the default business meal. Its neutrality implies neither the informality of a breakfast meeting nor the formality of a dinner meeting.

How about tea?

Business people, especially when they're from out of town and staying in a hotel, sometimes find afternoon tea in the lobby a relaxing option. Meeting for tea can be quite leisurely and social.

Afternoon tea is typically served between 3:30 and 5:00 p.m. Although you sometimes see this called *high tea* in America, high tea is actually a meal that nannies serve children in the nursery.

Unlike tea, meeting for coffee is quick and informal. Some people also like to meet for a drink between work and home, but the key words here are *a drink,* singular not plural. See Chapter 17 for more on combining alcohol and work.

The more formal the meal, the more emphasis there will be on the social aspects of your relationship. Informal meetings are for discussing business details, but formal dinners are for building personal rapport.

Assume you've decided to take someone out for lunch. Here are the steps to follow:

Step 1: Schedule the lunch

Choosing the restaurant is your business. Never ask your guest where she wants to go. Choose two different restaurants that you think will appeal to your guest. If you do not know your client well, check with his or her assistant to see if the person has particular dietary preferences or restrictions. See if reservations are available on the day that you wish to take your client to lunch. Ask for two times, noon and one o'clock. And the restaurant should be convenient to your guest, not to you.

The actual invitation can be phrased like this:

> *Chris, I'd like you to be my guest at lunch next week. Would Wednesday or Thursday work for you? Noon or one o'clock? Would you prefer Indian Garden or Chez Chez?*

Once you've worked the details out, repeat them at the end of the conversation:

> *Great talking with you Chris. I look forward to seeing you at Chez Chez at noon on Wednesday.*

Immediately call the restaurant to confirm your reservation and cancel any other reservations.

Step 2: Confirm

A day before the meeting, check with your guest and confirm the date, time, and location.

Step 3: Pay before you eat

On the day of the meeting, arrive early at the restaurant and ask the maitre d' to take your credit card and run it though for preapproval right away. Sign the receipt, add 18 to 20 percent gratuity, and, if you wish, request that the receipt be mailed to you in a stamped, self-addressed envelope that you provide. Or you can establish a house account at the restaurant. Either way, the bill never appears at the table, so there's no confusion about who pays.

Step 4: Be nonchalant

Do not remove your coat and do not eat or drink anything. When your guest arrives, you should look as if you've just arrived. Greet your guest warmly by name and with a handshake.

Step 5: Take the worst seat

Motion for your guest to follow the maitre d' to the table. Allow your guest to have the best seat. Guests should never sit looking at a mirror or toward the kitchen door.

Step 6: Order carefully

Take a couple of minutes to get situated. While you're perusing the menu, you can give your guest clues about the limits of your hospitality. You might say, "Hmm, I think I'll have a cocktail today," or "I think I'll have iced tea." You can also help your guest by suggesting items from each course on the menu. You might say, for instance, "The shrimp dumplings here are good and they're famous for their green chili corn chowder."

These suggestions allow your guest to gauge the prices you think are reasonable. But don't be stingy! Recommend one of the more expensive entrees. If your guest orders an appetizer, then you should too. Keep these tips in mind:

- Always order the same number of courses your guest does. This prevents the awkward situation that arises when one of you is eating and the other is not.
- If your guest is a light eater, then so are you. You won't starve.

Knowing When to Start Talking Business

Unless the need to transact business is urgent and you and your guest(s) have agreed to get right down to business, don't discuss business matters until the end of the meal. Yes, not until the *end* of the meal! Granted, in certain fast-paced businesses this rule is so frequently broken that it's no longer a rule. Nevertheless, there are still plenty of people who feel that business and dining don't mix. You should be able to get a feel for whether your guest wants to jump into business-talk right away, or would like to be social first.

During business meals, it's not uncommon to see memos and papers on the table. But resist the temptation to use wireless telephones, laptops, or palm pilots at the table — the restaurant is not your office. If you have to use all sorts of electronic devices to conduct the meeting, have the meal catered in a conference room.

Here are some more tips:

- Don't forget that there are other people dining. They don't want your business interfering with their meal. Try to find a table located at the edge or in the back of the dining area.
- Keep your voice low and pleasant.
- Don't load the table up with your sunglasses, keys, and plethora of electronic gadgets. Put these things in a briefcase or handbag and put the bag under the table or on an empty chair.
- If you have a beeper, turn on the vibrating option.

Planning the Perfect Social Event for Business

The time will come for you to welcome your business colleagues, bosses, or clients into your home. You'll want to make the experience as pleasant and as memorable as possible.

Whether your event is as simple as a weekend picnic for your colleagues and their families, or as complicated as a formal dinner for the President of Venezuela and fifty corporate titans, your test as a gracious host is whether you plan in advance and whether you can deal with unexpected disasters.

Your budget determines the kind of event you can host. If you have enough money, you don't need to worry about budgeting time and energy, since you can hire people to do everything for you. If you're considering a large, catered affair, read the suggestions in Chapter 18 about special events and catered affairs. If your goals are more modest, you can provide a gracious ambience and good company all by yourself by following a few simple guidelines.

Before pulling together your guest list, consider the reasons for the party. Is it to celebrate a promotion, to bid farewell to a colleague, or just to have fun with a Frisbee and some brews? Know your reasons, know your budget, and plan ahead.

Once you've determined occasion and style, make a schedule to keep yourself organized. At least a month before the party, you will:

- ✔ Determine the guest list.
- ✔ Plan the menu; prepare your grocery and beverage list.
- ✔ Select decorations and supplies.
- ✔ Arrange for a tent, tables, chairs, and other equipment, if necessary.
- ✔ Select linens.

At least two weeks before your party, you will:

- ✔ Mail the invitations.
- ✔ Check your dishes and glasses for chips and cracks and replace as necessary.
- ✔ Order flowers, if appropriate.

One week before the event, you will:

- ✔ Select platters and serving dishes, matching each menu item to a container and utensils. If you will be replacing buffet items, select the second set of serving pieces too.
- ✔ Choose appropriate music and confirm that your extension cords are long enough to reach the cabana!

One or two days before the event, you will:

- ✔ Wash dishes, glasses, and flatware.
- ✔ Call any guests who have not responded.
- ✔ Buy groceries and beverages.
- ✔ Polish the silver, if necessary.
- ✔ Clean the house and yard.

✔ Prepare any food items that can be made in advance and refrigerate.

✔ Coordinate last-minute arrangements with the caterer.

✔ Check the entry-closet for extra hangers or provide a coat rack.

✔ Put away valuable and breakable items.

✔ Order ice, if necessary.

Consider how much time you're going to have on the day of the party and arrange to have things delivered. And have enough help. Consider "hiring" your own teenager or her friends to help you serve and clean up.

Assembling the right crowd

Sometimes choosing the guest list is easy because it's clear that the whole company should be invited to the party. It gets tricky when some people will be invited, but not everyone. Try to make clear categories. For example, you invite the sales force and their spouses or guests, or you invite the company's clients, or you invite the people on your floor. The point here is to have a ready and justifiable explanation for including some people and excluding other people.

Some hosts like to invite folks they *know* don't get along "just to see what happens." Invite people who are not amicable with each other only if it can't be avoided.

Issuing invitations

An invitation is the first news of your intention to host an event. The way you word your invitations begins to set the tone for the affair. Invitations to casual events can be creative and unusual, but those to formal affairs should follow protocol. If there is a theme to the party, include it in the invitation.

Invitation basics: who, what, where, why, when, and RSVP. *Who* is doing the inviting and who is being invited; *what* you are inviting the person to do; *where* the party is to be held; *why* the party is being held; *when* the party will start and when it will end; and how to let your host know whether or not you will attend.

RSVP means respond either way, yes or no. RSVP stands for the French *répondez s'il vous plaît*, which means "please respond." *Regrets only* means the guest should contact the host only if not attending.

If you plan an informal gathering of business associates, you can issue your invitations orally, either in person or by telephone, but make sure that you're clear about the date and time of the affair. Say something like, "We'd love to have you join us for an informal brunch with a few others from work at our house a week from Sunday. We plan to get together at eleven, have brunch on the deck, and play a little croquet in the yard for an hour or so."

This invitation contains a lot of information. Your guests know how they need to dress and that others have been invited to the brunch. They know that the meal will consist of more than chips and dip, and they know that you expect them to leave by 3 p.m. Your guests will find all this information useful and will be grateful to you for providing it.

If you are composing a written invitation, make sure that it has all of the relevant information listed above.

For written invitations to business events, use titles on the envelope: *Mr., Mrs., Ms., Dr.*

Considering significant others and children

Always mention *exactly* whom you're inviting when you issue invitations. For a married couple, mention both names.

For a single adult whom you expect to bring a date, you do one of two things, depending on whether it's an oral invitation or a written invitation. If it's a phone invitation, call the person and say something like, "Hi Rex, this is Juanita. I'm having a luau next Saturday at the beach house from five to midnight. Please bring a guest, if you'd like, and let me know if you'll be able to make it by Wednesday. My office number is XXX-XXXX or you can reach me at home at YYY-YYYY. Hope to see you."

If it's a written invitation, call the person you're inviting and say that you're planning to send him an invitation and is there a guest he'd like to bring? If so, would he be kind enough to tell you that person's name? Then send a written invitation directly to the guest.

For couples who live together, both names go on the same line of the envelope. Roommate names are listed on separate lines.

Some people take their children everywhere, but unless you specifically mention them on the invitation, children are not invited. The only reasonable antidote is to be very specific in the way you address your invitation — make the envelope read *Ms. Dorothy Kwan-Smith and Mr. Edward Smith* instead of *The Smiths*. If you really want to include the little ones, address the envelope to *Ms. Dorothy Kwan-Smith, Mr. Edward Smith, and Miss Ruby Kwan-Smith* or to *The Kwan-Smith Family*.

Generally, children are not invited to formal parties, but sometimes they are there anyway. If you would like for them to attend, you can word an invitation simply by stating *children welcome* on your invitation.

For business functions, Romeo, if Juliet isn't invited, she isn't invited! Meet her under the balcony after the function.

Determining guest attire

A written invitation should include a freestanding line that specifies how you expect your guests to dress. If you want to see the gentlemen in tuxedos, your safest line is *Formal* or *Black Tie.* For suits and ties and cocktail dresses, people often use the phrase *Dressy* or *Semi-Formal,* although *Informal* is technically correct. For a reception after work at which you expect suits for all, use the phrase *Business Dress.* For slacks, sport coats, skirts or pants, use *Business Casual.* For Volleyball, use the phrase *Casual.*

Don't bother looking in Webster's for a definition of *casual.* Casual can mean whatever you want it to mean — just make sure that your guests are in agreement with you. In general, *business casual* implies a wardrobe suitable for a day at work. As people respond to the invitation, say, "I'm so glad you can make it. It really will be casual — shorts and T-shirts." Let people know how happy you are that they can come and let them know what they can wear.

If you're not sure what to wear to an informal or casual party, call your host and ask! Say something like, "Hi Sid. I'm looking forward to seeing you on Sunday, but I'm not quite sure what to wear. Any hints?"

Providing directions and parking

Don't make your guests search and fumble through an unfamiliar suburb or area of town. Enclose a separate sheet of paper with accurate directions. If necessary, make copies of a local road map and point out landmarks and distances. Many Internet search engines have mapping capabilities. Use this great service.

One of your responsibilities as the host of a large affair is to provide parking. You can hire someone from a valet parking service company to park cars if you live somewhere that has such a service. Alert your neighbors about the event and that there will probably be parking on the street. If the parking situation is difficult and your street or home cannot handle a large number of cars, consider limiting your guest list or hiring a shuttle for your guests.

If the event takes place at an establishment with valet parking, arrange beforehand to handle the fees and gratuities for your guests. Include on the invitation, *Valet Parking Provided.*

Dealing with RSVPs

If you're having a casual party, you can request telephone or e-mail responses to your invitations. Include your phone number and e-mail address.

If you're hosting an informal or formal party, send written invitations and request an RSVP. For all but the most formal occasions, a separate RSVP card may be included. RSVP cards are note-sized cards that allow the guests to quickly respond.

The *most* formal invitations, such as a white tie affair, require that you respond in writing, on fine stationery, echoing the wording of the invitation.

If you have not received an RSVP back from a guest within three days of the event, it's perfectly acceptable to call and ask if they are attending. A guest should respond to an invitation as soon as possible, certainly within a week of receiving it.

Finalizing preparations for the day of the event

On the day of the event, take care of last minute details. Mentally walk through the event. Review names of guests, spouses and significant others, company affiliations, and interesting tidbits from the week's newspapers. Allow plenty of time to set up and dress. Try to give yourself half an hour to relax before the party begins. If you have a nonsmoking household, now's the time to make arrangements for smokers by reserving a place for them outside somewhere.

Above all else, maintain your sense of humor in the face of adversity. The most important thing is your attitude, friendliness, and genuine pleasure in your guests' presence.

A senator's wife was hosting a barbecue to introduce the city's new symphony conductor to members of the business-arts coalition, a group of business and civic leaders dedicated to supporting the arts. An hour before the party was to begin, one of the catering equipment trucks was nowhere to be seen. No tables, no linens. She grabbed sawhorses and two-by-fours from the barn, covered them with blankets, and ripped up sheets to use as napkins. She greeted all of her guests with a big smile, and everyone found the rustic setting charming.

The uninvited guest

As a host, you face one of life's little challenges when an uninvited guest arrives at your carefully planned party. A guest may, for instance, arrive with someone you didn't invite. Perhaps a relative showed up from out of town and it seemed rude for your guest to leave her at home alone. Perhaps your cubicle mate shows up with his brand new girlfriend.

As a host, your job is to ignore your guest's breech of etiquette and to warmly welcome any uninvited guest as if you were hoping for just such a visit. Say how wonderful it is that she can join you all. Begin making introductions immediately. Rearrange the seating with a shoehorn. SMILE!

Greeting your guests

As your first guests arrive, greet them at the door. Use their names, shake hands, look them in the eye, and say "I'm so glad you could join us." As the party progresses, you may have an associate or your spouse greet people by saying, "Hello, I'm Joe Sixpack, Lynne's husband. Lynne is on the balcony." Make sure that you're close by and that the person welcoming your guests knows where you are.

Introduce newcomers all around the room until the number of guests gets too large. When that happens, introduce newcomers only to the people who are closest at hand. Keep an eye out for shy guests who plaster themselves to the wall. Engage them in conversation and introduce them to someone you hope can draw them out.

Offer your guests a drink or show them to the bar. Always have both alcoholic and nonalcoholic beverages, including water, available during cocktail hour. Keep cocktail napkins close at hand or offer them with the drink. Cocktails should be served for no more than an hour, and appetizers and snacks should be provided while serving alcoholic beverages.

Remember to serve the most senior guests first.

Running the meal

How you organize the meal depends on the number of guests and the atmosphere that you want to create.

The buffet meal

A buffet works for ten guests or one hundred. It is a great way to build cama-raderie and allow people to mingle. A buffet can be a bit formal or casual, depending on the seating arrangements and style of food. By all means, if women will be attending wearing dresses and business suits, provide chairs.

With a buffet, you can serve a group of guests without having to traipse back and forth to the kitchen. Arrange everything on a side table, stack up the plates and silverware, and let your guests help themselves. Buffets can work beautifully if you avoid a few hazards that can turn a party into a nightmare. Be sure to:

- ✔ Set up the bar away from the hors d'oeurves and the buffet table to avoid congestion.

- ✔ Provide a drop-off table for cocktail glasses before the buffet.

- ✔ Think about traffic flow. Make sure there's enough room for people to get to and away from the buffet table. Consider setting the buffet table up so that people can serve themselves from both sides.

- ✔ Set up glasses and dinner beverages on the dining tables so that people don't have to juggle food plates and drinks.

- ✔ Organize menu items in standard menu order — main courses first and desserts last.

- ✔ Be sure to have backup serving dishes of each menu item so that they can be easily replaced. Guests shouldn't have to scrape the bottom of a serving dish.

Without exception, provide adequate seating for everyone invited. Rent enough tables and chairs, or arrange your own furniture to accommodate small groups. For very casual occasions, the floor and some cushions or the lawn and a few hay bales are perfectly fine.

After you survive a few buffet luncheons and sit-down suppers, you may be ready for the daunting task of formal entertaining.

The dinner party

A dinner party is a small affair, with usually no more than twelve guests. Its business function is to provide a gracious climate in which to build relation-ships. The conversation at a dinner party should be general, social, and witty. The food at a dinner party should be prepared and served in courses — at least three, no more than five.

This is an opportunity to use your wedding silver, your fine china, and your crystal. If you don't have enough matching plates and silverware, mix and match and have a party rental company or your caterer provide extra pieces.

If you can't even remember what the inside of a grocery store looks like, let alone attempt a gourmet meal for twelve titans of industry, reserve a private room at a good restaurant or hotel. Or hire a caterer.

As the host, you are the leader. When the time comes, move toward the dining room — other guests will follow. Take your seat right away as a sign that others should do the same. As soon as all of the guests are seated, place your napkin in your lap. This is the signal to others that the meal has begun.

As soon as the wine is poured, offer a short toast. For example, you might say something like, "Here's to the great pleasure of dining with friends." If a special occasion has prompted the dinner, suit your toast to the event: "To a wonderful new vice president."

When it comes to serving food and drinks, if you remember only these three things, you'll do fine:

- ✔ Water glasses should be filled before your guests sit down at the table.

- ✔ Guests are served from the left and dishes removed from the right, unless the arrangement of the tables and chairs does not allow it.

- ✔ Make sure that all of the utensils for each course are on the table before the food arrives.

For further information about table manners, see Chapter 16.

After the meal, when you rise from the table after dessert, so will everyone else. Make sure that the slowest guest has finished eating before you stand. When you lead the way from the dining table to the living room or other conversation location, others will follow. Try to engage every guest in at least a short personal conversation after the meal.

Ending the party

One of the toughest challenges for a gracious host is the delicate process of getting your guests to go home. Moving your guests homeward is really a two-sided issue, because they are expected to exhibit their own good manners by knowing when it's time to leave. The party should be over an hour after dessert is finished.

If you're guests are lingering too long, there's no need to rely on hints or subtlety. Stand up, say, "This has been such a lovely evening," and begin thanking them for coming.

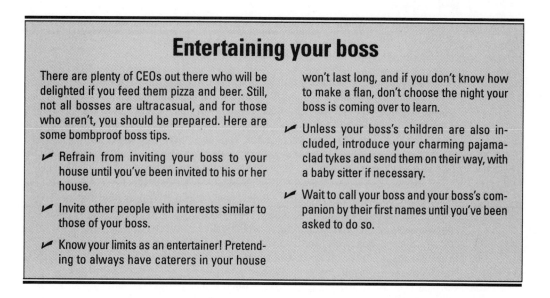

Entertaining your boss

There are plenty of CEOs out there who will be delighted if you feed them pizza and beer. Still, not all bosses are ultracasual, and for those who aren't, you should be prepared. Here are some bombproof boss tips.

✔ Refrain from inviting your boss to your house until you've been invited to his or her house.

✔ Invite other people with interests similar to those of your boss.

✔ Know your limits as an entertainer! Pretending to always have caterers in your house won't last long, and if you don't know how to make a flan, don't choose the night your boss is coming over to learn.

✔ Unless your boss's children are also included, introduce your charming pajama-clad tykes and send them on their way, with a baby sitter if necessary.

✔ Wait to call your boss and your boss's companion by their first names until you've been asked to do so.

Absolutely *perfect* manners require you to remain cheerfully hospitable until your guests leave without prompting. But absolutely *perfect* manners also require your guests to leave within an hour after dessert is finished or *digestifs* are served.

As guests begin to leave, station yourself at the door, accept their compliments, thank them for coming, and wish them a good evening. Don't apologize for the roast being overdone or for running out of tonic — just say how pleased you were to have them at your party.

Understanding Cocktail Parties and Receptions

Eating food while you're standing and have a drink in your hand can be a real nightmare. What are you supposed to do with those little toothpicks? Put them in that ficus pot over there? And how are you supposed to shake someone's hand when you're holding a plate and a glass of wine?

Cocktail parties and receptions are among the favorite events for businesses to host and yet they can be among the most difficult to navigate successfully. Not only are you hungry, you're often supposed to be mingling with people you don't know, and all of them are hungry and fried at the end of the day, too.

There are three kinds of cocktail parties: the true cocktail party; the cocktail buffet; and the cocktail reception. Each has its own function and structure, and each has its own wardrobe expectations.

A cocktail party is usually two hours long, starts sometime after 5:00 and ends sometime before 8:00 or 8:30 p.m. Dinner is not served at a cocktail party, but hors d'oeuvres are. A full bar is standard at a cocktail party, with nonalcoholic drinks for those who don't imbibe. This is the most flexible of the three, and can be casual to formal. Be sure to specify dress in the invitation. The primary function of a cocktail party is to provide a forum for mingling and meeting people.

A cocktail buffet is held typically between 6:00 and 9:00 p.m., during the business week. A buffet dinner is served (hence the name!). Tables, chairs, and silverware are provided. Often, the food is varied, copious, and served from different locations. The function of a cocktail buffet varies from mingling to announcing a new product to thanking long-standing clients. It usually requires business dress. Again, be sure to specify proper dress in the invitation.

A cocktail reception is traditionally held two hours before another evening engagement, say between 5:30 and 7:30 p.m. for an 8:00 p.m. theater curtain, or it can be held after an evening event, usually only for an hour and a half. Champagne is always served. Early cocktail receptions usually serve hors d'oeuvres; late cocktail receptions often feature egg dishes, such as omelets, fruits, and desserts. Cocktail receptions are the most formal of the three, usually reserved for making significant announcements, honoring someone, or celebrating an important event. Dressy or formal wear is in order. Again, be sure to specify proper dress in the invitation.

When you attend a cocktail party without seating, you will be challenged to hold onto your food and drink at the same time. Here's what to do.

First, hold your drink in your left hand, so that your shaking hand cannot be mistaken for a freshly caught mackerel.

Second, if you are holding both drink and food and someone approaches you, put the food down on a nearby table and offer your right hand, unless doing so would be awkward for the other person. With a little practice, many people can master the art of holding a small plate and a wine glass in their left hand. If you are unable to perform this astounding feat, try to stay near tables or other surfaces.

Third, if you cannot comfortably shake hands, smile and nod your head or shrug your shoulders in greeting. The other person will understand.

At some cocktail parties, little holders that attach to your plate and can hold your glass are provided.

Attending a Banquet

A banquet is a large luncheon or dinner typically hosted by a company or other organization.

At the event itself, your job as host is to ensure that all of your guests are satisfied. You will be milling, mingling, and massaging the situation most of the evening. You probably won't eat much. Don't fret it — your job is to talk to everyone, guarantee that they get what they want, and provide the necessary social skills to make the event a success for you and your company. You can help yourself to food and drink, but only so much as doesn't compromise your ability to be an effective host.

If you're the guest at a banquet, the guidelines that apply to any business function apply here as well. Don't overeat or overdrink, be polite to those whom you meet, and never forget that, as pleasant as the surroundings may be, this is a business function at which business conversation is going to happen. So be prepared to talk business at least some of the time.

Here's some more advice:

- ✔ As the host or coordinator of the banquet, you may not eat much. If low blood sugar is a problem for you, eat a substantial snack before the event.

- ✔ As a guest, leave before or at the stated ending time for the event. The polite guest knows when to leave.

- ✔ A great way to relax at a banquet is to really pay attention to others. Listen to what is being said. Enter into a conversation wholeheartedly. Ask questions of others and care about their answers.

- ✔ If you're very nervous and you're at an event with lots of new people, try introducing yourself anyway and then being quiet. Most other people will fill in the silence by talking about themselves.

Host and master of ceremonies

The host is the person who represents the organization having the banquet. It is often the President, CEO, or Chairman of the Board. The master of ceremonies announces and introduces speakers, those who offer toasts, and other entertainment. Sometimes the host is also the master of ceremonies, sometimes not. When distinct individuals fulfill the different functions, remember to direct your logistical questions about the event to the host's office and any questions about entertainment to the master of ceremonies.

As a host for an event, make the appropriate contact people available to your speaker and guests.

Many professional speakers travel with an *aide de camp* or an entourage. Figure out who is in charge and talk to that person. Some speakers like to make the decisions themselves; others prefer to delegate these matters to their handlers. Know your speaker's preferences.

If you are the host for a dinner speaker, your primary responsibility is to ensure that the speaker is at the right place at the right time and has everything he or she needs. This means making sure that the master of ceremonies knows how to introduce the speaker, that the speaker is aware of all details of the scheduled appearance, and that any technology the speaker will be using has been tested and is ready to go.

Remember to do the following:

- Before the event begins, check that projectors, laptops, microphones, overheads, or any other technology are in fact working and are fully functional.
- Ask if the speaker would like instructions for using any of the technology.
- Ask the speaker if there is anything else that is required.
- Introduce the speaker to important audience members during cocktails.
- Supply the speaker with water for the speech.

As master of ceremonies, you introduce the speaker. Introductions need not be long — good introductions are usually two minutes or less — but they should be prepared. Recognize that your impromptu witticisms may desert you as you face a thousand people in a brilliantly lit banquet room. Write something down ahead of time in a font large enough to read.

Dinner speakers are common at large banquets. They are often members of the company itself. Sometimes they are famous people or speakers from other walks of life. The purpose of dinner speakers varies enormously, from providing reports on technical matters to offering comedy for the evening's entertainment.

Toasts

Toasts can be made with wine or any other beverage. Traditionally, you do not toast to yourself, although some people now think that it's okay to raise your glass in response. In either case, you do not drink if you're the one being toasted.

Toasting was once only a man's job and only the men drank the toast, while the women nodded and smiled. Now, it is perfectly appropriate for anyone to make a toast and for anyone to respond to the toast, regardless of gender.

Are there any rules left? A few:

- ✔ The host or hostess can and should propose the first toast to begin the dining. This is a welcome toast.

- ✔ If there is a guest of honor, it is again the role of the host to propose a toast to that person.

- ✔ If the guest of honor is a dignitary, a very important person, or a distinguished elder, it is a sign of respect for everyone to rise with the toast.

The guest of honor, regardless of gender, responds to the toast by toasting the host, thanking them. In fact, guest of honor or not, if you are toasted, you should always respond with a toast.

At large events where you wish to command the attention of a room or more than one table, it is traditional to rise for the toast. At smaller occasions, rising is not necessary. Simply ask for everyone's attention. Once you have the floor, be respectful, take a minute or less to make the toast, and be seated.

Clinking your crystal with a fork to get attention is gauche and potentially dangerous.

Uh-oh, you're giving a speech?!

If you're the speaker, you are well advised to do a little research ahead of time. Your favorite speech containing the metaphor about the old-growth forest may not play too well at the annual banquet of Clear Cut Logging Corporation! Know your audience.

Once you arrive, make yourself available to the host and introduce yourself to others. Review any special arrangements with the host. When it comes time to give your speech, wait for the master of ceremony's introduction to be complete. Amateur speakers are routinely so nervous that they stand up in front of the crowd before they've even been introduced.

Thank your introducer and your host upon reaching the podium. When you speak, do so slowly, with a combination of voice inflections and emphases. Speak from your voice box and not the back of your throat. If your voice starts to crack, find a suitable stopping place and have a sip of water.

At the end of your speech, thank the audience. Thank your host in person. The next day, thank your host again in the form of a thank-you note — you may be on your way to being a famous speaker, but it's a privilege to be given a podium from which to speak. Don't abuse it!

Chapter 16

Mastering Table Manners

• •

• •

*W*ell done — you've been invited to the company's annual awards ceremony at the ritziest room in town. But instead of thrills, you've got chills. They didn't teach you how to go to one of these affairs in business school. When you ask your parents how to go to one of these things, they just laugh, recalling that "formal" in the commune meant wearing shoes. No help there!

You need a quick course in dining etiquette. Not just in basic eating, either — you've got to know what to do with that place setting from *Titanic*. You don't know a Chardonnay from a Beaujolais, let alone how to locate your bread plate. Relax! Meals are supposed to be fun and entertaining. Of course, they often aren't, but by the end of this chapter, at least you'll know how to handle yourself with grace at a business meal.

The Pregame Show: Making Arrangements and Greeting Guests

Whether you're having lunch with well-known business associates or you're sitting down to a formal dinner with complete strangers — who just happen to be your company's most important clients — knowing dining etiquette will help put you and others at ease. Good manners are like the handrails on a rope bridge — you may not be dashing across the chasm like Indiana Jones, but if you hang on tightly you won't fall off!

Attending to preliminaries

As already noted in the last chapter, if you're the host, arrive early to make arrangements for paying the bill. Make sure that the table or room is what you had arranged and decide on the seating plan. The guest or most important person sits in the best chair (normally the one with the best view and location). The maitre d' can help you identify that seat. Everyone should be able to see everyone else and converse easily. Have large flower arrangements or other obstacles removed from the table by the waiter or maitre d' if you think they will be distracting. Return to the bar or waiting area to greet your guests.

Do not order a drink before your guests arrive. Even if you have arrived twenty minutes earlier to make sure everything is in good order, it should appear to your guests that you, too, have just arrived. Don't start off by making your guests uncomfortable thinking that they are late or have kept you waiting.

If you are hosting a group, wait in the bar area until your party is complete. As each guest arrives, get off to a good start by making formal introductions. Unless it is unwieldy, everyone should stand for an introduction and exchange handshakes (and business cards, if the parties are being introduced for the first time).

Mentioning the purpose of the gathering is appropriate. Try something like, "I know we're all thinking about the roll-out schedule, which we will get to. But, first, I'd like to invite you all to just relax. We'll save that discussion for the end of the meal."

Coming to table

Once introductions, cocktails, and pre-dining chit-chat are complete, you just sit down at the table, right? Wrong. At business meals, the host or lead business person should seat clients first and her business associates second. In formal business occasions, the seating is predetermined by place cards. In such a situation, no one sits down until the host or guest of honor is seated.

Never switch place cards at a business function. You may be more comfortable, but considerable thought involving business strategy has probably gone into the seating plan. Moving the cards around might be a ticket to Palukaville!

Before sitting down, make sure you know everyone at the table. If you don't, make last-minute introductions. Unlike social situations, it is not necessary for men to seat women at a business meal. However, whether you are a man or a woman, if you are to the left of an elderly woman or man or someone who requires assistance, you may always draw the chair and assist as needed.

Excellent Etiquette for Dining

Once seated, wait for your host to take up his or her napkin and place it on his or her lap. Then, place your own napkin in your lap. Unlike a social situation, where guests wait for the hostess to touch her napkin, in a business situation hierarchy replaces gender.

It's not necessary to fully open a large napkin, and you should avoid flourishing it like a bullfighter. The purpose of your napkin is to dab the corners of your mouth, not to wipe off lipstick or blow your nose. If you leave the table during the meal, place your napkin on your chair. When you've finished your entire meal and are leaving the table, place your napkin to the left of your place.

Sit up at the table throughout the meal, and remember not to support yourself with your forearms or elbows. You may rest your wrists on the edge of the table, but lightly. Even though it may be tempting, don't rest your head in your hands between courses.

And no fidgeting! Don't plink on the table with your cutlery, fidget with the tablecloth, your napkin, cocktail stirrers, appetizer picks, your hair, your fingernails or anything else close to hand.

As soon as you're seated, informal conversation is in order. You may talk about the town you or your guest are visiting or a widely publicized sporting event in the news and ask for an opinion. If some of the participants traveled a significant distance, inquire about their trip. Listen carefully to responses and indicate your interest by asking pertinent follow-up questions.

Avoid discussing your personal life, sex, politics, or religion — you want cordial conversation, not controversy.

A drink or two before dinner as an icebreaker is perfectly acceptable and, for some, a way of life. However, if you intend to conduct business, protect your mental clarity. There's nothing wrong with ordering mineral water or iced tea, regardless of the choices others make. When you are the host, it is best to follow the lead of your guest. You can offer a cocktail, but if your guest doesn't order one, abstain as well. If you're a non-drinking host, suggest to your guests that they have a cocktail and offer to order wine during the meal.

It takes time for a productive discussion to develop. One purpose of chit-chat during the meal is to warm up. If you've had a lively conversation during the meal, everyone will be primed to talk about the business plan over coffee. Be prepared to spend as much time as necessary at the meal. Don't book an appointment too close to the time you think the meal should end, because you don't want to be rushed or appear preoccupied to your guests.

Bring on the meal!

When should you start to eat? Almost every meal has a host (the person who invited you to the meal or the person in whose home you are dining). It's your turn to eat when and only when your host begins to eat. You don't even have a sip of water until your host does!

If you're at a banquet or other group situation, wait until all those around you have been served the first course and begin to eat together. If the first course is brought out in twos or threes to the table and not everyone has food yet, wait until everyone has food. Sometimes the host will encourage you to "Go ahead, please don't wait." In this case, begin eating. Or, if you wish, you can still wait for everyone to have their course before you begin, chatting with the other guests in the meantime.

The host may offer a toast before the meal. It should be simple and short. Something like, "Here's to dining with esteemed colleagues" is fine.

A Primer on Table Settings (Basic and Formal)

The first step to intelligent utensil use is learning where the basic utensils and dishes go on a dining table and how to use them. Then, you'll be ready for advanced utensil information — those additional utensils and china you may encounter in formal dining. At every meal, you have a plate, a napkin, several utensils — usually consisting of a knife, fork, and soup spoon — and at least one glass. Sometimes you have a bread-and-butter plate. When you add a salad fork, you've filled out the simple place setting that most Americans recognize. Sometimes a salad plate rests on the table rather than being delivered with the salad, and sometimes the dessert utensils, dessert plate, and coffee or teacups and their spoons appear after the meal. See Figure 16-1 for an illustration of a basic table setting.

The basic setting is an abbreviated version of a full or formal place setting, which can have any number of other utensils, plates, and glasses.

The two most important rules to learn in dining, whether casual or formal, are:

- ✔ Drinks right, bread plate left
- ✔ Start by using the utensils placed farthest away from the plate and work inward with each course

By examining the formal place setting in Figure 16-2, you get a good idea of what each course will be.

Figure 16-1:
An
American
basic table
setting.

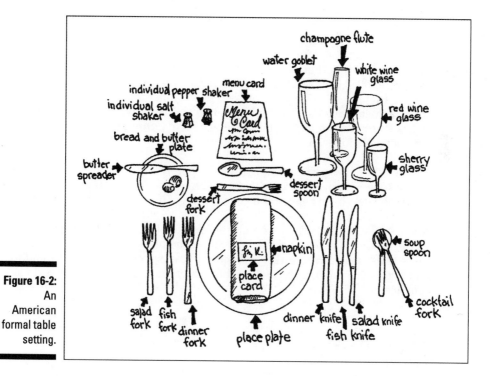

Figure 16-2:
An
American
formal table
setting.

Plates

The place plate or main dinner plate is in the center in front of each chair setting. In formal dining, there is usually a *charger,* or under plate, as well. The bread plate is always to the left, slightly above the forks. It has a small knife across the top. That's the butter spreader. If soup is served as a first course, the soup bowl will be on a service plate. A salad, if served as a first course, may be placed upon the service plate and will then be removed. Toward the end of the meal, you may find a small plate with a doily and a small bowl above your dinner plate. These are the finger bowl and a dessert plate. There may also be a small fork and spoon resting on the edge of this plate — your dessert spoon and fork.

Utensils

Forks are to the left of the plate, and knives and spoons to the right (with the exception of the tiny cocktail fork, which is placed on the soup spoon or to right of the soup spoon). The dessert fork and spoon are above the dinner plate.

If a salad is the first course, as is often the case in the United States, but rarely the case in other countries, the salad fork, which is smaller than the dinner fork, will be farthest to the left. If fish is being served as the first course, there is a fish fork first. Next is your dinner fork for the entree. Salad is sometimes served as the third or fourth course, in which case your salad fork is closest to the plate. The bread plate and butter spreader are on the left above the forks.

To the right of the plate, starting from the outermost utensil, are a cocktail fork, a soup spoon, a fish knife, a dinner knife, and then a salad knife nearest the plate. The sharp edge of the knife is always turned in toward the plate.

A dessert fork is placed horizontally above the place plate, tines *right;* a dessert spoon is placed horizontally above the place plate, bowl *left.* All these additional knives, forks, and spoons have specific functions — and to add to the confusion, a few look slightly different in Europe than they do in America.

Glassware

In a formal setting, you usually have lots of glasses at the table. These are to the right. Each glass is slightly different in shape and size. This is fairly easy to master — your waiter will fill the glasses with the correct beverages in the right order. As long as you are not drinking from an empty glass, you will be fine!

The glass farthest to the right may be a sherry or apéritif glass, if one is served to accompany the soup course. This will be the first glass you use. When each course is finished, allow the waiter to remove the glass for that course as well as the plate. Next is the white wine glass, which is used during the fish course or appetizer. Behind the white wine glass is the red wine glass. This glass is larger, with a fuller bowl that allows the red wine to "breathe." The largest glass is the water goblet, which sits just above the dinner knife. Finally, behind and to the right of the water goblet is the champagne glass, if champagne will accompany dessert. You may also find a champagne glass in the first position, perhaps served with oysters as an appetizer.

Salt and pepper

Most table settings include salt and pepper shakers or grinders. At formal meals you'll see individual salt and pepper dishes with tiny spoons.

Thoughtfully taste your food before you add any seasoning. The chef has tried to achieve perfect seasoning, and when you immediately reach for the salt and pepper, you indicate that perfection was not quite achieved. Pass the salt and pepper as a pair, so that they can stay together throughout the meal.

The Meal: Managing Basic to Formal Dining

As noted in the previous chapter, you may suggest items from the menu for the guest but, when it comes to ordering, follow the lead of your guests. Order an item similar to theirs and in the same price range. If they order appetizers, you should order one, too, so your guests don't have to eat alone. In a formal dinner, a menu card will be presented to you on which each course served will be printed. The date, location, and purpose of the dinner will be on the card at the top — this is the only, or main, keepsake for guests.

Avoid selecting the most expensive item on the menu. If a client or your employer will be paying for the meal, it's best to order from the mid-priced offerings on the menu. If you dine in restaurants that specialize in international cuisine and you don't speak the language, take the time to learn four or five food items ahead of time. It's also acceptable to request assistance from the waiter.

During a business meal, your mind is on business, even if the preliminary chitchat is about Tiger Woods. Don't overburden yourself by ordering foods that challenge your table manners and your wardrobe. As you survey the menu, be alert to the following hazardous foods: deeply colored sauce or gravy; spaghetti; food that requires on-the-plate management, such as whole lobster, crab, and spare ribs; finger foods such as hamburgers or french fries; unfamiliar foods that may challenge your digestion or allergies. If you have special dietary needs and you know in advance where you will be dining, call ahead and discuss your needs with the restaurant personnel. Conversation will continue during the meal, so be prepared to participate. Don't get caught chewing a large hunk of pork chop when the company president asks you how your children are doing in school. Remember the sage advice of president George Washington: "Put not another bit into your mouth till the former be swallowed. Let not your morsels be too big for the jowls."

If the food or the wine is especially good, mention it to your host, but keep complaints to yourself. If you must leave the table, for any reason, rise from your seat, put your napkin on your chair and say a simple "excuse me" as you depart. When you return, resume your seat without comment.

Don't announce a visit to the "john" or the powder room, or the need to make an important phone call.

If the occasion arises in which you must quit the meal permanently before it is over, make a brief apology, indicate when you will next talk with important guests or clients, then leave with as little interruption as possible. Everyone else should return and gracefully re-enter the meal and conversation.

Silence your gadgets! If there's an emergency, briefly explain the situation to the others before excusing yourself: "I regret the interruption, but my wife has been involved in a traffic accident. I'll be in contact as soon as I take care of the emergency."

American and Continental dining styles

There are two methods of handling and using the silverware at a meal: the American style and the European, or Continental, style. Either version is fine in America.

In both the European and the American style, you cut your food as follows. First, you hold the knife in your right hand. Place your index finger on the handle and a little of the blade, if necessary. Hold the fork with your left hand, prongs facing down (with the curve pushing up) as shown in Figure 16-3. Then you may eat your food one or two bites at a time.

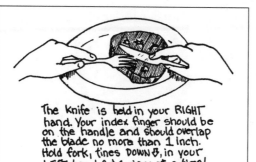

The knife is held in your RIGHT hand. Your index finger should be on the handle and should overlap the blade no more than 1 inch. Hold fork, tines DOWN &, in your LEFT hand. Cut 1 piece at a time!

Figure 16-3:
Cutting food.

In the American or *zigzag* style, once you've finished cutting, you lay the knife on the plate near the top of the plate, cutting edge facing in, and switch the fork to your right hand after cutting your food. Holding the fork with your thumb over the end and your index finger underneath and the prongs up, you pick up the food, either with the prongs or slipping the food onto the prongs, as shown in Figure 16-4.

Hold your fork like a pencil. Steady it between your middle and index fingers. (Turn your thumb up, not down, like you would a pencil.)

After you cut the meat, lay your knife on your plate. The cutting edge should always face the center of the plate. Switch the fork to your RIGHT hand before you raise it to your mouth.

Figure 16-4:
Cutting and eating American style.

When you finish a course, you place your knife and fork side by side, knife on top, in the 4 o'clock position on the plate, the blade of the knife facing in. (See Figure 16-5.) This way, your server knows that you have finished this course and can remove those dishes and utensils.

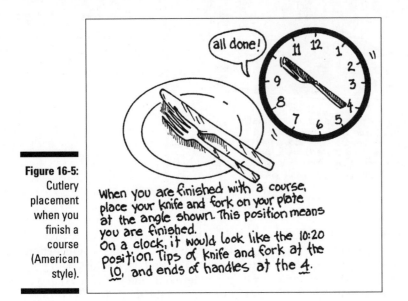

Figure 16-5:
Cutlery
placement
when you
finish a
course
(American
style).

If you wish to rest between courses, you use the same position, but space the utensils farther apart and slightly higher on your plate, as shown in Figure 16-6.

Figure 16-6:
The rest
position
when eating
American
style.

In the European or Continental style, you simply use the fork to prong the bite and bring it to your mouth with your left hand. Raise the fork to your mouth with the tines down but turning your forearm toward your mouth. The knife can stay in your right hand, ready to be used again, as shown in Figure 16-7. If you put something onto the tines of your fork, use a gentle nudge from your knife. You may also rest your wrist on the edge of the table while you hold your cutlery.

Figure 16-7:
Continental
style of
eating and
placing
utensils.

Raise fork, tines down, to your mouth.
Twist the wrist and raise your forearm
slightly. Keep the knife in your RIGHT hand.
You may add a small amount of the other
food to your meat on the tines of the fork.

To rest your cutlery in the European or Continental style of eating, you cross the fork (tines down) across the knife, cutting edge in, in the 4 o'clock position, as shown in Figure 16-8. Place your utensils in either of these positions if you must leave the table, take a drink, or use your napkin. The finished position is the same as in the American style, but with the fork tines down.

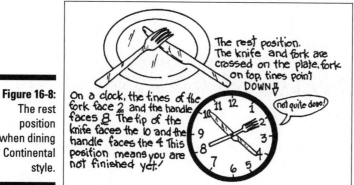

The rest position.
The knife and fork are
crossed on the plate, fork
on top, tines point
DOWN

not quite done!

Figure 16-8:
The rest
position
when dining
Continental
style.

On a clock, the tines of the
fork face 2 and the handle
faces 8. The tip of the
knife faces the 10 and the
handle faces the 4. This
position means you are
not finished yet!

Do not wave your utensils around while you're talking. You're not conducting an orchestra!

At no time should you hold your utensils in any other fashion than those suggested. It doesn't matter whether you're left-handed or not. Never saw your food; simply request a steak or meat knife. Never cut your meat into bites all at once. And don't place your utensils by their tips on the edge of the plate, letting them hang onto the table. After you pick up your utensils, they should never touch the table again.

Eating french fries in France

American table manners allow for considerable latitude in the use of fingers while dining informally. European etiquette, however, is much more formal, even during a casual meal. For example, Americans will eat French fries with their fingers. But in France, *pommes frîtes* are eaten with a knife and fork. When you dine overseas, or with an international group, be especially watchful for the behavior of your companions. When in doubt, use a knife and fork.

Serving food

In banquets or banquet-style serving, platters of food are served from the left. A serving spoon and a serving fork are usually on the serving platter, spoon with bowl up and fork with tines down. Take the fork in your left hand, tines remaining down, and use it to steady the food. Using the spoon in your right hand, lift the food and steady it with the fork while bringing it to your plate.

Serve the food in individual portions, as it is presented on the platter. Don't take more than one portion. If the food is presented as a whole — mashed, grouped, or in gels — take a portion with the spoon, using the spoon sideways to cut, if necessary. Return the spoon and fork to the serving plate as they came to you: spoon bowl up on the right, fork tines down on the left.

Eating the meal

This section covers the basic courses diners encounter most often.

Bread

Bread is placed on or passed around the table. If a bread basket or bread plate is sitting in front of you, you generally begin by passing (but not taking). If the table is round, offer the bread to the person on your right and wait to take bread until the bread comes back around. If the table is rectangular and you can see that the bread may not come back your way, help yourself first and then pass to your right.

When bread is served half-sliced in a basket with a napkin, take the portion of the napkin with your left hand and hold a section of the bread, without touching the bread, while you tear off one piece with your right hand. The napkin is in the basket to cover or protect the remaining bread.

Place butter from the serving dish on your bread-and-butter plate, not directly on the bread. Never use the knife with the butter dish to butter your bread. If there is no knife with the butter dish, you may use your own butter spreader.

Break off a piece of bread only when you're ready to eat it. Do not butter the entire slice or roll at once. Break off one piece, butter the piece held over the plate, and eat it. If it's a crunchy hard roll, keep it as close to your bread plate as possible — it's not the end of the world if a few crumbs get on the table. The wait staff will take care of them later in the meal.

Dipping, dunking, or wiping sauces with your bread is not polite, except in the most informal gatherings or with certain dishes that are designed to do just that — such as fondues, certain *au jus* dishes, and olive oil. If you are dipping your bread into communal olive oil, never, ever double dip!

Soup

Soup is served in a variety of bowls and cups, hot or cold. Clear soup is served with a small round soupspoon; cream soup with a medium, more oval soupspoon.

Occasionally, you may be served consommé, served in a small bowl with handles on each side, without a spoon. Pick up the delicate bowl by the handles and sip.

All other soups should be handled like this: Hold your spoon the way you would hold a pencil, between your index and middle fingers with your thumb up. Spoon the soup away from you toward the center or top of the bowl, and then sip the soup from the side — not the point — of the spoon. You may rest the spoon in the soup bowl while you pause. After you have finished, place the spoon on the saucer or plate beneath the cup or bowl. Don't leave the spoon in the bowl or cup.

A sherry or apéritif may be served with your soup.

Blowing on your soup to cool it down is not polite. You may gently stir it or spoon from the edge of the bowl first.

Entree

Your main course is normally beef, chicken, duck, or lamb, and you eat these foods with a knife and fork. Finger foods, such as fried chicken or barbecued ribs, are not served at formal occasions.

If you happen to be served a very large steak, it is permissible to cut it into two or three sections, but not into many small pieces all at once.

A sorbet or intermezzo may be served between courses to cleanse the palate. You only need to have a small taste; it's not necessary to finish the entire dish.

If planning a personal menu card for your guests, it is not necessary to include the intermezzo with the menu. However, if you think that some of your guests may be confounded by the course, list it. Think of their comfort.

Salad

Salad may be served before or after the main course — the placement of the salad fork will tip you off. In a basic American table setting, there is usually only one knife. For this reason, some Americans seem to think that the knife is for the main course and that they cannot use it for the salad.

A fine restaurant or considerate host always serves the lettuce in bite-sized pieces. However, if you're served large pieces, cut one bite at a time by using the knife provided. Using your knife to cut lettuce is perfectly fine — just request a clean knife when the main course arrives.

If salad is the main course, such as at a luncheon, use the entree fork. If the salad is served prior to or after the main course, use the smaller salad fork. When a salad is served during a formal meal, you always have a salad knife. Notice that it is usually smaller than the dinner knife.

The trick to eating cherry tomatoes without making them fly off the plate: pierce the top where the stem was located with your fork.

After finishing a course, don't push your plate or bowl away. The way your cutlery is placed informs the wait staff you've finished. If placed properly in the 4 o'clock position, it also allows the staff to pick up your plate easily.

Never "help" the wait staff by handing them plates or holding glasses for them to fill, unless asked to do so.

Finger bowls

A finger bowl is presented after the main course and before your dessert arrives. It is placed in front of you on a plate, usually with a doily under the bowl. The bowl contains warm water with a slice of lemon and occasionally a small flower. A small dessert fork and spoon are on the plate.

Dip just your fingertips in the water and dry them on your napkin. Remove the doily and bowl and place it to the left. A server will then remove it.

Dessert

When the main-course plate is removed, you may have a spoon and a fork left above it. It is your responsibility to move the fork down to your left and the spoon down to your right. If you do not have silverware above your plate, it will be brought to you prior to your dessert. If served ice cream, just use your spoon; if served cake with a sauce, use both the spoon and the fork. In a Continental-style setting, you hold your spoon in your right hand and the fork in your left, tines down.

Fresh fruit and cheese are sometimes served as dessert. You eat these foods with a knife and fork.

Polishing Up Your Wine Savvy

Wine enhances food. Like music, wine can be as much a pleasure for the blissfully ignorant as for the expert. The only danger with wine is knowing that your knowledge is so limited that you won't order the right one! Relax! Nearly everyone is curious about wines and most people are delighted to try new kinds. You can read more about choosing the right wine for your meal in Mary Ewing-Mulligan and Ed McCarthy's *Wine For Dummies,* 2nd Edition (IDG Books Worldwide).

Selecting a wine to complement your meal

Think of wine as the final seasoning of the dish. Normally, you order red wines with red meats and other robust dishes and white wines with fish and other delicate entrees. Delicate foods are usually better with delicate wines. But some of these rules are changing. Wine experts sometimes simply drink what they like. What if you order oven-roasted sea bass served with a veal-reduction sauce? If a dish has a wine base, say a Pinot Noir, a buttery Chardonnay is an excellent choice, or try to choose an appropriate Pinot Noir to match the sauce — you will find it a sure hit. If you're not certain, ask the waiter to make a suggestion.

Wine and food go together. The key to choosing a wine is to find one that won't overpower the food, or be overpowered by it. In general, the following are examples of wines that complement certain foods:

- Light meat dishes (such as pork), poultry, or full-flavored fish (such as salmon) go well with a red wine such as a light-bodied Pinot Noir or Burgundy.

- Lighter fish and shellfish dishes are fine with a light-bodied white wine, such as Chenin Blanc, Sancerre, Pinot Grigio, or German Riesling.

- Lobster or richer fish dishes are complemented by a full-bodied Chardonnay, Semillion, or Viognier.

- Chicken and pasta can take either red or white wine, depending on the sauce. A heavy meat sauce will be better complemented by a medium-bodied red wine, such as a Merlot or Cabernet Franc.

✔ Stews, roasts, game, duck, and other full-flavored dishes go best with full-bodied red wines, such as Cabernet Sauvignon, Petite Sirah, or Zinfandel. Some foods were not designed to go with wine. So try to be creative and experiment with different varieties. With Cajun food, try Alsatian white wines or Champagne. Chardonnay often goes surprisingly well with Mexican and Indian dishes. Sushi is nicely complimented by a good Sauvignon Blanc. And sweeter rosés go well with spicy Chinese or Indian food. Chefs across the country pour champagne with everything from Asian-influenced main courses to Indian curries. The effervescence of champagne can refresh the palate and cut the spices. The right sparkling wine makes a meal memorable and creates a festive mood.

Sparkling wines

Champagne is for celebrating and is normally served before a meal or with dessert. However, champagne is the ultimate "power beverage" and can complement appetizers and first courses. Just opening a bottle of champagne injects zest and signals the importance of the meal and your guests.

Champagne is distinguished by its degree of dryness: Brut is very dry, Extra Dry is slightly sweet, Sec is medium-sweet, and Demi-Sec is sweet. Dry champagne and rose wines are served chilled. Champagne is bottled in various sizes of bottles which, with the exception of magnum, all come with biblical names: Magnum, Jeroboam, Rehoboam, and Methuseleh. You are unlikely to need more that a magnum, which holds about one and a half liters.

Everyone loves hearing the "Pop!" upon opening a bottle of Champagne, but you need to open the bottle with a minimum of fanfare to protect your guests from a flying cork. Holding the bottle at a 45-degree angle from your body, making sure not to point it toward anyone, follow these steps:

1. **With your thumb over the cork, remove the foil and wire cage from around the cork. Cover the top of the bottle loosely with a clean cotton napkin.**

2. **With one hand about two-thirds of the way down the bottle and the other over the cork outside the napkin, twist the bottle (not the cork) while pushing down on the cork.**

3. **As the cork emerges, continue putting pressure on the cork so that it makes only a quiet hiss as it's released from the bottle.**

Dessert wines

Dessert wines often go unnoticed or neglected. These rich-flavored sweet wines go well with desserts of cheese, nuts, and fruit and are served best at room temperature, with the exception of champagne, which is served chilled. Particularly outstanding are sweet Chateau Y'quem, Marsala, Angelica, Tokay, Malaga, Cream Sherry, Port, and Madeira.

Holding the glass: Stem or bowl?

Wine is served in clear glasses to show off its colors. The type of wine served determines which glass to use.

Many restaurants preset the tables with at least two wine goblets — a long-stemmed glass for white wines and a tulip-shaped glass for ordinary red wines. When you order wine, the server leaves the appropriate goblet on the table and removes the other.

✔ Rhine and white wine glasses have longer slender stems so that you can hold the stem and avoid warming the wine with the heat from your hand. The bowl of the glass is smaller than a red wine glass with a more fragile look to complement the wine's delicate flavor and clear color.

✔ A red wine glass has a shorter stem with a bulbous bowl. The bowl is larger to allow the wine to breath. Hold the glass close to the bowl.

✔ Sherry and port glasses are small and open since these wines are more potent in aroma, flavor, and alcoholic content.

✔ Champagne glasses are tall and narrow and are designed to emphasize the effervescence and flavor of sparkling wines.

Mastering the ritual of ordering wine

You and your guest have been seated and you've been presented with a wine list. Uh-oh! All those French words! All those grape varieties! All those fancy descriptions! Now what?

Deciding who selects the wine

In business settings, the official host or hostess navigates the wine list and orders the wine. You may pass the wine list around the table for others to inspect or offer to have a guest select. If you conduct business regularly at a favorite restaurant, consider calling ahead and having them plan a menu and select the wine, or arrive early to discuss the menu, wine choices, and prices.

Wine adds flair to a meal and communicates to your guests that they are valued and important associates. The effort you put into wine selection not only helps you entertain successfully, but it helps you appear confident and in charge. Do your homework!

Deciding how much to spend

If you are a beginning wine drinker, you may want to enlist the help of your waiter in making a selection. Fine restaurants will have a wine steward, or sommelier, on hand to assist you.

Have a price range in mind before you order. A sensible guideline is to spend about as much on a bottle of wine as you spend on one complete dinner. Fine wines can vary in price from a few dollars to many hundreds of dollars, so make sure that you know what you're doing if you select an expensive wine.

Most restaurants price their wine by doubling the retail price and adding ten dollars. The most expensive wine on the wine list isn't always the most impressive. When looking for value, don't follow the trends — select lesser-known varieties or local wines; these are normally priced lower.

Taste, learn, and drink what you enjoy. Personal preference should be the final deciding factor.

Asking what your guests want

Ask if your guests have any preferences. It is fine to offer or make suggestions on an apéritif, champagne, or white wine to be served with the first course.

Ask about their meal choices. If everyone decides to have a rich red meat entree, then a red wine would be appropriate. If guests are having lighter chicken or seafood dishes, suggest a lighter-bodied white wine. Occasionally, there may be a guest who does not drink red wine. If the majority prefer red wine, suggest individual glasses of white wine, or order one bottle of white and one bottle of red for the table.

Handling the presentation

The server will present the wine to you. Now is the time to examine the label, making certain it is the correct wine and vintage. If acceptable, the next step will be for the server to remove the seal, take out the cork, and place it on the table. Visually examine the cork. It's not necessary to sniff or smell to see if the cork is in good condition. Unless the cork bears a different name from the label or is dry and crumbly, there is nothing to worry about. If the cork is crumbly, that is a sign that air may have leaked into the wine and spoiled it. The bottle should be replaced with another.

Tasting the wine

The person ordering the wine is normally the taster, although the host may ask one of the guests to taste instead. A small amount of wine will be poured into your glass. Color tells you a lot about the age of the wine, so look carefully before you taste. Red wines lose their color when aged — the younger the wine, the brighter the color; the older the wine, the deeper the color and the more concentrated the flavors. White wines become deeper yellow or gold with age.

Gently swirl the wine by holding the stem firmly and rotating the bowl. This is a small motion, not at all akin to preparing to lasso a steer. Swirling wine provides it oxygen, which assists in releasing its aroma or *nose*. Now sniff. Most of what you need to know about wine can be determined by its perfume. If you'd like, take a small sip. Although it's not necessary to swish the wine through your mouth, you may want to hold the wine in your mouth for a moment before swallowing.

Tasting allows you to discover the overall impression of the wine. If the wine has been spoiled — or, as it is commonly known, *corked* — you will know it upon tasting. It will taste *terrible,* not just strange. If the wine tastes "off" to you, don't hesitate to say so. The waiter or sommelier may also taste it to confirm. They will then bring another bottle of the same wine. If that vintage is not available, the waiter or sommelier will suggest or bring a similar wine. Establishments do not ask guests to pay for spoiled wine. Fine restaurants will always replace truly spoiled wine without hesitation.

Returning a bottle of wine only because you dislike it is gauche!

One bottle of wine contains approximately four glasses. Make sure to request an adequate number of bottles for the number of guests. If there are more than four guests, order a second bottle.

Finally, remember that red wines are normally served room temperature and white wines chilled, so that their flavor and aroma are at their peak. If it's hot in the restaurant, a slightly chilled, light red wine may be more desirable than a heavy Margaux.

Coping with Difficult-to-Eat Foods and Unusual Utensils

Some foods are tough to eat without looking too much like an animal gnawing away at bones or tubers. In this section, we offer some advice on how to eat these difficult foods while maintaining your dignity.

A couple of general tips to begin with: When eating fowl of any kind, separate the bird at its major joints. With small animals such as frogs and game hens, pick up tiny legs and wings by a protruding bone and eat the meat as finger food. And once you have finished, place all bones to one side of your dinner plate.

Specific foods

Here is a listing of the biggest troublemakers for those of us unsure about dining etiquette.

Peas

There are a number of ways to get peas onto your fork. Either move them against the meat and scoop them onto the fork or use a crust of bread to help "push" the peas on the fork. If eating Continental style, use your knife or other food on your plate and push or smash them on to the back of the fork tines.

Pitted foods

Olives are a finger food. Large stuffed olives are best eaten in two bites. You may pick up olives and other foods with pits with your fingers once they are on your plate. Discreetly remove pits with your forefinger and thumb.

Shellfish and mollusks

✔ **Lobster and crab:** Whole lobster and crab are almost always served in informal situations. The host provides bibs. Everyone accepts that a lot of finger work is forthcoming. When in doubt about the correct method, ask your host for guidance. If you're unfamiliar with the procedure for tackling a whole lobster and you find yourself confronted by one, the other guests are likely to have plenty of good advice. Don't be shy about asking for suggestions.

✔ **Mussels:** Steamed mussels may be eaten with a fork and spoon or a cocktail fork. Spear the mussel, dip it into the sauce provided, and eat it whole. Place the empty shells in the shell bowl.

✔ **Oysters:** Oysters are attached to the bottom shell by a slender membrane. To free the meat from the shell, slip your oyster fork underneath the meat and wiggle it back and forth a time or two. If you wish, you may dip it into the sauce on your plate. Eat the oyster in one bite, usually more of a swallow. You may pick up the shell with your fingers and drain the juice directly into your mouth. Try not to slurp.

✔ **Shrimp:** If shrimp is served ready-to-eat in a cocktail appetizer, pierce the shrimp on a little cocktail fork and bite off a succession of manageable pieces. If the shrimp are large, place them onto the plate and cut with the provided fork *before* dipping them into the sauce. Steamed shrimp served in their shells, however, are definitely a finger food. Before you tackle a serving of shrimp in their shells, make sure that you have a large fabric napkin on hand. Ask for a bib if you fear for the safety of your shirt or blouse. Usually, a large bowl is provided for the empty shells. Otherwise, neatly pile them on your plate.

✔ **Snails (Escargot):** Using the escargot tong to secure the snail in place, pick up one escargot at a time, and remove with a cocktail fork prior to dipping into butter sauce. Many restaurants serve escargot already removed from the shell and placed in special dishes with sauce or melted butter.

Spaghetti

It may look difficult, but it is easy to eat spaghetti. Spaghetti is normally twirled on the edge of your plate with your fork. However, a fork and a place spoon may also be used (though you rarely see this method in Italy). The place spoon serves as a base of operation. Place a forkful of spaghetti strands, not too much, into the bowl of the place spoon. Then twirl it around until the strands are firmly wrapped around the fork in a bite size portion.

Sushi and sashimi

Sushi was created as a way of preserving fish, presenting raw or cooked fish along with cold, cooked rice flavored with vinegar. It is served in hand-shaped bite size pieces which can be eaten using chopsticks or a fork. Many aficionados use their fingers. No matter how you choose to eat sushi, it should be eaten in one or two bites. Sushi is served with soy sauce and various condiments, with ginger provided as a refresher for the palate between courses.

Sashimi, a dish of thin slices of fresh raw fish, is the crowning glory of the formal Japanese meal. The soup and raw fish are so important that other dishes are merely decoration. Sashimi is arranged artfully on beautiful plates, with a variety of garnishes, and is usually eaten early in the meal while diners are hungry. It is typically served in individual shallow plates, in small slices or bite sized pieces to be eaten with chopsticks.

Japanese soups and noodles

Soups are often served after the appetizer as the first course. The soup should not be so hot that you have to imbibe quite a bit of air with your sips to avoid being scalded.

Noodles are often served so hot that they can't be eaten in puckered silence. Open your mouth wide to accommodate the slippery pasta and suck in with a fair amount of gusto! For a Westerner, picking up the knack of noodle eating depends on how quickly you can abandon the American taboo of noisy eating!

Using chopsticks

In many Asian countries, chopsticks are used instead of the Western knife, fork, and spoon. Chopsticks come in a wide variety of finishes, from plain wood to ornately decorated lacquer.

There is a certain technique to using chopsticks: Hold them between your index finger and thumb, with the lower stick resting still in the web of your hand and the top stick being held like a pencil. (See Figure 16-9.) The top stick does most of the moving. Your two middle fingers are used to maneuver it. Holding chopsticks too tightly restricts mobility; holding them too close to the tip makes you lose leverage.

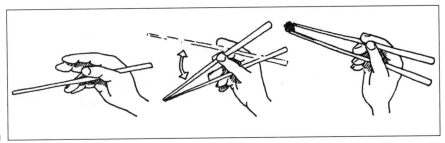

Figure 16-9:
Holding and
using
chopsticks.

If your food is too big for a single bite, you may use your chopsticks to cut it or hold the food with your chopsticks while you take a couple of bites. Between bites, either place your chopsticks on the rest provided or lay them across the lower dish, or plate.

Here is a brief list of chopstick don'ts:

- ✔ Never point, gesture, or talk with chopsticks
- ✔ Do not leave chopsticks pointed upright in your rice or soup bowl
- ✔ Never take food from another person's chopsticks

And remember, if you're not ready to tackle chopsticks, it is perfectly fine to request a fork and knife if you are in the United States.

Managing Dining Mishaps

Eating in any social setting may result in mishaps. The following tips may help you steer yourself out of common mishaps that can occur:

✔ **You drop a utensil onto the floor.** Never lean over and pick up the utensil. Beckon a waiter and politely ask for a new one.

✔ **You're served a piece of food that is not cooked properly.** This situation particularly calls for action when meat is involved. Call a waiter and quietly explain the situation in a whisper. Trust the waiter to reappear with a different plate of food for you.

✔ **You find a foreign object in your food.** Again, find a waiter and tell him or her about the problem in a very discreet manner. Rest assured, your meal will be replaced quickly.

✔ **You dislike the food that is being served, or you are allergic to it.** Of course, the polite thing to do is try a little of everything; however, if you are allergic to a food, just smile and say no thank you. It's not necessary to say anything critical.

✔ **You have a piece of bone, gristle, or some other unwanted food item in your mouth.** Discreetly place the item onto the tines of your fork and lay it on your plate, hiding it under something if possible.

✔ **You notice that your dining partner has spinach in her teeth or a crumb in his beard.** Catch your dining partner's attention and discreetly motion to that part of your face where the offending morsel is lodged on his or her face.

That's a lot of information for one chapter. But you're ready to go anywhere now! *Bon appetit!*

Chapter 17

Outings, Sports, Retreats, and Sporting Events

In This Chapter

▶ Hosting business outings

▶ Going over special etiquette for golf and sailing

▶ Finessing the fine points of tennis, racquetball, and squash

▶ Being safe at skiing and extreme sports

▶ Having fun at retreats

▶ Covering your bases at sports events and private clubs

*W*ith the new flexibility in the workday, it's not surprising that business isn't restricted to the office or the restaurant anymore. In the contemporary workplace, there are as many venues for business as there are activities that are shared by colleagues and associates.

Whether you and your best client are avid ice climbers or fanatic golfers, you're likely at some point in your career to find yourself in a situation in which you never thought you'd be doing business. In this chapter, you'll get advice on some of the more frequently used out-of-the-office venues for business: outings, golfing, retreats, and sailing. There are plenty of others. Your list might include paragliding or heli-skiing in the Bugaboos. But take heart: At least for now, trips to Everest are not *de rigeur*.

Hosting Group Outings

Just as the workday is more flexible than it used to be, so too are the places where you are can conduct business. You might work for an engineering firm that encourages its employees to take after-lunch group bike hikes to the city overlook. Your boss might like to take small groups to her house so that you can discuss strategy in the privacy of her back yard. You might visit a high-tech firm in Portland and be invited on a walking tour of Horsetail Falls in the Gorge. In these and all other cases, there are acts of consideration you can take as the host and good and bad ways to act as the guest.

If you're the host of such an off-site outing, take care to think things through *ahead* of time. Make the invitation in advance and clearly state the equipment needed (if any), the purpose and the length of the outing. Unless you provide ample warning, respect people's right to decline if the outing radically deviates from the time and place of the regular workday. That way, an employee won't be stranded on a granite face ten minutes before he needs to pick his daughter up at day care.

Schedule off-site outings in advance if you can.

Also take the time to learn whether there are other personal or practical impediments to the off-site outing. Perhaps your guest is asthmatic and the trip you'd hoped to take to the sea lion caves would only make her miserable. Perhaps reservations have to be made months in advance to go on that ferry ride through Puget Sound — if you show up without reservations, you'll embarrass yourself and your guest. Whatever it is, think things through.

A new hire at an engineering firm in Denver spent a day interviewing on site and enjoyed an evening dinner with the interview team. On the following day, her interview team offered to take her up into the mountains. They had a lovely time together. Then the driver decided to take an alternate route down from the town they had been visiting, an unholy dirt road that descended 7,000 vertical feet in five miles. Without asking the boss, the driver started down the exposed and devilishly twisty road. Within three minutes, the driver's boss ordered him to stop. He had to get out of the car . . . pronto! He emptied his stomach, got back in the car and was green and silent until they reached level ground again. By the time they got back to their building, he had recovered, but he was furious at the driver for embarrassing him like that in front of a new hire!

Combining cruises and business meetings

An increasingly popular place for off-site business meetings is, believe it or not, the cruise ship! And it's not just conventions and trade shows that are happening on board. Day cruises for business meetings from major and minor port and river cities are at an all-time high.

The reasons for the new-found popularity of business cruises aren't hard to find. Unlike hotels and convention centers, once you're on the boat, there are few distractions. Executives and managers alike find that business meetings held on board are well-focused and efficient. And everyone has a good time to boot, at least as long as the weather is good!

If you are hosting a guest from out of town and would like to take her to see some of the local sights and landmarks, discreetly inquire as to his willingness to undertake such an excursion. Say something like, "Mr. Ferrari, I would like to offer you the opportunity to see our wonderful art museum and the local arboretum tomorrow. Would that be of interest to you or is there something else you would prefer?" If Mr. Ferrari has some restrictions that would prevent him from enjoying walking, this phrasing of the question allows him to back away gracefully. And it prevents embarrassment to you as well, for the way you've phrased the question doesn't put him in the position of having to admit that he'd rather not join you for reasons he'd rather not reveal!

CAUTION

Avoid strenuous outings unless your guest is a health nut. There's no point in jeopardizing a business relationship by possibly humiliating your guest!

TIP

Being in the shade at an outside restaurant on a beautiful day is one of the best off-site outings you can have.

Going Golfing

Golf and business are like hot dogs and baseball — they naturally go together. The relaxed pace, bucolic surroundings, and handsome appointments of the clubhouse provide an elegant way to get to know other people and to strike deals.

Of course, golf works well as an icebreaker and dealmaker only some of the time. That's because golf is an immensely frustrating game on occasion, so it's a remarkably accurate test of a person's stress-management abilities! If your partner doesn't lose her cool after a quadruple bogey on the par-3 fifteenth, chances are pretty good that she'll be cool under other kinds of fire.

As old as the game is, golf is loaded with expected behavior and attire. Except on public courses, it is, for example, rare to see jeans on a golf course. About as casual as things get is business casual.

There are two codes of conduct to keep in mind when golfing — the etiquette of golfing and the etiquette of combining golf and business.

General golf etiquette

When you golf, you should know that:

- Women wear knee-length skirts or long shorts or pants, shirts with collars and sleeves, and golf shoes with soft spikes.

- Men wear slacks or long shorts, shirts with collars and sleeves, and golf shoes with soft spikes.
- Colors never found in nature or in the office are acceptable on the golf course. However, many clubs favor more muted, conservative attire. If in doubt, call the club and ask.
- You don't talk when someone else is playing a stroke.
- You should be ready to play when it's your turn.
- The player with the lowest score on the previous hole is first to tee off on the next hole.
- Everyone in your group should be behind you when you hit.
- You let faster groups play through. Take your practice swings before you get to the tee.
- You repair divots and pitch marks and rake away your footprints in sand traps.
- You don't stand with your group on the green after you've all holed out.
- You put no more than two people in a cart and you drive it slowly. Keep your cart on the cart path and off the green, unless you have special needs and have made special arrangements.

- Never, ever scream obscenities or throw your clubs.

Business golf etiquette

Putting golf and business together is supposed to be fun and productive at the same time. You can do that more effectively if you remember that the golf outing is first and foremost a business event and that your boss and clients have to look good if you're going to get what you want. Keep these tips in mind:

- You don't outplay the boss or client, even if he's a 15 handicap and you're a 4.
- Avoid talking business until the group is settled into the game and is comfortable with each other.
- Keep your dirty jokes to yourself. The same rules apply to conversation on the golf course as apply to conversation in the office.
- Avoid talking business if a companion is facing a difficult shot.
- Avoid offering bets, but accept them if offered by your client or boss. Win graciously and pay promptly if you lose.
- Don't cheat on your scorecard.
- In general, the host tips. But if you have a personal caddie, you may tip your caddie even as a guest.

Sailing and Motorboating

Sailing and motor boating can be opportunities for the boss or client to show off their latest toys. But they can also be enormous fun, so long as you know what you're doing on the boat.

Never call a yacht a yacht! All boats, from the smallest motorboat to the largest yacht, are simply boats to their captains.

Sailing takes years of practice to become proficient. If you are a novice, no amount of confident bluster will cover for your ignorance of the difference between a line and a halyard. It's simply not in your strategic interest to fake it. Better to admit your landlubber status and ask for directions. Most captains will be more than willing to tell you what to do.

If the captain asks you to just stay put and stop helping, stop helping. Uninformed "helping" on a sailboat can result in an unintended swim!

If you're the host of a day at sea, advise your guests ahead of time as to what they should wear and whether it's likely that they will get wet. Let them know whether they will be sailing, motoring leisurely, or attempting to break the sound barrier. Don't invite more people than your boat can accommodate. If you're a guest, remember that the boat is your captain's. The captain is boss at all times on the boat: It is not a democracy. Follow directions.

If your work will involve frequent sailing or boating expeditions and you grew up in Nebraska or some other landlocked area, browse through an introductory handbook on sailing or boating to familiarize yourself with terms.

Here are some other guidelines to know:

- Wear clothes that will protect you from the elements and can get wet. Layer! If the weather is reasonably warm, wear a bathing suit, shorts, T-shirt or polo shirt, a hat, and sunglasses. Bring a windbreaker and a sweater or sweatshirt if you will be out in the evening or out on the ocean. You may take most of your clothes off, but having the right kind of clothes on hand can help if the weather goes bad or you're out after dark.

- Wear deck shoes or simple tennis shoes like Keds. Sandals, hiking shoes, or leather-soled shoes are inappropriate and sometimes dangerous.

- If you don't know how to help, stay well out of the way of those who do.

- Never smoke below deck; ask if you may smoke above deck.

- Bring only gifts that can be shared while you're on board. If you're not sure about the galley facilities, ask.

- If you fear that you'll be seasick, take medication for it.

Playing Tennis, Racquetball, and Squash

Racquet sports are popular in large cities because they happen inside and don't require a lot of space. As inside sports, there is usually a dress code attached to playing them. Make sure that you know ahead of time what the dress code is for the club you are going to attend.

White is always appropriate at a racquet club. You will always be dressed correctly if you wear a white knit shirt with a collar and sleeves tucked into white shorts. Women may also wear tennis dresses. Tennis shoes are the appropriate footwear.

Some dress codes are less restrictive than others. When in doubt, check with the club.

If you're hosting a guest at your club, be sure to arrive early so that your guest will not face quizzical looks from the staff. Escort your guest to the locker room, supply him with towels and a locker, and allow him some privacy when changing.

As a guest, you should arrive with the right gear and the appropriate attire. This means that you bring your own racquet, balls, and protective eyewear and that you check ahead about the club's dress code.

John McEnroe notwithstanding, racquet sports are known for their genteel play. And with the exception of professional or refereed competition matches, racquet sports rely entirely on the honesty of the players to enforce the rules. This feature has the following implications:

- ✔ You show up on time.
- ✔ You call out-of-bounds on your side of the net.
- ✔ You don't return serves that are out.
- ✔ If your opponent makes a lousy call, you say nothing.
- ✔ You say the score after every point.
- ✔ You return stray balls from other courts when there's a break in your game.
- ✔ You stay in your court and you don't interrupt other players while they're playing. Wait for a break in their game.

- ✔ Never, ever scream obscenities or throw your racquet.

Although it's more fun to play someone at your own level, you will not always have this luxury. If you are playing with someone at a different level, try to make it enjoyable for your guest. That means that if you're a beginner and your guest is an accomplished player, let her know about your status and ask for advice. On the other hand, if you're an experienced player and your guest is not, don't destroy her in the game. Be encouraging. Remember — the point is to have fun.

Skiing and Snowboarding

The rules of skiing and snowboarding are, like many other etiquette guidelines, based on safety — yours and others. Begin by acknowledging that skiing happens in winter and requires warm clothing. You have to be properly outfitted to enjoy skiing. Thermal underclothes, pile shirts and sweaters, wool/nylon blend socks, moisture wicking pants, breathable waterproof parkas and ski pants, gloves or mittens (or both!), hat, sunglasses or goggles (or both), and sunscreen are all *necessary* clothing items.

If you've never been on skis or a snowboard, then, by all means, do the sensible thing and take a lesson or two. With parabolic skis now the norm for recreational skiers, learning to ski is easier than ever before. Counting on your natural athletic ability to get you down the slope is not smart. The same goes for boarding. Skiing and boarding may look easy, but they aren't. Ask any orthopedic surgeon!

If you're a skier or a boarder, you'll know these etiquette rules. If you're a beginner, memorize these:

- ✔ Do not crash the lift line. Stay in order. Offer to ride with singles or offer a ride to a single.

- ✔ If you've never been on a lift, tell the operator at the bottom of the lift, who will slow it down and show you how to get on.

- ✔ If you've never gotten off a lift, motion to the operator at the top to slow it down for you to get off. Move away from the off-ramp immediately.

- ✔ Ski and board under control at all times. Skiing and snowboarding can be lethal sports. Don't go on runs you're not prepared to ski or board all the way down under your own power.

- ✔ The skier or boarder below you has the right of way at all times. If you want to pass, yell "Left!" or "Right!" before you do so.

- ✔ If you get in over your head on a slope, side slip down the edge of the slope to safer ground.

As a skiing host, be aware of the situation with your guests. Do not cajole them onto a double black diamond run to impress them with your skill. Always be prepared to ski well below your level to assure the comfort and safety of your guests. Again, remember the point is to have fun. You're not at the Olympics.

Undertaking Extreme Sports

The etiquette of extreme sports is, more than most other sports, a function of safety concerns. These are, after all, *extreme* sports to which a significant risk of injury or death is attached. Your strict adherence to the sport's etiquette may well save your life and almost assuredly will save you from injury. Whether you are mountain biking or kayaking, your knowledge of a sport's specific safety concerns will help you enjoy the sport more and make it an effective social activity for business.

Each extreme sport has its own set of etiquette guidelines. We won't cover them here. But we can say that the key business etiquette issue is, again, to take care not to outdo your guest or boss. If you're both kayakers, but your guest is capable only of Grade IV water and you're capable of Grade VI water, then either don't take her on a river with Grade VI water or confirm that the Grade V and VI rapids can be portaged. Not only will your guest be humiliated if she tries to run water she can't run, she may end up seriously injured or worse. It is always advisable for the host to introduce the etiquette of a particular sport to her guests. And if, as a guest, you're uncertain, don't hesitate to ask.

If in doubt about this advice, reread *Into Thin Air,* by Jon Krakauer. Need we say more?!

Going on Retreats

Corporate retreats — for brainstorming sessions, for entertaining clients, for relaxation — should be treated like extended home entertainments. That means that, if you're the host, you are responsible for putting the retreat together and making sure that everyone has what they need to have. If you're a guest, you are responsible for enjoying yourself, getting your work done, and being grateful to the host for the trouble he or she has gone to in putting it together.

A retreat is not an episode of *Survivor.* Resist the temptation to bare your soul, or anything else for that matter.

Some retreats are multi-day affairs at lodges or private homes. If you're invited to such an affair, you will have to spend the night at the lodge and see your colleagues or clients early in the morning. This wouldn't be so bad were it not for the fact that there are people who just don't get going until they've been awake for a couple of hours. At home, this poses no problem, since you can pad around in your bathrobe until you've had those two triple lattes.

What are you supposed to do at a lodge if you're a slow riser? We recommend that you get up early enough that you clear at least some of the cobwebs before confronting anyone at the breakfast buffet. Do as much of your morning routine in your room as you can. If possible, force yourself to take a brief morning walk. The fresh air will help revive you. If you're desperate about the prospect of seeing *anyone* without at least one cup of coffee, you can pack your own instant coffee and drink a cup in your room or call room service.

Remember the movie *City Slickers?* Coffee grinders can cause stampedes, so don't be so rude as to wake others up with yours! If you're an early riser, be quiet.

Retreats often come packaged with arranged activities and entertainment. These activities can range from planned strolls and fishing afternoons to team building exercises that run the gamut from preschool art projects to boot camp. This is, for better or worse, the stuff of the modern workplace.

If you end up participating in team building exercises, remember always that the point of these exercises is to cultivate productive cooperation within a group. You may be faced with a blank wall that everyone has to get over or a zip line at twenty feet over a nasty looking mud pot. Your team's cooperation and mutual trust in this kind of situation is supposed to transfer to the workplace when you return.

You do yourself absolutely no good by expressing your disdain for these exercises. You might be right, of course, but that doesn't mean that you should say what's on your mind. Instead, try to be a productive member of the team, even if it is painful for you to do so. After all, it only lasts a couple of hours, but your whininess may be remembered for a *very* long time.

Attending Sporting Events and Private Clubs

Corporate boxes at football and baseball stadiums and at basketball arenas are more popular now than they have ever been. They are impressive ways to entertain clients, and companies in major cities spend lavishly to impress clients with their firm's prestige. In fact, they are now as popular as the old-line country club. But both venues are bound by the same guidelines.

As host, you invite a client, employee, or friend to your box or club expecting them not to pay. Your invitation carries with it the presumption that you will pay for the time your guest spends there and for her food and drink, if any. This extends to tips.

The presumption that the host pays does not, however, extend to buying equipment for your guest. If you invite a client to a game of tennis at your club, you will pay for her time on the court and for her refreshments, but your guest is expected to arrive ready to play.

As a guest, keep it in mind that you are at the box or the club at your host's expense. Your presence is a privilege and should be treated as such. Do not embarrass your host by arriving in anything less formal than business casual, and have the right wardrobe and equipment for the sport you will be playing.

Wearing cutoffs, jeans, T-shirts, or halter tops to a private box for a sporting event or to play sports at a private club is inappropriate.

And remember, it's perfectly all right to admit that you don't play the sport you've been invited to play. Rank beginners and fakes are not appreciated. It's better to decline than embarrass yourself at a sport you don't know how to play at least proficiently.

Chapter 18

Marking Life's Major Events and Passages

*W*hen the heat is on and everyone is working full bore, a break to celebrate a colleague's new baby can seem superfluous, but it may be just what everyone needs. There is a tendency to dismiss office celebrations or to look at them as contrived affairs that no one really enjoys. But recognizing major events in the life of your colleagues helps establish camaraderie and cooperative working relations as well as acknowledge your colleagues as individual human beings.

People often feel uncomfortable at such gatherings, not because they don't like their colleagues, but because they're not sure what to talk about. In this chapter, you'll come to see that the social gatherings that occur in professional life can be handled with grace and genuine pleasure or sorrow for events affecting others.

Office Parties

General office parties are useful for building morale and celebrating accomplishments. They can also be held for special occasions, such as a beloved boss's retirement or a colleague's fiftieth birthday.

However, holding too many office parties or holding office parties for obscure reasons tends to undercut the whole point of giving them in the first place. The impetus for parties should be genuine and sincere.

Office parties should be given for a reason and be reasonably short. Once or twice a year is plenty for the entire company to celebrate together with a big bash.

The first thing to do when planning an office party is to verify with your boss that the time and day you would like to have the party are open. Failing to do this can make the party happen under a cloud of your boss's displeasure, and you wouldn't want that.

If your division or department is going to host an office party, send invitations out in the form of memos or e-mail if the party is in the office and send real invitations if the party is to be outside of the office (see Chapter 15 for more details on invitations). The invitation should include the reason for the party, where it's to be held, and its commencement time and duration.

Delegate the details of the party as you require, but guarantee a successful party by putting one person in charge to whom the others report. If there are to be donations, designate one person to collect the money, and specify whether the money is to be used for a gift, refreshments, or both. Don't ask for too much — if you can't get by with less than $5 or $10 from people, look for some other way to supplement the party kitty. Here are some more delegation tips:

- Try not to overburden your colleagues by asking for too much for office celebrations or by asking too frequently for contributions. In a large office, there are bound to be quite a few birthdays, babies, weddings, and parties, and the constant solicitation for money can be annoying.

- Try having an office kitty to which people contribute as much as they can when they can. This helps provide a ready source of money for small employee gifts and helps prevent frequent requests for more money.

Hosting a restaurant gathering

If you're having the party at a local restaurant, then, as host, you are responsible for the reservations. When you arrive at the restaurant, make arrangements to pay the bill privately, so that no one else has the opportunity to dispute your generosity. If everyone is pitching in for the meal, then the bill can come to the table. But remember to clarify this matter *before* the meal.

On the day of the party, check with everyone early in the day for any last minute business emergencies and do what is needed to take care of them.

As host, you are responsible for making sure that no one gets out of hand and that even the wallflowers have as good a time as they can. And look out for those habituated show-offs in every office who relish their time in the limelight, even if it's from a lava lamp! If you sense that someone is trapped by one of these hams, intervene politely and ask the trapped person to accompany you on some needed errand. Make sure, too, that no one drinks too much of the punch. Being drunk on company time is a very bad idea, and you as host can try to prevent it.

Being a guest

As a guest, your normal guest responsibilities are in order at the office party too. Stay sober and don't imbibe any illegal drugs. And, even if everyone is feeling giddy, stay away from baring your soul to your favorite shipper, displaying a little too much affection for your romantic partner — or that attractive new accountant you wish were your romantic partner — or making aggressive sexual advances to any of your colleagues.

An economic research firm in Nashville had two summer interns, Romy and Kim. On Labor Day weekend, the company had its annual picnic by the pool at the home of a board member. Romy was advised by her mentor to avoid getting drunk at all costs. She was told that her first drink should be water; her second drink could be alcohol, followed by two more glasses of water, and so on. She was warned that things could get out of hand at this party, and told that self-control was in order. Kim was given no such advice.

The day of the party arrived, and the mentor's predictions were true. Many members of the upper management were extremely drunk. Many people ended up in the pool, fully dressed. By the end of the party, many people ended up in the pool, fully undressed. Romy, heeding her mentor's advice, spent most of her time talking with the sober managers, their spouses, and teenage children. Kim, on the other hand, led a strip hula dance on the diving board and was later sick in the Jacuzzi.

On Tuesday morning, Romy received a call from the president of the company, who had been quite drunk, asking her if she would like to take a permanent position with the company after her graduation.

Employee Birthdays, Weddings, Babies, Retirement, and Deaths

Although many people keep their work life separate from their private life, everyone has a birthday, everybody eventually retires, many people get married and/or have babies, and most people will lose someone dear to them while you know them at work. What are the best ways to mark these milestones with colleagues, clients, and bosses?

Birthdays

There is no general requirement to mark every coworker's birthday. But significant ones — the decade birthdays are the obvious example — call out for recognition. A card signed by everyone in the office, and perhaps a gift, are in order.

Birthday gifts from boss to employee are always acceptable, but a birthday gift from a subordinate to a boss at the office is not advised. Others may perceive it as sycophantic behavior. A group card or group gift for a special birthday is better.

Weddings

Colleagues, clients, and bosses get married. And you won't be invited to all of the weddings. Unfair? Maybe, but not everyone shares everything with coworkers: Plenty of people draw a sharp and bold line between work and home. Rather than being hurt, acknowledge that some people are just plain different from you. If you are invited, send a gift by all means. But even if you're not invited, it's a nice gesture to organize an office gift for your fellow worker.

A couple in the plastics manufacturing business held a small wedding, inviting only family and a few close friends. They sent announcements to coworkers and other friends. Upon seeing the new bride for the first time since the wedding, a coworker immediately blurted out, "You got married and you didn't even invite me! How could you?" No congratulations, no happiness for the bride, just pure, self-pitying narcissism.

Try to be gracious, even if you're hurt not to be included. Often a wedding budget is tight or the couple has their own reasons for limiting the guest list. Assume that the omission was not personal.

If you are invited to a colleague's or client's wedding, remember that it is an honor to attend. Act accordingly. This means, among other things, responding to the invitation promptly and with the same amount of formality as found in the invitation, as well as buying a gift and sending it either to the bride's parents or the bride herself *before or shortly after* the wedding. Do not bring gifts to the wedding. If the invitation is to you alone, go alone. Do not bring uninvited guests. And be on your best behavior at the wedding.

A gift of money in the form of a check is always proper for weddings. On the other hand, asking for money as a wedding gift is always wrong.

Babies

Anticipating the birth of a baby can bring out the very best in people; unfortunately, it can bring out the weirdest in people too. The office shower is occasionally a painful experience for all involved. The reason is simple: Having a baby is necessarily an intimate affair, and you may not be — in all likelihood, are not — on intimate terms with your coworkers. And yet there you are, discussing things with your colleagues that even some of your closest friends don't know.

Avoid the following mistakes:

- Touching a pregnant woman's stomach.
- Asking a new parent detailed questions. Demanding a play-by-play description of the delivery or subjecting others to every detail of your own experience is not appropriate.

Unless you and others in your office are *good* friends with the person having the baby, group gifts are preferable to office baby showers.

Retirement

Everyone retires at some point. If your company has a party-giving culture, you might plan a retrospective of the person's time at the company — slides, anecdotes, and photographs can be fun and warmly appreciated. A group gift or a charitable donation is appropriate. Often, the retiree is also presented with a personal gift from the president or CEO. Be grateful for whatever effort your company makes. And enjoy your retirement!

Funerals

At some point in your career, either you or someone you work with will lose someone dear. The death of a loved one is a wrenching and debilitating event for the survivors, as they confront not only their loss but also their conflicted feelings toward the person who has died.

It is not at all unusual for survivors to go through a prolonged period of mourning after the death, during which sociability and probably even performance will lag. As a coworker or superior, you can help the grieving person by offering to help, either in a condolence card or in person.

As soon as you hear about the loss, draft a letter of condolence in black ink on a plain white fold-over card or a plain monarch sheet. (See Chapter 8 if you need to brush up on your business stationery needs.) In this letter, your compassion for the survivor should be apparent, as should your own lack of ego. You should focus on the loss of the loved one and offer to do what you can to help the survivor through their period of mourning. Be prepared never to get any such request. Most people mourn alone.

Don't get caught making these mistakes:

- ✔ Talking about *your* loss of a loved one in a letter of condolence is uncaring and mean.
- ✔ Offering ribald memories of the dead person is inappropriate.

As a manager or boss, watch the griever carefully. Offer to help with the griever's job if necessary, and, if it's clear that he or she cannot work, offer time off. It will be welcome.

At funerals or memorial services, your dress should reflect the somber nature of the occasion. Wear a dark gray, black, or navy blue suit with a white shirt and dark tie if you are a man, or a dark dress or suit with subdued jewelry if you are a woman. Now is definitely not the time for your Bugs Bunny tie or your sandals! And check with the funeral home or church for the appropriateness of flowers. Often, the obituary will explicitly state that flowers are not preferred. Please take that advice seriously. If a memorial is suggested, send your donation to the given address. You do not need to mention that you have done so. The organization receiving the gift will send an acknowledgment to the bereaved.

If the funeral is at a funeral home, certain other formalities are typically observed. At all times, your comportment should be quiet and dignified. If there is a receiving line, shake hands with everyone in it. If you are unknown to the family, identify yourself and your professional relation to the deceased. If you don't know them, say something simple and genuine, such as, "I am so sorry for your loss."

Widows and widowers often forget to eat in the weeks following their loss. It is a charity to bring food to them. You don't need to spend long delivering it. You can even call ahead and leave it on the porch.

To Give or Not to Give

Giving and receiving cause a considerable amount of concern in business, for obvious reasons. Gifts can be used appropriately to thank clients for business, to reward someone for a job well done, to celebrate a promotion, or to commemorate a long-term relationship. But gift giving can also veer into undue influence and bribery.

There are two kinds of gift giving in business. The first kind, between colleagues and/or supervisors, is easier to justify and is less fraught with danger than the second kind, gift giving between companies. This second kind of gift giving is sometimes cause for concern.

Gifts in the office

Gift giving between coworkers, especially during the holiday season, is a common practice found at many companies. If you work for such a company, you will be considered churlish if you don't participate. This is one of those coercive acts of generosity that really can't be ignored or belittled, so bite the bullet and join in.

Avoid making holiday gifts explicitly religious.

The gifts for your coworkers don't have to be lavish and they ought not to be too personal. Something a colleague can use in the office, such as a coffee mug or a picture frame, is just fine.

Group gifts for weddings, babies, and retirements are the norm. Here, again, don't presume to know your recipient so well that you get her something personal. Focus on the utilitarian and the practical, not the exciting or the alluring.

Gifts for bosses are a different matter altogether. There is a serious problem with giving a gift to a boss: It may look like you're trying to curry favor with him or, worse, bribe him. Besides, if you spend too much, your boss — who, after all, knows what you make — may decide that you're a toadying fool. Follow these simple guidelines:

- Extravagant gift giving is both bad strategy and in poor taste. Others may not share your love of lavish gifts and it makes them resent you for going overboard.
- Send group gifts rather than individual gifts to bosses.
- It's all right to send a card or flowers to your boss if she has been ill or in the hospital.

Gifts between companies

Gift giving between companies or between individuals in different companies is a thorny issue, so thorny in fact that most organizations have explicit rules governing the practice.

Here, again, there are two kinds of gift giving to look at. First, there is the gift you or your company presents to others; second, there is the gift you or your company receives from others. In the last section of this chapter, we'll consider the different kinds of gifts that are appropriate to give professionally.

Giving gifts to companies or individuals in other companies

It is a common practice for companies to give gifts to clients and customers during the holiday season. So long as the gift is not ostentatious, this practice avoids the appearance of attempted favor-currying, and so long as it is reasonably well-made, it avoids the appearance of trying to dump promotional items.

There are other occasions for professional gift giving. Birthdays are an obvious opportunity, but so too are significant business-related events shared between you and the other company. Just be careful to abide by your company's policy concerning gifts when you consider what to give.

Be careful with humorous gifts! If you are not sure the recipient will be pleasantly amused, don't send it.

Receiving gifts from other companies or individuals in other companies

There is really only one thing to consider here: Know your company policy about receiving gifts! Some companies do not allow their employees to receive any gifts worth more than, say, $50. Others require all gifts worth more than a specified amount to be automatically disclosed to your supervisor or some other manager.

Problems arise when you receive a gift that violates company policy. If you receive season tickets to the Green Bay Packers and your company forbids acceptance of any gifts worth more than $100, then you are painfully obliged to decline the gift. Ouch!

If you are in this predicament, you will probably have to write a letter declining the gift.

Compose the letter in which you decline a gift carefully, focusing on the company's policy on receiving gifts rather than your personal feelings. It's the company's policy that prevents you from accepting the gift, not your own displeasure. Say so.

Finding Appropriate Gifts for Every Occasion

Now that you know when it is appropriate to give and receive a gift, you may still be mystified by the prospect of choosing a gift. Luckily, there are only a few choices to make here.

Make a distinction between a personal gift and a business gift. If you know a client or colleague well, socializing outside a business context on a regular basis, you may want to give a personal gift for a birthday, promotion, or holiday. Send or deliver such a gift to the person's home.

If you wish to give a business gift, first familiarize yourself with your firm's gift policy, if there is one. Professional gifts can be quite varied, from food or wine to small conveniences, such as a business card holder or a new pen, to office items, such as a frame or a computer accessory. If you know your client well enough to have visited her office many times, you may have had the opportunity divine a welcome addition.

Consider giving someone who writes a lot a hardbound thesaurus, good dictionary, or foreign phrase book.

Perishable gifts

Just as there is a distinction between personal and professional gifts, there is also a distinction between perishable and lasting gifts. Perishable gifts are, as the name implies, gifts that have a short life, such as food, flowers, and wine. Lasting gifts are intended to last longer, perhaps even a lifetime.

Perishable gifts are just fine for most professional gift giving between companies and between individuals who don't know each other well. Lasting gifts are better reserved for especially significant events and for those events you want the other company or individual to remember for a long time.

When choosing a perishable gift, there are some guidelines to keep in mind. Take flowers, for instance. Flowers can be a great gift, but if you send long-stemmed roses to an administrative assistant as a thank-you for her outstanding accomplishment in getting everyone organized, you send the wrong message. Roses traditionally have romantic overtones, and that's not a professional message. Tulips, a tasteful mixed bouquet, or a flowering plant are better choices.

If you enjoy sending flowers, develop a relationship with a good florist, who can provide guidance.

Food can be just as tricky. Everyone laughs about fruitcake at Christmas, but there's a reason people are so fond of it — it travels well and doesn't go bad out of the refrigerator! But it's not the best gift because it is hackneyed. A gift of gourmet or regional food is preferable. Of course, check before you give it — giving the best turkey you can find to a vegetarian is a bad choice.

The language of flowers

Sending flowers as a professional gift is constrained by a couple of simple rules. First, never send roses. Perrin once received a dozen red roses from a customer as a thank-you at the end of a project. Her boss told her to return them immediately and composed a letter to the customer explaining why the gift was inappropriate! Second, remember that cut flowers are good as host or hostess gifts and as a gift for someone in the hospital. However, arrangements or potted plants are preferable for an office colleague.

Finally, you can always give wine or stronger spirits, so long as you know that the recipient imbibes and would enjoy the gift. But be careful — never present a gift of alcohol at the office and don't send alcohol to the office either. Even a whiff of impropriety with alcohol may leave a permanent scar on an otherwise unblemished record in some environments.

Lasting gifts

Permanent gifts require a good deal more thought — after all, you want it to be remembered favorably. You can err in one of two ways: Either the gift is not appropriate to the person or the gift is not appropriate to the relationship you have with the person. The first is easy to remedy — choose the gift more carefully! The second is a little trickier. There might not be anything wrong in giving one of your very best clients two tickets to the opera, but giving those tickets to a client who gives you little business would be inappropriate.

Finally, if you order a gift to be delivered, either from a brick and mortar store or over the Web, double check with the company you ordered from in a few days to make sure the gift has actually been delivered.

Whether temporary or permanent, personal or professional, take care to present the gift competently wrapped and with a card. Otherwise, your intentions will be sabotaged by your shoddy presentation. If you can't wrap a box, get someone else — such as the customer service counter at the store where you purchase the gift or someone you know — to do it.

And, remember, it *is* better to give than to receive. For, in giving, you extend your everyday kindness to an act whose *only* goal is kindness.

Chapter 19

Handling Alcohol

• •

• •

*P*lenty of opportunities to combine alcohol and business exist, and there are lots of strong spirits and lots of ways to enjoy them. Making blanket statements about the etiquette of serving and accepting drinks is difficult. However, good hosts and guests behave differently than their boorish counterparts when it comes to alcohol.

In this chapter, you find out that there is an art to being a good host and an art to being a good guest with drinks. We show you how to temper your drinking (and what to do if you forget).

Drinking Alcohol while on Business

Business is stressful. Alcohol is relaxing. You don't have to be the CEO of an Internet start-up to figure out why the two sometimes are paired. Of course, more sinister reasons exist for why alcohol and business are partners, the most obvious being the link between alcohol and impaired judgment — something that some take advantage of in business.

If you are the host and you want to offer liquor to your guests, do so graciously. If you're at home, a tray, table, or bar displaying a selection of liquors and glasses, along with a container of ice, will show them what you stock. Ask how your guest prefers the drink to be served — straight in a tumbler, with ice, or perhaps diluted with water, seltzer, or some kind of mix.

If you're the host at a restaurant or a cocktail lounge, offer liquor to your guest. If he accepts, join him by having an alcoholic drink. If you don't drink alcohol, join your guest by ordering a nonalcoholic drink.

As a guest in someone's home, survey the possibilities and make your request within the available choices. Save the fancy mixed-drink-served-in-a-coconut-with-lawn-furniture for the Polynesian Room. As a guest at a cocktail lounge or at a reception, your fancy requests can more likely be accommodated, but oversized drinks or outrageously expensive drinks are best avoided in most business situations. See the section on types of drinks, later in this chapter, for more information on drinks that are always safe to order.

Whether host or guest, whether at home or in a restaurant, you are representing your company and doing business. It's in no one's best interest that you over-indulge. Know your limits and stick to them religiously. Remember, you can always drink water or another nonalcoholic beverage for a while.

Knowing the Types of Drinks

If you find that having an occasional drink other than at dinner is a part of doing business, then knowing what to drink and when should be of some help to you. The following sections provide some guidelines. For wine at dinner, we refer you to Chapter 16.

Drinks before dinner

Before dinner, one drinks cocktails or *aperitifs*. Cocktails are mixed drinks made with gin, vodka, scotch, whiskey, bourbon, or rum. Cocktails consumed before dinner should not be overly sweet or contain milk or cream. The idea here is to stimulate the appetite, not provide enough calories to replace dinner. Some people prefer a before dinner drink of straight liquor on the rocks, such as vodka or scotch.

Here are a few tips to keep in mind when drinking or serving cocktails:

- ✔ Some drinks have a season. Like white bucks, gin-and-tonics traditionally appear only between Memorial Day and Labor Day. This rule applies to all drinks mixed with tonic.

- ✔ When in doubt, a blended scotch (with soda or on the rocks), a martini, a glass of dry white wine or champagne, or a sparkling water with lime and a dash of bitters are all safe bets before dinner.

An aperitif is a more particular choice — it's intended to precede the dinner and stimulate the appetite, without overwhelming the palate. Popular aperitifs are typically grape-based, with a medium-high alcohol content. Dry sherry, Campari, Lillet, Dubonnet (red or white), and dry champagne are all excellent, sophisticated predinner drinks. Campari, Lillet, and Dubonnet are great mixed with soda water and served with a slice of orange, lemon, or lime.

For casual situations, white wine and beer are often served before dinner. A light red wine, such as Beaujolais, may also be served, but save heavier reds for the meal itself.

For information on wine served with the meal, see Chapter 16.

Drinks after dinner

After-dinner drinks or *digestifs* can provide a nice touch to your evening. Some claim that they're necessary aids to digestion after a rich meal. Perhaps. But what is unquestionable is that after-dinner drinks are strong: high alcohol, high sugar, strong taste, or all of the above! Port, cognac, brandy, or cordials traditionally follow a fine meal, although many people would add single-malt scotch and stout to this list.

In case you're wondering, here's how some after-dinner drinks are served:

- ✔ Ports and cordials are served in small glasses with short stems.

- ✔ Cognacs, Armangnacs, and brandies are served in short-stemmed goblets with very large bowls.

Liqueurs — spirits that have been sweetened with fruits or herbs — can sneak up on first-timers who mistake their sweetness for innocence. Keep a watchful eye on your guests. Many an evening has been ruined by too much port.

If prices are not listed on a wine or dessert menu, discretely ask your waiter about the price of individual glasses of port, cognac, or dessert wine. Some of these can be shockingly pricey — over one hundred dollars a glass in some cases!

Drinking Sensibly and Saying "No"

A surprising amount of pressure exists to drink when doing business. Although the three-martini lunch is a thing of the past for most people, you may still be tempted — or pressured — to drink at lunch or dinner. At plenty of business dinners, the gentle twist to be part of the team or to celebrate with your colleagues can be applied. And when you're away from the home office at a convention or a sales conference, you may end up in a happy hour where drinks are two-for-one and there's no one around to know the difference if you have four instead of two.

You don't have to drink if you don't want to. And you don't have to cave in to other people's pressure to drink more than you want to. A clear-headed strategy is probably your best line of defense if you feel pressured to drink more than you're comfortable with. If you're getting the none-too-subtle suggestion that it's time to drink and that "no" is not an option, but you want to say "no" anyway, find a way. If necessary, citing religious grounds for not drinking will get most people off your back.

Occasionally, you'll end up in a situation in which you can't win. For example, in some cultures, it's rude not to finish a drink once it's been ordered. If you've been at the bar for three hours, have already had six beers, there are still three left in front of you, and you've got a 7 a.m. tee time with your most important customer, you're going to have to leave even if it means hurting your host's feelings. Apologize for your "early" departure, thank him for the evening, and leave without looking back.

If you're hosting an event, keeping an eye out for any sign of accidental overindulgence is one of your duties. Before-dinner cocktails, wine with dinner, and cordials afterward may sneak up on guests and impair their ability to make a safe trip home or back to their hotel. Be sure to monitor your guests' conditions and, if you're serving mixed drinks, make adjustments to the strength of follow-up servings if necessary.

Offer more nonalcoholic drinks as the evening progresses. If you have a guest who is not fit to drive, you can enlist the assistance of another guest, call a taxi, or as a last resort, provide a guestroom for an overnight stay.

When you are a guest, take care not to overindulge. Nothing is less mannerly than losing control after drinking too much — and nothing can ruin an evening more quickly for everyone else. Make sure you're eating while drinking, and pace yourself by alternating alcoholic beverages with water.

Some things to remember:

- Keep in mind that drinking any alcoholic beverage causes dehydration; so be sure to drink enough water.

- Making strong drinks pleases no one. If you're the bartender, don't do this in an attempt to make the party more fun.

- Be considerate of those who do not drink. As a host, offer juice, soft drinks, or sparkling water. Never push anyone to have "just one little drink."

Part V
Meeting Etiquette and Boardroom Protocol

The 5th Wave — By Rich Tennant

"GET READY, I THINK THEY'RE STARTING TO DRIFT."

In this part . . .

We help you shine in the boardroom. From seating arrangements to chairing a meeting, we'll hit the potential highs and lows of group gatherings — including the latest information on video and teleconferencing. Then we give you words of wisdom on surviving trade shows and conferences and on representing yourself and your company to your best advantage. Finally, we show you what to do if the responsibility for planning a special event falls to you. We give you checklists, creative ideas, and all the information you need to make your event a success.

Chapter 20

Meeting Manners

*I*f you've been in the work world for very long, you know that meetings are the butt of frequent jokes. What do you do when you don't know what to do? When you're lonely? When you want to seem diligent without actually performing any work? Have a meeting!

In many cases, the bad reputation that meetings have is well deserved. However, conducting efficient and effective meetings is possible. If you can master the art of the meeting, you will be a powerful asset to your organization. And even if you're not planning the meeting, you still need to know what the proper etiquette is for your role as a participant.

Planning a Meeting

Planning a meeting can be a thankless job. Your work often goes unrecognized unless something goes wrong, in which case you become the object of intense scrutiny. If you're lucky, though, your boss will recognize and appreciate your skill.

Perhaps the single most important element of a good meeting is *purpose*. You must know why you're holding the meeting and what you hope to accomplish. If you're initiating the meeting yourself, spend a few moments clarifying the purpose in your mind. If you're asked to plan a meeting for your boss, ask her to take the time to explain her expectations.

A clear purpose is essential for a successful meeting. Ask yourself or your boss: What goal (or goals) do we hope to accomplish? How will a meeting help accomplish this goal?

After you've determined your purpose, make sure that a meeting will help achieve your goal. A meeting can be a good way to disseminate information to several people at the same time. While e-mail or other means can also be effective, a meeting allows for eye contact, body language, and opportunities to ask questions in order to clarify the information. On the other hand, a meeting may not be a good idea if the information is unlikely to generate discussion.

The next step for putting together a successful meeting is an agenda outlining what the meeting will cover. An agenda helps participants prepare before the meeting, which minimizes choruses of the always popular, "I'll have to get back to you on that." Ask participants to review the agenda and to come prepared. No one likes to look disorganized and incompetent in front of a room full of people. If you provide your coworkers with an opportunity to prepare ahead of time, they'll take advantage of it.

A complete agenda includes a list of topics to be covered, assignments of who should be prepared to cover each topic, time estimates for discussion of each topic, and start and end times. Be sure to leave a little more time than you think you'll need — you find out later in this chapter how to control the musings of those long-winded bores in your office, but you should still build in plenty of time for discussion. Your agenda should also include the meeting location and a list of attendees so that they can discuss items before the meeting if necessary (or gird themselves for verbal battle with each other). Including all this information means you'll have to hold off on your meeting announcement until you have the details. Resist the temptation to shoot out an e-mail prematurely, or you'll end up having to send two or three, and people will start to think of you as the proverbial boy who cries "whoops!"

If you don't set an agenda, participants may arrive at the meeting with their own hidden agendas, possibly ones you don't like. A written agenda puts you in the driver's seat.

Scheduling the meeting can be tough, and it gets more complicated with every added participant. In some cases, you may have to schedule a time that's convenient for the most important players, and ask the other participants to rearrange their schedules. One strategy is to come up with three meeting times on different days and at different times of day, then propose those times and ask people to respond with their availability. E-mail is an excellent tool for this task, as are calendar-sharing software programs.

In many corporate situations, a meeting is actually part of a larger event. Large corporations with employees in several locations often host combination meeting/social events to get managers or employees together in one place. If you're in charge of putting together this kind of awards banquet/golf outing/Cajun cookout/all-night dance party, read the section on special events in Chapter 21. With any luck, you can get help from a consultant or another employee who can show you the ropes.

Taking a Seat

At a company that makes a point of minimizing hierarchy, seating arrangements are probably no big deal. Even in many larger companies, seating arrangements are often inconsequential at internal meetings that do not include vendors or clients. In more formal sessions, however, you may need to be aware of possible seating rules that affect where you should sit after you've confidently strolled into the meeting.

Many people have theories about the psychology of seating arrangements: that you should sit directly across from the most important attendee in order to be noticed (or sit behind a large person if you don't want to be noticed); that you should sit at the right hand of the important person; that the right hand of the important person is less impressive than the left hand; and on and on. There are probably even those who recommend sitting in a lotus position with your fingertips pressed together for greater meeting harmony.

In fact, there are just a few basic guidelines:

✔ Don't sit where the host or most important attendee plans to sit, which is usually at the head of the table. This is easy if that person is already seated. If not, you can remain standing until he or she arrives or, depending on the situation, take a seat that you know the boss won't desire.

✔ If the host or the most important attendee has an assistant coming to the meeting, he or she will probably want to sit directly to the right of the boss.

✔ If you start to suspect that you have chosen the wrong seat — for example, if your boss is suddenly giving you that look — say something like, "Would you like to sit here?" and make getting-up motions. This is far preferable to having your boss ask you to move.

Always be flexible — for example, if the room is small and the last arrival will have to navigate around you to get to the last available seat, you might offer to move.

If you are the meeting planner, you may give polite direction to attendees about where to sit. For example, "Sebastian, why don't you sit at this end," or "Miss Brightenshiney, I think Dr. Dullendrab may prefer to sit at the head of the table, but this seat is available."

Being an Effective Chair or Participant

The meeting is starting now. So it's time to take charge of the situation and make sure that the meeting runs smoothly.

When you're running the meeting

Your first job is to begin the meeting promptly if you're in charge, and to arrive at all meetings on time or a little early whether you're in charge or not. Part of civility in the workplace is respecting the value of everyone's time. Those who sit around while waiting for latecomers to show up are understandably peeved. Their schedules are also full, and they don't deserve this kind of treatment. If you develop a reputation as a person who starts meetings on time, people will be more likely to arrive on time to your meeting. Conversely, if you develop a reputation as someone who always starts late, people will start showing up late, and the situation will spiral downwards.

In some cases, you may need to bend your starting-on-time rule if the boss or some other very important attendee is late. Even so, you probably shouldn't delay for more than about 10 minutes. This person may exercise his or her prerogative to repeat the part of the meeting that was missed. If you're lucky, this person will call in advance to warn you, apologize profusely upon arrival, and not make this behavior a habit. Most people are late at least once in a while, but frequent lateness is a subtle way of telling others that they're not important — not a good management strategy!

Another important job for the meeting host is to stick to the agenda. Though you've sent the agenda to all participants in advance, you may want to bring along copies to distribute, ensuring that everyone knows what's about to happen. You should then keep an eye on your watch so that you can hold up your end of the bargain — participants arrive at your meeting on time, and you do your best to get them out on time.

To run a meeting effectively, you should be at least somewhat familiar with Robert's Rules of Order. These rules are a system of parliamentary procedures first published in 1876. While this sounds daunting, Robert's Rules are simply a system for agreeing on how meetings should be run. Some of the rules are extremely detailed, but it's not necessary to know all of them. You should, however, be familiar with the basic concepts of procedure.

Not all meetings are formal enough to require Robert's Rules. Many of the meetings you'll run will be entirely informal affairs in which people get together to hash things out. Yet even here some procedure must be followed. Everybody can't talk at once, and you'll have to agree on some method for discussing the options, reaching a decision, and implementing it. Knowing the basic steps of procedure as Robert's Rules spells them out can help here, too.

✔ The *moderator* — usually the same person as the host — is in charge of keeping the meeting on track and preventing participants from interrupting one another.

✔ Participants generally raise their hands when they wish to speak. The moderator then *recognizes* a speaker. If the meeting is a small one, you don't actually have to raise your hand above your head — a small hand gesture will do the trick. Even a particularly earnest look may get across your desire to speak.

✔ Once a participant is recognized, she is said to *have the floor*, meaning that she can speak for a reasonable amount of time about her suggestion or point of view. If someone attempts to interrupt, the moderator has the right to remind that person — politely — that someone else has the floor at the moment. The moderator should, of course, eventually recognize everyone who wishes to speak.

✔ In addition to preventing interruptions, the moderator should prevent speakers from repeating themselves or blathering on for too long. An appropriate comment might be, "Gene, I think we have heard enough to understand your position. I'd like to recognize Jezebel now and hear what she has to say."

✔ The speaker should voluntarily yield the floor when finished speaking by sitting down (if she is standing) or simply saying, "I'm finished."

Some organizations have been known to have an object of some kind that is passed from speaker to speaker. While this method makes it patently obvious who has the floor, it also has the disadvantage of reminding people of the humiliating potty pass from grade school.

In some cases, a meeting will include voting:

✔ Once ideas have been discussed, a participant can make a *motion* (an idea to be voted on) by saying, for example, "I move that the water cooler be filled with sparkling wine." While you as the moderator usually will not actually make a motion, you can start the process after you feel there has been adequate discussion by saying something like, "Do I have a motion to fill the water cooler with sparkling wine?" At that point, someone who advocates that position should jump in and make the motion.

> ✔ Another participant should then second the motion.
>
> ✔ You, as the moderator, ask if there is further discussion needed. You then say, "All in favor say 'aye,'" count the votes, then say "All opposed say 'nay'" and count those votes, if necessary.

If you are the chairman of an organization or find yourself leading frequent meetings, you may want to pick up a guide to Robert's Rules for easy reference. Even if no one else knows them, your familiarity will help you run an efficient meeting.

If the discussion starts wandering far from the central topic, the moderator or host should suggest that the new topic be *tabled* for another meeting. Most participants will acknowledge the need to stay on track and finish the meeting on time, even if they are very concerned about the new topic.

Finally, you, as host or chair have to take notes. Glamorous it's not, but taking notes is an important part of a successful meeting. Though other participants may take their own notes, they may not be comprehensive. You, as the meeting host, want to make sure that everyone who attended the meeting ends up with the same record of what happened. If you're lucky enough to have a secretary or other assistant at your disposal, you can ask that person to take the notes and you can simply approve them. If not, then it's your job to do it.

Unless your organization has a specific format for meeting notes, you can include this information:

> ✔ Time and date of the meeting
>
> ✔ List of attendees
>
> ✔ Agenda and notes of the discussion for each agenda item
>
> ✔ Notes of any motions made and the resulting decision

Meetings aren't football games, so not every meeting requires formal rules. Knowing the rules can be helpful, however, in politely corralling boorish (or simply inexperienced) colleagues and letting them know they are out of line.

When you're participating in but not running the meeting

As a meeting participant, your first rule is to follow the procedures that the chair or host adopts. If your host is running an informal meeting, your points of order are unnecessarily rigid. If your host is running a formal meeting, learn enough about Robert's Rules of Order to be able to participate effectively.

Of course, you should never interrupt other speakers. You should also avoid the temptation to sigh loudly, roll your eyes, or otherwise express your contempt when someone else is speaking. If you have a colleague who incessantly interrupts others, please refer to Chapter 10.

You're obliged to stay for the entire meeting unless you have another appointment or another commitment. If so, at the beginning of the meeting let your chair know at what time you'll have to leave and then leave quietly at that time. If you're unlucky enough to be a participant in a meeting whose chair has not set an adjournment time and the meeting is dragging on and on, pass a note to the chair explaining your other commitment, stand up, excuse yourself quickly, and leave without making a show of it.

If you like taking notes, by all means do so. If you're not fond of note-taking and it looks like someone else is, then don't. You'll know after a couple of meetings how accurate other people's notes are. If you're concerned that the decisions made during the meeting diverge from the decisions reported in the notes and subsequent memoranda, then offer to take notes for the meeting. You'll be doing your chair a favor.

Some people arrive late at meetings, come in loudly, and start asking questions about topics that have already been covered. Don't ever be that person. If you've arrived late, keep quiet and ask a sympathetic soul to catch you up later — not while someone else is talking.

Participating in Conference Calls and Video Conferences

Teleconferences — also known as conference calls — and video conferences are wonderful tools when used properly. A few moments of real conversation over the phone or through video can be worth a thousand e-mailed words. As with all meetings, however, these electronic get-togethers require attention to etiquette.

Some conference calls, usually for smaller groups, consist of several people calling into one participant's office. The central person manually conferences everyone together by pressing the conference button for each addition. Other types of calls are monitored, meaning that all participants call into a central number and are placed into the conference either by speaking to an operator or by entering a password.

You should always identify yourself when you join a call, but you must do so with caution. On a monitored call, you may not be able to hear other speakers for a few seconds, so don't announce yourself immediately or you may step on another speaker. If you join the call late, other callers will usually hear a beep of some kind. Don't announce yourself immediately; once there is a break in the action, the host will probably say something like, "who just joined the call?" You can then announce your name and apologize profusely for your tardiness. Don't ever sit in complete silence on a call without ever announcing yourself. The other callers deserve to know everyone who is in the "room" listening to them. Not announcing your presence is akin to hiding behind the curtains in the boardroom!

In general, every additional person on a phone call adds an extra layer of background noise. When you're on a conference call, put your phone on mute unless you're actually speaking. Your heavy breathing adds nothing to the conversation. Don't forget to take yourself off mute, however, when you have something to say. This is amazingly hard to remember — fortunately, it's immediately obvious when the other callers start saying things like, "Hello? Are you still there?"

It's fine to listen to the call on speakerphone, but for heaven's sake, pick up the handset when it's your turn to talk. When you yell into the phone during a conference call, background noise can make it sound like you're at a truck stop with 18-wheelers whizzing past in the background.

You should not carry on side conversations during a conference call, but if you do, make absolutely certain to mute the phone. (Putting your hand over the receiver is not adequate.) Others on the call will not be amused by your Saturday night date report in the middle of the meeting. Nor will they be amused (well, some of them might!) by your disparaging remarks about the speaker. Likewise, never type when others will be able to hear it. The tapping sound comes across like gunfire.

Marvin, fresh out of graduate school, had little respect for his boss, Ms. Ironfisted. One day Ms. Ironfisted was out of town and was calling in from the airport for a meeting with several other people. Marvin took the call from a conference room with another junior employee and couldn't resist showing his impression of Ms. Ironfisted's Kentucky twang. Besides being impertinent, Marvin was forgetful — he didn't mute the conference room phone. He got to hear what Ms. Ironfisted's accent sounded like when she's really, really mad.

It's also a good idea to say your name before you begin talking. If you think everyone will recognize your voice, you're probably wrong. You should introduce yourself before the first time you speak and then again if you haven't spoken for a while.

Since you can't see the other speakers, it's easy to accidentally talk over someone (or have someone accidentally talk over you). When this happens, simply apologize and offer to let the other person speak first. You'll get your turn in a moment.

Video conferencing is an entirely different ballgame, and it can be a little disconcerting the first few times you participate. On most systems, there is a slight delay between sound and motion. As a result, you have to be careful to wait a few seconds before speaking to make sure you won't talk over the person on the other end. In addition, you will probably look at the monitor while you're speaking, because that's where you see the other people. You naturally want to look at them while talking. You should look at the camera instead (usually located above the monitor), otherwise you will seem to be speaking to the midsections of the other participants. Though the people on the other end of the conference are seeing you on a delay, they are still seeing you — and that means that you should pretend they are right there in the room. No slouching, smirking, looking up at the ceiling, or other behaviors that you could get away with during a phone call. Some systems automatically focus the camera on whoever is talking at that moment, but don't be lulled into false sense of security while you're not talking. Cameras have been known to switch focus for no particular reason.

A manager at a large company had a terrible cold, but she dragged herself into the office anyway for an important video conference. Each time she sneezed, the camera would immediately focus on her — and each time, she was wiping her nose in a most unattractive fashion. Moral: Stay home when you're sick, and always be aware that you could be on camera at any moment during a video conference.

Chapter 21

Conferences, Trade Shows, and Special Events

● ●

In This Chapter

▶ Mingling at social events

▶ Remembering that you represent your company

▶ Being social after hours

▶ Planning or attending a special event

● ●

Most people end up attending work-related special events at least once in a while. Depending on your perspective, these events are enlightening and energizing, or they're a big, fat bore. Regardless of how you feel about these events, certain guidelines exist for how to act when you're at one of them.

In this chapter, we show you how to mingle at conferences and conventions, how to be a good company representative, and how to avoid embarrassing yourself after hours.

Networking and Circulating

Industry events are a great place to make contacts in your field and to find out more about what's going on at other companies. In fact, your company may be paying your way to the event in part so that you will learn more about your industry. If you're naturally confident and outgoing, the social aspects of work probably aren't that difficult for you. If you're a little shy (or a lot), the idea of navigating a room full of new faces may be terrifying. Instead of hiding in your room watching HBO, take a deep breath and try these strategies.

First of all, slap on a name tag. These events almost always provide them, and they make you more approachable. The name tag should go on your right shoulder, the idea being that when you shake hands, the other person's eyes will be drawn up your arm to your name tag. If the tags are the self-adhesive kind and you're concerned about damaging a silk blouse, ask if any pins are available. Better yet, try to remember this problem when you're packing and bring something a little sturdier.

Next, you should establish some goals for yourself. If you're in sales, your goal might be to gather as many business cards and sales leads as possible. If this is your first conference, your goal might be simply to practice introducing yourself. If you don't have a specific need to meet people, your goal might be to have a good time and sample the shrimp toast.

If introducing yourself to a stranger is daunting, keep in mind that saying hello and telling someone your name is not a major commitment. For some people, speaking to a stranger is as scary as asking for a first date. It shouldn't be. Everyone in the room has at least something in common with you — they don't know many people, they're a little nervous, and they're not sure what to say. They will be very grateful if you break the ice by starting the conversation. All it takes is extending your hand and saying, "Hi, I'm Otto Phin." This will prompt the other person to respond with his or her name. Then, you can say, "What did you think of today's speaker?" or "What company do you work for?" or even "How's the artichoke dip?" It doesn't have to be something profoundly interesting; it just has to be something. The other person will respond, and then you're off.

Unless you're attending a convention of Nobel Laureates, no one is expecting you to be outrageously witty or wise — just friendly.

If someone approaches you and starts the conversation, good for you! Smile and be pleasant. Share some information about yourself and ask questions in return. If you have a business card, give it out. You're doing great!

Now it's time to remember your goal. If you're trying to meet the maximum number of people, stay on task. While you want to be polite, you don't want to spend too much time with any one person. After you've chatted with someone for a few minutes and have learned a little bit about him or her, it's all right for you to move on. You can say something as simple as, "Mary, it's been nice getting to know you," hand her your business card, and ask if she has a card. If it makes you feel more comfortable, you can make up some small excuse, such as, "I really wanted to make sure I met this afternoon's speaker, and I see him over there." That's really not necessary, though; there's no need to apologize for wanting to meet a variety of people at the event.

If you're not concerned with making lots of contacts, you can be a bit more relaxed. An interesting conversation could last all night. You can end a boring one and move on.

Whatever you do, avoid the temptation to look around the room while you're talking to someone. This can be difficult at a busy party, because there is so much movement going on — like sitting at a sports bar and trying not to watch the hockey game. You have to discipline yourself, though — it's very disconcerting for the other person to see your eyes darting around the room.

If you have a friend or a colleague at the event, you may want to buddy up, provided you don't talk only to each other. When you're introducing yourself to someone, introduce your friend at the same time. What you shouldn't do is stand together in the corner like cellmates looking out at the world. You're there to meet new people and expand your boundaries.

Representing Your Company

It may not be fair, but it's true: when you're at a conference or a trade show, your actions are not completely your own. If you are an employee of Big Fish Corporation, the people you meet will see you as a Big Fish representative, even if you see yourself as a guppy. Make sure you conduct yourself in a way that's fair to the people who sign your paycheck.

Perhaps your most important responsibility is to avoid making negative comments about your company. You don't have to lie, but you shouldn't slander your employer, either. Even if you hate your job or think the company is mismanaged, it's not your place to say so in this environment. Politely change the subject. If someone says something like, "I had a friend who worked for Big Fish, and he says the CEO has spent all the company's money on exotic sharks for his personal pool" you could respond with, "Hmm, I haven't heard that. Did you say you work for Mega Minnow? I've heard lots of interesting things about your new product — is it really going to revolutionize the frozen burrito industry?"

Come up with a few stock answers for questions about your company — explanations of what the company does (if this is a frequent question), positive comments about the new CEO, or information about new products.

Obviously, you should never reveal any kind of confidential information about your company. If you're not sure whether something is a secret, assume that it is. What you're saying may not seem especially important, and the person you're talking to may seem inconsequential, but you can never be sure. You should, however, discuss interesting and exciting news that's public information. Making comments about how much you like working for your company or other positive comments, is always appropriate.

Your behavior at meal times, during meetings, and after hours also reflects on your company. To be a good representative, follow the other rules you learn throughout this book.

Socializing after Hours

Whether you're at an industry conference or at a meeting that's only for your company's employees, work only lasts for so long. In many cases, you will be on your own in the evenings. You may want to use this opportunity to get to know the people you work with — or want to work with — a little better.

Before you get down to serious socializing, you should first decide whether you want to attend any social event at all. If your boss or another influential person asks you out to dinner, don't say no, even if you have a stack of work and a big headache. While such opportunities are not strictly part of the workday, they're an important part of your career. Even if the invitation is from a peer, you should usually accept. If you routinely turn down opportunities to socialize with your colleagues, you risk getting a reputation as aloof or not a team player.

On the other hand, if you're craving an evening alone, you may not make a very good dinner companion. Particularly on long trips when you're working long days, you may be tired, cranky, and overwhelmed with work. On those occasions, it's alright to tell colleagues, "I'm really not up to dinner this evening — I'm planning to get some work done and turn in early." Politely stick to your guns if they try to change your mind. You have every right to use your evening the way you want to.

A busy executive for a telecommunications company travels frequently, and she almost always has dinner with colleagues. She's learned to recognize her own limits, however, and sometimes lets others know that she's going to *slam and click* — shut her hotel room door, click the lock shut, and open it for no one but room service! As long as you don't use it too often, the slam and click can be a great strategy for renewing your energy.

When dining with colleagues, you should follow the standard rules for business dining outlined in Chapter 15. When you're with people from work, the conversation often drifts toward office gossip. Watch your step, keep your own comments to a minimum, and resist the temptation to say anything vicious or untrue. While you may be forced to respond to a question — "is it true that you heard Sam getting chewed out because he screwed up on the IPO?" — avoid wallowing in your own contempt for Sam and his incompetence. Just say something like, "I heard that he and Sue had a big talk about the offering, but other than that I don't really know what happened." Your colleagues may be disappointed if they can't get some good dirt, but that's their problem, not yours.

If you're with your boss or some other senior person, you should follow that person's lead in ordering. If she orders an appetizer and an additional side dish, you should too. Remember, keep courses balanced, so that everyone is eating at the same time.

While you can always drink less than the senior person, you should not drink more. Two or three glasses of wine during a business dinner is plenty for almost everyone. Chapter 19 is all about alcohol. Let us summarize the contents: Be careful! Getting drunk in front of your colleagues will make you look pathetic and out of control, not fun and sophisticated. Know your limit, and stay well under it. If you're having drinks at cocktail hour or later in the evening, drink slowly, and have at least one glass of water for each alcoholic drink. When drinking wine or beer with dinner, savor it slowly. If you feel even close to woozy, stop drinking and keep eating.

In addition to keeping your conversation under control, staying sober can keep you from doing things you will regret back at the office. Even if you haven't had a thing to drink, however, being out of town can make you feel that a liaison with that attractive coworker isn't so far out of reach. Resist, resist, resist! You shouldn't do anything out of town that you wouldn't do back at home. First, if your colleague isn't interested in your advances, you may find yourself facing a sexual harassment claim, or at the very least an awkward situation. Second, keep in mind that you have to work with this person for the foreseeable future. Third, stories about your after-hours activities may — and probably will — find their way back to the office gossip, and possibly to your boss or members of your family. Even if you think you're being very discreet, you may well be the subject of next week's nudges and smirks. Questionable behavior with consenting adults from other companies may be slightly less risky, but not much.

Special Events

Myriad reasons exist for having special events in the business world — boosting employee morale, celebrating company successes, recognizing employees, entertaining and impressing clients, launching new products, and many more. When you're on the planning end of these events, you play a key role in their success. Even as a participant, you are an important part of the proceedings. This section gives you some guidelines for each role.

Planning a special event is a huge task — some people make a career of it! A few simple tips exist, however, that go a long way towards helping you plan a successful event.

When you're the planner

Start as far in advance as you can. In many cases, you don't have much control over the schedule — many an executive has said something like, "I'd like to take our top 10 clients ice fishing in Alaska two weeks from Saturday — get on that, won't you?" — but you should control it as much as you can. For example, if you know that there is an event coming up and that you will be in charge of organizing it, get as much information as possible right away. What's the purpose of the event? Approximately how many people will be there — 50 or 5,000? Will it be casual or formal? Where will it take place? Is there a budget allocated? Take a cue from the experts — planning for some huge events, such as the Olympics, begins years in advance.

If someone is reluctant to discuss the event with you because they don't have all the facts yet, explain to them that you will get started with whatever facts are available now. The earlier you begin planning, the greater chance you have of success.

Be as organized as possible! You can't put together a successful event by keeping everything in your own head and on those tiny sticky notes. Professional event planners are known for their extensive, detailed to-do lists and ubiquitous clipboards. Many professionals start a project by putting together a huge list of every single thing they can think of that will need to be done. From that list, they develop:

- ✔ **A timeline, working backward from the event.** The timeline includes a list of tasks from booking the location (months in advance) to sending out invitations (weeks in advance) to having fresh flowers delivered the morning of the event. The timeline must include reminders to get the necessary approvals: everything from your fireworks permit from the city to your boss's okay on the menu.

- ✔ **A list of assignments.** With any luck, you'll be able to find someone to pick up the keynote speaker from the airport while you're busy cutting 10,000 egg salad sandwiches into the shape of the company logo.

- ✔ **A list of the vendors needed.** Caterers, limousine services, travel agents, sound system experts, florists, belly dancers, balloon-animal technicians, and so on. Even if you don't know right away who these vendors will be, you should make sure you have all the categories in mind.

- ✔ **A list of contingencies.** What if extra attendees show up? What if the speaker is late? What if it rains?

Share your big list of things to do with at least one other person, who will act as your backup if needed. And have a list of contact persons at the various service providing organizations, including notes about what's been arranged with each of them. As the event gets closer, you may want to review this list with the other person, or at least send it to them, on a weekly or even daily basis. Most events require lots of last-minute preparation and on-site management. If you wake up with a debilitating rash on the day of the event, your backup will appreciate having this list.

Thinking through every aspect of an event in advance is also important. Walk through the entire event in your mind, and if possible, walk through it physically. How long does it take you to walk slowly from the conference room to the gazebo? Take that figure and multiply it by four — that's how long it will take you to herd your guests.

A new employee at a large company thought she had planned for everything — prompt airport pickups, vegetarian meals for those who didn't want Iowa beef, fresh flowers on every table, and welcome letters in each room. What she didn't plan for was a hog auction in the conference room next door. For her next event, she added "check on other events in hotel" to her big list.

You dramatically increase your chances of pulling off a successful event if you take into account that people will act the way they want to, not the way you want them to. For example, most people cannot sit still for three hours without a break. If you plan a meeting without sufficient break time, you can be assured that it will be interrupted with a steady stream of participants leaving to smoke, powder their noses, and make phone calls. Many others will not eat certain foods, especially red meat, so you should always offer at least one vegetarian choice. Most people will also refuse to wear bathing suits, sing, or do the limbo in front of coworkers.

When you're an attendee

When you're a guest in someone else's home, you're probably gracious and polite by instinct. Your instincts at a special event should be no different. Even in a hotel ballroom or in the middle of a wheat field, you're someone's guest, and your behavior is important.

- ✔ **Do what's asked of you.** If a chair is marked "reserved," don't sit in it. If someone asks you to move into the dining room, don't keep standing right where you are. Even if you're used to being in charge, take this opportunity to see how the other half lives.

- ✔ **Be on time.** If the event starts at a certain time, you don't want to be the one walking in late and disrupting the speaker. Be sure to allow time for getting a name tag and finding a seat, as well as the regular concerns like traffic and parking.

- ✔ **Stay seated and pay attention.** If the event involves a meeting or a sit-down program, sit down and do your best to pay attention. Turn off your pager and cell phone, just as you would during a business meeting or meal, and refrain from jumping up to make calls. You should also avoid talking during the presentation. It's distracting both to the speaker and to those around you. These rules go for outdoor concerts, too!

- ✔ **Be polite to the staff.** If you have a problem that can be fixed, mention it politely to your server. A knife if you didn't get one and refills of coffee should be easy. Some food-related requests, however, just don't make sense at a banquet. For example, your server will probably not be able to correct an overcooked steak while taking care of 79 other guests in a fixed period of time. Accept that fact and give thanks that you don't have to eat in a hotel ballroom every night of the week. Likewise, ask the buffet attendant if there will be more shrimp coming out, but don't complain to him if there's not. He can't do a thing about it.

✔ **If you're at an outdoor event, don't leave your manners inside.** Paper plates and napkins belong in the trash, not on the ground. Your mouth should be firmly closed while chewing, even if you're eating corn on the cob and fried chicken with your fingers. Casual dress doesn't mean frayed, see-through, or tight, at least at a business function. When you're back in the office next week, you don't want your colleagues contemplating the image of you in a Metallica T-shirt with the arms cut off.

Unless you've been given very special treatment of some kind, thank-you notes are usually not required for business special events. However, a nice note to the host and/or event planner will be treasured for a long time and is preferable to an e-mail.

When you're part of the action

If you're an important part of the special event — a speaker, entertainer, or guest of honor — congratulations! You've obviously earned the respect and admiration of your hosts. By following a few simple rules, you can be sure that they will still respect and admire you after you leave.

Try not to be extraordinarily high maintenance. Asking your hosts to pick you up from the airport — which they will probably offer to do, anyway — is well within bounds. Asking them to pick you up, drop you off for an afternoon of skydiving 40 miles in the opposite direction, and then pick you up again later is out of bounds. If you want to combine the event with other personal business or pleasure, offer to arrange your own transportation. If your hosts are in a position to assist you, they will offer to do so.

When traveling long distances for an engagement, plan extra time for travel delays. If that will leave you with an extra half-day of down time, ask your hosts to help you out with finding temporary office space, setting up a video conference room, or whatever you might need. They would much rather do that than have you arrive after the event because of a weather delay.

Don't commit to an engagement unless you're sure you can make it, and don't cancel unless the circumstances make it absolutely unavoidable. A parent's sudden hospitalization is a reason to cancel. A golf game with an old buddy at a really great course is not. It's never polite to cancel plans because you get a better offer, but it's especially impolite when hundreds of people have arranged their schedules to hear you speak.

If you have a problem with your accommodations, speak up, but know when to quit. It's one thing to call the front desk of your hotel and complain about the temperature, cleanliness, or smokiness of your room. It's another thing to rant at your host about the inferior quality of the hotel she chose. At that point, it may be too late for her to do anything about it and she'll only feel guilty (or annoyed). After the event is over and her stress level has receded, you could follow up with a polite note to let her know that a different hotel might be a better choice for the next speaker.

Don't be the boring presenter that everyone talks about for years to come. If you've agreed to be the keynote speaker, you've agreed to do your very best work onstage.

It seems elementary, but it's important — prepare for your presentation! If you're the main event, your audience expects an interesting, articulate, and enlightening presentation. Unless you are extremely good on your feet — and most people aren't — don't plan to get on stage and wing it. Outline your presentation and practice it as many times as needed to make it shine. In addition, having an outline may make it possible for a colleague to do your presentation in case of an emergency.

Part VI
Going Global: Manners for a Small World

The 5th Wave   By Rich Tennant

"It's the crew Captain Columbus—they want to know what our flat-world contingency plan is."

In this part . . .

We give you some universally helpful pointers on all facets of travel. From surviving airline travel to knowing what to pack and how to speak when you get there, we'll get you through international business travel with dignity.

Chapter 22

Traveling Comfortably

• •

In This Chapter

▶ Going out of town

▶ Keeping your cool while flying

▶ Using ground transportation

▶ Playing the host

▶ Traveling with coworkers

• •

*B*usiness travel doesn't have to be drudgery and, although some stress is inevitable, it doesn't have to make you miserable either. The key is knowing that, in all probability, something will go wrong: Your hotel will be next to a construction site, your luggage will be lost, your flight will be cancelled, or you'll forget your favorite shoes.

Once you expect something to go wrong, you won't be upset when things go awry.

Yeah, right.

It may still annoy you when your flight is delayed or the hotel doesn't have a record of your reservation, but at least you'll be better able to adapt a stoical attitude if you know that these things are perfectly likely.

Good travelers are ready for the unexpected. They appear to take the inconveniences in stride, cope with the disasters, and are amused when something goes wrong in a way that they might really be able to laugh about later. In this chapter, you find out what it takes to be a good traveler. We show you how to cope with airlines and airports, how to travel with your colleagues, and how to handle your accommodations once you get to your destination. We also offer some tips on how to host the guest from out of town — and how to be that guest.

Going Out of Town on Business

Your job may take you all over the city, country, or world. If you travel on a regular basis, you will eventually learn what all good travelers learn — on the road, being self-reliant, and having a routine are essential.

Plan your itinerary and hold on to whatever shreds of your daily routine you can. Having a familiar routine helps you better cope with the inevitable onslaught of new and unfamiliar people, places, and information.

Self-reliance, a routine, and a sense of humor are the traveler's highest virtues.

Tickets and itinerary

When you travel, you may be making your own plans, relying on the in-house travel department, or using an agency.

You can begin to guarantee a good business trip by planning it as soon as you know the dates of the trip. Car rentals, airline tickets, train reservations, and hotel rooms aren't any cheaper the longer you wait, and they don't become more available. So get on the ball. And don't rely completely on your company's overwhelmed travel agent, either. Some Internet research on your part might help.

Once you've made your travel and accommodation arrangements, put together an itinerary. On this itinerary, list:

- Departure flight information: flight number, departure and arrival times, departure and arrival cities, airline name, and airline telephone number
- Ground transportation information: car rental agency name, telephone number, and reservation number, or limousine confirmation, or other ground transportation information
- Hotel name, address, telephone number, and reservation number
- Meeting times and places, with telephone numbers if possible
- Host name(s), telephone and fax numbers, e-mail address(es)
- Meal arrangements
- Scheduled entertainment
- Return flight information: flight number, departure time and city, arrival time and city, airline name and telephone number

Once you (or your host) has composed your itinerary, make copies of it; give a copy to your supervisor or assistant and give one to your family or to a friend. If something goes wrong and you don't arrive back when you say you will, someone will be able to initiate a search with accurate information about you.

Taking what you'll need

The rules are simple here: Pack what you'll need and leave everything else at home. You have to take your laptop, phone, Palm Pilot, reports, contracts, brochures, clothes, a shaving kit or cosmetic bag, and your vintage cowboy boots. Oops, leave that last item at home (unless they fit into your carry-on and you really like them).

The key to travel clothing is to keep it simple, lightweight, and wrinkle-free. You can achieve the first goal by taking no more than two changes of clothes per day — and try to recycle clothes if you can. The second goal is easily achieved by leaving your heavyweights — the overcoat and ballroom gown — at home. And the third goal is achieved by taking as many no-wrinkle items as possible.

Don't forget to take clothes for evenings and outings. If you're in doubt about what to bring, ask your host. And don't assume that because your company has Casual Friday, the company you're visiting next Friday has one too. Ask your host whether his office has casual dress on Fridays.

In addition to your business clothes, you'll also want to take one change of underwear per day, a comfortable pair of shoes for the trip and a good pair of shoes for your meetings, your workout clothes or swimsuit, a complete shaving kit or cosmetics kit, and a collapsible umbrella and a hat. Don't forget your medication and your eye prescription if you wear contacts. Being stranded without your Prozac can be devastating, and if you lose a contact in Albuquerque without your prescription, you'll be sorry.

Take a credit card with an open balance and cash if you will be in a rural area. You may also want to bring traveler's checks. Buy an expense book or envelope and use it assiduously. If you're going overseas, be sure to have enough currency from your destination country to pay for small expenses before you get a chance to get to a hotel or bank exchange window. And ask your host if your ATM card is going to work for getting destination currency at the hotel where you'll be staying or a nearby bank.

Avoid exchanging your money at airports. Airport exchange windows are more expensive than money-exchanges at hotels or banks.

No matter where you go, you'll want to take enough identification to allow you to drive. You never know when you might want to take a quick tour of the countryside. And if you are a frequent overseas traveler, consider getting an international driver's license.

If you're traveling overseas, get your passport or visa at least six weeks in advance. You have to supply either an old passport, a birth certificate, or a baptismal certificate, as well as two passport photos.

Coping with Planes and Airports

Airline travel has never been more convenient, in theory, or more harried, in practice, than in the last few years. The number of travelers who opt to fly has been increasing so rapidly that many airports and airlines have been working beyond capacity for the last couple of years. Pilots, staff, and ground crew are stressed — that translates into rudeness and anxiety.

Most airport employees *are* trying hard to do their jobs, often under far-from-ideal circumstances. Weather, late connecting flights, problems at other airports, and ongoing labor disputes conspire to make flights late and everyone exasperated.

Planning well

As a traveler, you expect the airport to be efficient and the flight to go smoothly. Do yourself a favor — modify your thinking. Be prepared for a flight that's delayed or an airline that loses your baggage. Being prepared means avoiding scheduling meetings within two or three hours of your arrival, and having enough money and food on your person that you can survive if the plane gets in after all of the local banks, restaurants, and stores have closed. It means carrying all of your luggage with you onto the plane, or at least carrying a bag with a change of clothes and your essential toiletries.

Double-check the size of your carry-on suitcase. Be sure that it will fit the new, smaller carry-on size limits, *even when the suitcase is completely stuffed!*

Skycaps are tipped $1 per bag; they're tipped $2 per bag if they carry it into the terminal.

Remember Dad's advice before those long family trips in the station wagon? Make sure you "go" before you leave the terminal. You may be parked on the tarmac for quite a while with the restrooms off limits.

Staying calm

Air travel is stressful, no doubt about it. Unfortunately, some people seem not to be able to handle stress without lashing out. Everyone who has been in an airport or on an airplane has probably seen someone lose it at the check-in desk or on the plane. If you can't control your temper when you're stressed out, do what you can to prevent the conditions in which you get stressed out. Confirm your reservation and seat number ahead of time. Get to the airport early. Avoid the luggage check-in line by carrying your luggage. Avoid sugar; eat something with protein in it. Drink enough water. Take your medication. Breathe.

Once the plane is in the air, you will probably be served drinks and may even be even served "food." Here, as much as anywhere, your good table manners are in order. Try to adhere to standard table manners as much as your tiny space allows. If you have dietary restrictions or preferences, you may want to request a special meal, such as vegetarian or kosher, when you book your ticket.

Keep these tips in mind when dealing with fellow passengers:

- ✔ At least nod and say "Hello" to your row mates. You don't have to carry on a conversation if you don't want to, but it is polite to acknowledge others, especially in such tight quarters.
- ✔ Ask your neighbor if working on your notebook computer is a bother.
- ✔ Keep your work off of your neighbor's lap and tray.
- ✔ Be considerate to airline attendants and thank them, and the pilots, when you deplane.

And avoid these mistakes:

- ✔ Premature boarding
- ✔ Cutting in any line
- ✔ Crushing or relocating other people's belongings in an overhead bin in order to accommodate your own baggage
- ✔ Talking on and on to the person in the seat next to you while she's trying to work, read, or sleep

Remaining sane on overseas flights

On overseas flights, you need to remember a few additional things. First, when you are on a plane for more than six hours, you're likely to get tired. Ask for a pillow and a blanket, and try to arrange yourself so that, when you awake, you won't find your head in your neighbor's lap! If a sleeper leans onto you, gently push the person into another position. If you snore, either don't sleep or try to position yourself to minimize the din.

Next, if you're flying for more than six hours, you're going to have to use the facilities. Be considerate of those who follow you by not taking an undue amount of time in the bathroom and by cleaning up after yourself when you leave.

Finally, you may find yourself getting a case of cabin fever on a long flight. The aisles and galley areas are acceptable areas for low-intensity stretching as long as there's no service underway, and you're not attempting your full tai chi routine.

Using Taxis and Limos

Once you've arrived at your destination, you need to get from the airport to the hotel and check in at the hotel.

If you're budgeted for it, taxis are a convenient way to go. But be aware that taxi lines at busy airports are often very long. If you're in a hurry and are sufficiently familiar with the public transportation system, you can often shave time off your trip from the airport to the hotel by taking the subway or an express bus.

Keep these tips about taxis and public transportation in mind:

- ✔ If there is a dispatcher, let him get the cab. If your host has met you at the airport and there are a lot of cabs around, the host hails; if cabs are scarce, both host and guest hail.

- ✔ The host gets in first, so the guest doesn't have to slide across the seat. If there are three or more, the tallest or the heaviest sits in front.

- ✔ CEOs and other big wigs rarely carry cash. If you're traveling with your superiors, be prepared to pay the bills.

- ✔ Be courteous to the driver. The driver may snarl back at you. If so, continue to be polite, but give a smaller tip.

- ✔ On public transportation, you may ask people to move items on an otherwise available seat so that you can sit.

- ✔ On public transportation, it is polite to give up your seat to the elderly or persons with disabilities if you are not disabled.

The other alternative is, of course, a driver and a limousine. Limousine service isn't cheap, but it is pretty darn convenient. Once you or your host has hired a car, you can count on the driver to meet you at the arranged location, usually holding a little sign with your name or your company's name.

If you hire a limousine, remember that, as with taxis, the best seat is the rear seat closest to the curb. So that's where the muckety-mucks go. If you're a personal assistant or an associate sales representative for the Yukon, you go in the jump seat or up front with the driver. Both seats have their advantages and disadvantages. If you're in the back, you can talk to the muckety-mucks, but if you're in the front, you can get the lowdown on things to do from the driver.

- ✔ Refer to a limousine as a *car,* not a *limo.*
- ✔ If the car has been hired for you, you do not tip the driver, unless he/she does something special for you, such as lugging your sample cases up four flights of stairs.

Navigating Hotels

Most business people stay in commercial hotels, which are designed specifically for business travelers. They are less expensive than luxury hotels, because commercial hotels have fewer services.

This isn't to say that commercial hotels have no services. You can rely on commercial hotels to have meeting and conference rooms, computers, fax machines, copiers, and other business amenities. Commercial hotels also have concierge desks, where you can get advice on things to do in town, look at menus from selected restaurants, purchase tickets for local entertainment, and make car rental or child-care arrangements.

If you're a very important person or someone is trying hard to impress you, you may be lucky enough to be staying at a luxury hotel. Luxury hotels have most of the services found at commercial hotels and many others as well. While you're less likely to find thirty conference rooms at the Ritz, you're more likely to find doormen, bellmen, and your own bathrobe hanging in the closet of your room.

Once you know what kind of hotel you're staying in, you'll know how many dollar bills you're likely to dispose of before you get a chance to lie down on your bed. Commercial hotels rarely have the staff of a luxury hotel. You're likely to find a maid and a concierge at a commercial hotel. But, at a luxury hotel, there are, in addition, valets, doormen, porters, bellmen, and sometimes elevator and bathroom attendants, dry cleaners, tailors, and shoe shiners.

- ✔ Doorman hails a cab: $1
- ✔ Doorman carries your bag: $1 per bag
- ✔ Bellman arrives at your room with your luggage: $1 or $2 per bag
- ✔ Parking valet retrieves your car: $1 or $2

- ✔ Maid cleans the room: $3 per night
- ✔ Concierge shows you a map of the downtown area: no tip
- ✔ Concierge gets you into the wildly-popular-don't-even-think-about-it Ethiopian restaurant you've heard so much about: $10 to $20
- ✔ Concierge gets you and your colleague into opening night of an eagerly awaited opera production: $20 per ticket

Now that you're at the hotel, check in, find your room, and take a breather. If your host has done his job correctly, and your flight was on time, you won't have to be anywhere for at least a few hours. Take the time to have something to eat, exercise, snooze, or prepare for your meetings.

Hosting the Out-of-Town Guest

If you are hosting business guests, do your best to make their trip as pleasant as possible. If your company or organization has a policy of paying for travel but requests that individuals make their own plans, inform your guests of the policy and offer to do what you can to assist them. If your company allows, but doesn't require, you to handle your guests' plans, begin by asking whether they would prefer to make their own plans or have you make them. Most will opt for making their own plans. If so, clarify your company's policies.

Some visitors will take you up on your offer to plan their trip for them. If so, ask them about their preference for accommodations as early as possible. If your company is handling their airfare, inquire about your guests' preferences for airlines and flight times. If your company will be reimbursing your guests for expenses, let them know what documentation will be required.

Don't assume that the friendly person you met at a trade show will want to sleep in your living room. Always offer business guests private hotel accommodations.

Once accommodation plans are firm, inform your guests and begin compiling their agendas. On their agendas should be listed everything they will likely need for their visits, including:

- ✔ Flight information: flight number, departure and arrival times and cities, airline name and telephone numbers
- ✔ Ground transportation information: car rental agency name, telephone number, and reservation number, or limousine confirmation, or other ground transportation information

✔ Accommodations information: hotel name, location, telephone number, and reservation number

✔ Meeting agenda

✔ Meal arrangements

✔ Brief background information on people they will be meeting

✔ Contact name(s) and telephone number(s)

Here is some advice that will help you put together your guests' agenda:

✔ If at all possible, arrange for your guest to arrive a day before any meetings. And then arrange the first day's meetings sometime late in the morning to allow your guests to recover from their travels the day before.

✔ Try not to overburden your guests with too many things to do. If they're in meetings all day, a quiet dinner and an early evening is probably better than dinner, the theater, and a late reception.

✔ Once the agenda is finished, fax it or e-mail it to the guests as soon as you can so that your guests can finalize their plans.

As the day of your guests' visit approaches, you might call them to assuage any concerns and to update them on any changes in their agendas. For example, you can give them a heads up on any additional activities.

If you're hosting an out-of-town business guest, your duties are similar to any host's duties. Take care of your guests by making sure that they're taken care of from morning until night. That means, among other things:

✔ Confirm travel arrangements from the hotel to the office and back.

✔ Provide maps to and from the office if they are driving themselves.

✔ Meet them at the door and escort them to the meeting room.

✔ Ask them if they would like something to drink.

✔ Direct them to the facilities.

✔ Thank them for coming and listen to them closely when they speak.

✔ Give them some down time. Many people appreciate a break between late afternoon meetings and dinner.

If you are the guest, your responsibilities are less onerous. However, you do have to be grateful for the arrangements made on your behalf; it's better to keep your complaints to yourself. At the end of the visit, thank your host again for all that he has done, and send a thank-you note upon your return.

Traveling with Colleagues

Traveling with colleagues, especially those you like, can add immeasurably to your trip. Conversely, traveling with those you merely tolerate or those you dislike can turn a pleasant trip into something trying.

You and your colleagues don't become friends just because you sit next to one another on a plane or share a hotel room. Sharing close spaces creates an opportunity to share other things as well, but you don't really want your colleague to know that you sleep with a stuffed monkey, do you? Probably not. Leave it at home. And you would be better off back at the office if you remained the model of discretion even as your colleague blathers on and on about his childhood pets after one too many in the hotel bar.

You may be tempted to go everywhere with your colleague when you're in a strange town. But your insecurity is not an excuse to do something you probably wouldn't do at home. That means if your colleague wants to go visit friends, you do not have to tag along just because you're lonely. And it means that if your colleague wants to go to a bar or find some entertainment for the evening, you do not have to tag along just because you've got nothing else to do.

If you're thinking of sharing a hotel room, find out ahead of time if your colleague snores or walks in her sleep. Both can be unnerving and can lead to loss of a good night's sleep. Make other arrangements if necessary. Of course, you have to be polite about this. If your colleague doesn't volunteer that he snores, you can ask: "Are there any reasons why we should get separate rooms?"

For more on sharing the company of colleagues when you're not at home, see Chapter 21.

Chapter 23

Interacting Overseas

- -

In This Chapter

▶ Avoiding insulting your host

▶ Understanding etiquette around the world

▶ Being safe if you're a woman

- -

*T*he ugly American is not just a creation of fiction. Perhaps no culture on Earth sends more rude or inconsiderate visitors overseas than the United States. The reasons are not difficult to uncover. America is the most powerful nation on Earth and we all too often assume that since we are the most powerful nation, our customs and codes of behavior are the best. We then take those customs and codes overseas and are shocked when not everyone acts as we do and when some people have the effrontery to dislike us for acting as we do!

Imports of the ugly American, although still found, are increasingly shunned in the global economy.

In this chapter, we show you how to develop enough awareness of cultural diversity to avoid exposing yourself as a "typical American." We also show you some of the more common etiquette issues that you're likely to encounter when doing business around the world. Finally, we offer some cautionary advice for women travelers.

Avoiding Foreign Faux Pas

Volumes have been written about how to behave in other countries, from attire to hand gestures to eating habits. The "Examining Etiquette by Region" section later in this chapter addresses a few of these pitfalls, and you may want to purchase a book addressing the specific culture of the area you're visiting. A few simple guidelines exist, however, that can carry you through a variety of cultural situations without offending your hosts or damaging a business relationship.

First off, erase any sense of xenophobia or cultural superiority from your mind. If you were born in the United States, you may — as many Americans do — believe that American culture is the best in the world. Drop that attitude! In order to do business in other countries or with representatives from other countries, you must realize that their cultures are different, not inferior. In fact, words like *good* and *bad* really have no place at all in describing cultural differences. While your reaction to someone else's culture may be positive or negative, the culture itself simply is what it is.

Are your hosts taking long lunch breaks when you think there's work to be done? Bowing when you're expecting a handshake? Offering you a glass full of goat's blood? Remind yourself: Your way is *not* necessarily better, and every new experience you have makes you not only a greater asset to your company, but a better global citizen.

Along the same lines, never assume that you're doing someone a favor by accepting his or her culture. In fact, accepting and attempting to appreciate another country's way of life and business is something you *must* do to succeed — just like learning to deal with other people in your office. The attitude that people are lucky to have you around so that they can learn how to act like Americans will not make you many friends around the world.

Alicia, a sales rep from the United States, was visiting Spain to train the sales force there. After several days of enduring mid-morning arrivals and long lunches, Alicia lost her temper. "You need to learn that you can't just waste all this time every day," she told the sales team. "If you're so lazy that you can't get here by 8:30 and get back from lunch in an hour, you're all fired." Alicia's mistake was in believing that the company culture she was used to — starting early, eating lunch at one's desk, and working through the afternoon with no breaks — was superior. Not wanting to lose their jobs, the employees played by her rules the next day. As soon as she left Madrid, however, they resumed their standard procedures — and never gained any respect for Alicia.

Heated discussions about politics should be avoided — in the United States, in the country you're visiting, or pretty much anywhere in the world. You never know when you may say something that will offend, even if it seems like a harmless remark to you. If your associates begin criticizing other countries or governments, you may find yourself in a no-win situation. If you defend the country, you may end up offending someone. If you join in the criticism, your colleagues may lose respect for you and wonder why you would ever say something so negative about your own country. Either way, it's a conversation best avoided. If someone tries to engage you in a political debate, politely deflect it. "I've learned never to discuss religion or politics. Now, what can you tell me about the history of your city? It's so lovely," will probably work.

Keeping an open mind

Learn as much as you can about the cultures of others you work with. If you're traveling to another country for business, you should start by doing some research. The state department Web site at `www.state.gov` is an excellent place to start, and plenty of other resources on-line and in bookstores exist about customs and business around the world. If someone at your company has visited the country you're traveling to before, or if your company happens to have employees there, tap those resources for information.

If possible, begin reading newspapers from your target country before you leave for your trip, and read daily newspapers once you arrive. The Internet also makes it very easy to keep up on relevant news. Many major newspaper sites and news portals offer search services that allow you to specify search terms and get daily feeds of news about other countries.

Bridging the language gap

Even if the people you're visiting speak perfect English, it never hurts to learn at least a few words and phrases in their native language as a show of respect. Though they may snicker at your pronunciation behind your back, or even to your face, they will appreciate the effort. You should also realize that English speakers around the world use very different words and expressions, not to mention different accents. With a little research, you won't be alarmed when someone offers you a rubber for your pencil or Spotted Dick for dessert, and you won't make your English hosts blush by describing your shag haircut.

You should also make yourself familiar with the various types of personal address used in a country. Many languages use forms of *you* that are either singular or plural, masculine or feminine, and formal or informal. Even when you're speaking English, however, forms of address are often much more formal in other countries. For example, your pal Sol, the guy who writes the software in your office, might be Engineer Solomon in some other countries.

Never begin using first names until someone else takes the lead. While telemarketers in the United States feel free to call and ask for Al, and physicians invite the elderly to "take off all your clothes, Peg, and put on this paper gown," most other countries are much more formal. Don't even ask someone's first name. *Mr.* and *Ms.* are the norm until someone tells you otherwise, and often forever.

Getting to know foreign attire

Office attire, as well as dress for after hours, can pose a conundrum in other countries. When visiting a country whose people are strongly religious, you can assume that dress will be more conservative, particularly for women. Find out the rules before packing your suitcase. In all countries, you should dress on the conservative side until you're able to size up the situation and see what your colleagues are wearing. While many cultures have adopted Western styles of dress, you should never assume that it's alright to wear a skirt above the knee or troop through the subway in your running shoes and a suit. In some countries, dress is largely dictated by weather. If you feel comfortable trading your pinstripe suit for a *guayabera,* ask your host first if it's appropriate.

Tip-toeing around religion

Religion is perhaps the most delicate of all subjects. Before you visit a country, find out what its major religions are and learn at least something about those religions. When people around you begin pulling out their prayer mats, you shouldn't look stunned. It goes without saying that you should never, ever say anything disparaging about another religion, even if you consider something to be weird, and even if your religion advocates converting others. Remember, you're there for business, not as a missionary. Don't make jokes about religion, either — just as many Catholics don't want to hear jokes about what happens when the president, the prime minister, and the Pope are stranded on a desert island, your colleagues may not be amused by a joke that begins, "So, Buddha walks into a bar . . ."

You probably shouldn't ask any questions about religion, either, unless you know someone very well and are certain that they will not be offended. Though your curiosity may be genuine, questions like "I don't understand why you pray so many times each day. Can you explain it?" may be interpreted as rudeness or criticism. If you're really interested, pick up a book on the subject or visit your local university.

Frieda, a software engineer, was working on a project in India. In an attempt to lighten the mood, she referred to herself one day as the "Swami of Software," a nickname her Silicon Valley friends found hilarious. Several Hindu colleagues, however, were appalled by her lack of respect — not exactly her intended result.

Wining and dining

Of course, dining is also something to be careful about. If the country you're visiting is very different in other ways, you should brush up on its cuisine and dining etiquette so that you'll be ready, if necessary, to sit on the floor, eat with your hands, not eat with your hands, or swallow some new foods. Will you offend your host if you refuse to eat slimy things, things with eyes, things with more than four legs, or things that look just plain weird to you? Better find out in advance so you can be prepared.

With all these opportunities for confusion, you're bound to make a mistake at least once in a while. That's where your humble and respectful attitude come into play. Let the people you're around know that you don't know everything and that you would appreciate being corrected when do you something wrong. When you can tell from someone's expression or body language that you've made a mistake, address it immediately. "I'm afraid I may have done something to offend you, and I'm so sorry. Please let me know if I've made a mistake so I can avoid it next time." If someone said this to you, wouldn't you forgive an offensive remark or two?

If you happen to be visiting with other Americans, agree to help each other out. When you make a blunder at the big meeting, let your colleagues know so they can avoid doing the same thing the next day. While it may be embarrassing to share your blunder, you'll help raise the cultural literacy of the entire group, and therefore your group (including you) will earn more respect from your hosts.

Understanding Foreign Visitors

Now that you've read about the many mistakes you can make abroad, you should be much more sympathetic to the many people who travel on business to the United States. In most cases, these people have made a diligent effort to learn American English and American culture. Even so, mistakes and misunderstandings are bound to occur.

In many cases, visitors are anxious to follow American customs while their hosts are anxious to make the visitors comfortable by following the visitors' customs. For example, American business people may be practicing their bows in anticipation of Japanese guests, while those guests are practicing shaking hands and making eye contact. Absolutely nothing is wrong with meeting your foreign counterparts and finding out that everyone is trying to adopt the other's customs. In fact, knowing that each participant is interested in making the other comfortable is a great way to start a business relationship. In general, however, business people follow the customs of the country they are in.

When employees at your company make mistakes with American etiquette, you should help them, but with care. Never embarrass anyone by pointing out the mistake in front of a room full of people. Instead, pull them aside later and let them know that, "our custom here is to eat almost everything with a knife and fork, with a few exceptions," or whatever it is. If the employee makes many mistakes, concentrate on the biggest ones. You want him to be successful, but you can't expect him to learn everything at once!

Idioms can be confusing to foreign visitors, even if they speak the King's English better than you do. For example, the expression "how's it going?" doesn't make much sense to someone who doesn't understand what *it* refers to, let alone where it would be going. A sentence like "The printer works 24/7, so I'll get you that report ASAP unless the finance guy is AWOL again today" could be difficult even for a native. If you say something and get a puzzled look in return, don't keep repeating it more and more loudly — think of another way to say it.

If you're a manager and employees are coming to you with cultural conflict, consider educating your team on the differences and having an open discussion about how to minimize discord. Foreign employees may not realize that they're annoying someone else, and local employees may not realize that the source of the annoyance is a cultural difference, not a deliberate act. You have to do this with care, because you don't want to single out the foreign employee as "different" and cause a problem.

Remember that even on your own turf you have many opportunities to learn from foreign employees and visitors. Keep an open mind, and when you notice behavior that seems unusual to you, ask about it (respectfully and with humility). The more comfortable you make people feel, the more willing they are to explain. You may end up expanding your knowledge — and becoming a better employee, to boot.

Examining Etiquette by Region

Your best source of etiquette information for countries other than the United States is a country-specific book. We can introduce you to some of the most common etiquette issues you are likely to face, but certainly not all of them and certainly not some of the more unusual ones, either! However, the following list is a great place to start.

Europe

Europe ranges from the cold northern countries of Norway and Sweden to the warm Mediterranean countries of Italy and Greece. Some customs and mores vary as much as the topography, while others are shared across all of Europe.

Handshakes

Handshakes are standard business greeting gestures throughout Europe. However, the European handshake is usually exchanged before and after every meeting, no matter how many meetings you've already had. An exception is Great Britain, where, as in the United States, an initial handshake is often the only one you'll receive.

European handshakes are more formal and less buddy-buddy than those in the United States. You will not find a lot of back-slapping at handshaking time. Nor will you often find the extended handshake. A quick grasp and release is the norm. In most European countries, handshakes are firm. An exception is France, where a lighter grasp is customary.

Finally, it's customary to let women and those of higher rank extend their hands first in Europe.

Business cards

In Europe, the business card has a historical connection to the social card. As a result, their proper exchange at a meeting is significant.

Most European business people speak English, so your English business card will probably suffice for most places that you go. However, you do yourself a real favor by printing your business card with English on the front and your host's native language on the back. Present the side printed in his language to your host. And in some countries, such as France and Germany, any advanced academic titles you hold that are printed on your business card carry a certain cachet.

Names and titles

It's unusual in Europe for people to use first names immediately. It is, therefore, never appropriate to assume that you will immediately be on a familiar basis or that, because the person you've just met is named *Johann,* you may call him that. Wait until he asks you to call him by his first name or uses a familiar form of address with you.

Titles, especially academic titles, are always used in Europe. In the United States, it's unusual for a professor to be called *Doctor* or *Professor* outside of the classroom, but in European countries, professors, along with lawyers, medical doctors, and others, are introduced with their title(s).

Meeting times and style

In general, meetings in the northern countries of Europe begin promptly and the tone is businesslike, while meetings in the Mediterranean countries of Europe begin late and are prefaced by seemingly irrelevant banter. But this banter is considered part of business, for it's the best opportunity for your host to get to know you, and that is a prerequisite for business dealings in the Mediterranean countries (and many other places, for that matter).

That meetings in the Mediterranean countries typically begin late doesn't mean that you arrive late — it means that your host will typically arrive late. And, although your presentations should be precise, detailed, and logical everywhere, their reception will vary. In the northern countries, you're unlikely to be interrupted. Don't expect the same elsewhere. Your beautiful presentations are likely to be regularly interrupted in Italy, Greece, Spain, Portugal, The Czech Republic, or the countries of the former Yugoslavia.

Business attire

Throughout Europe, business attire is, in most businesses, formal. That means dark suits, subdued ties, and lace-up shoes. In some countries — Germany, Great Britain, and Denmark, for example — dress is ultraconservative and polished, while in other countries — France and Italy, for example — greater personal style within the uniform is tolerated and appreciated. Women's clothing follows suit.

The Netherlands is an exception. The Netherlands is a famously egalitarian society, and this egalitarianism extends to business attire. Although you'll find plenty of conservative suits in some circles, you'll find business casual up and down the hierarchy.

Dining and entertaining

Expect enormous variation when it comes to dining and entertaining. But one virtually universal practice exists — Europeans don't do business breakfasts.

In France, Austria, Germany, Great Britain, The Netherlands, Norway, Denmark, Sweden, Finland, Portugal, Poland, and Spain, talking business over lunch is not a violation of etiquette. In The Czech Republic, Italy, and Greece, on the other hand, you do not talk business over lunch unless your host initiates it.

Dinner in Europe is usually reserved for social entertaining. Depending on the country, you may start dinner as early as 6:30 p.m. or as late as 11:00 p.m. Depending on the country, your spouse may be invited.

Dining is taken seriously in most of Europe as an expression of generosity. In some countries, such as Italy and Greece, this generosity can reach stupefying levels; it can be virtually impossible to pick up a check in Italy and virtually impossible not to overeat or overdrink in Greece. But it's rude to refuse dinner invitations or any of the sumptuous items proffered to you at a dinner.

Here are some general dining rules:

- In Norway, Sweden, Finland, Denmark, be on time for dinner. Elsewhere, being fashionably late is acceptable.
- No host gift is expected in Great Britain.
- Do not take wine to a dinner in The Netherlands, France, or Belgium. It insinuates that you think the host's cellar is lacking.

Gifts

Business and social gift giving varies from country to country. In most countries, for instance, a small host gift is appropriate if you are invited to someone's home for dinner. But not in Great Britain — here, no host gift is expected.

Across most of Europe, business gifts should not be too personal and should be wrapped professionally. Try not to use white wrapping paper, and use brightly colored ribbon.

Social taboos

In many European countries, asking people what they do or asking them a personal question as an opening conversational gambit is a serious mistake. Europeans are, for the most part, more formal and reserved about such matters than Americans are.

Watch out for these gesture-related mistakes:

- ✔ The American gesture for "OK" using a circle formed by forefinger and thumb is offensive in Germany.
- ✔ Showing your palm to someone is offensive in Greece.
- ✔ Keeping your hands in your pockets is rude.
- ✔ Back-slapping is out of place in northern Europe.
- ✔ Having your hands below the table while dining in France, Germany, and Austria is rude.

The Middle East

Much more than in Europe, the Middle East is a region in which religion plays a significant cultural and social role. The dominant religions are Judaism in Israel and Islam in Egypt, Syria, Lebanon, and the Arab countries. Some Christians are found in Turkey and Israel.

Since religion is so much a part of daily life in most Muslim countries, you can expect certain differences, some mundane, some extraordinary. For example, neither alcohol nor pork is consumed, the workweek in most Muslim countries runs from Sunday to Wednesday or Thursday morning, and prayers are said five times a day, during which time business stops. Period. But the most extraordinary difference is the rigid separation of men and women in the vast majority of Muslim countries (Bahrain, Kuwait, and Oman being exceptions). In Arabic countries in particular, women are rarely seen, and when they are, they're heavily veiled.

For Christians, Sabbath is Sunday; for Jews, Sabbath is Saturday; for Muslims, Sabbath is Friday.

Handshakes

Among Jews, handshakes are standard greetings. Among Arabs, hugs and kisses are standard. If you're not Arab, you may get a handshake, but it's less like a handshake than it is a handhold, usually with both hands. Don't get nervous and don't move away. And remember that Arab men often hold hands as a gesture of friendship.

Business cards

Expect to exchange business cards with everyone. In Arab countries, it's polite and expected that your business card will be English on one side and Arabic on the other. Present your card Arabic up. In Israel, engraved business cards are preferred to printed ones.

Names and titles

Use full names and all appropriate titles upon meeting.

Meetings

Meetings can be long, chaotic, and even pointless to an American sensibility. In Turkey and Israel, punctuality is prized, and meetings typically start on time. But "meeting time" is a rather loose term in Saudi Arabia, where you may wait an hour or more before your host appears.

When he (or in Israel, sometimes, she) arrives, you will begin with banter and conversation centered not on business but on many other topics. Once you get down to business, you may be overwhelmed by the amount of argument and haggling. And in Arab countries not only will there be miles of discussion, but many discussions will occur at once. Be patient. Whether Jew or Muslim, people in the Middle East love to talk, discuss, wrangle, and argue.

And if no decision is made on the spot, do not be disturbed. The decision will come, sometimes weeks, sometimes months later.

The following are some general rules for meetings:

- ✔ Never say *no* directly; it causes shame. Find other ways to express disagreement.
- ✔ Age is important in Turkey. Defer to the oldest person.

Business attire

In Israel, business casual is acceptable in a wide range of businesses. In Turkey and the Arabic countries, go conservative with dark suits and subdued ties. Business women may have a hard time in the Middle East, in Saudi

Arabia in particular. If you're a woman brave enough to risk being ignored or shunned, remember that your knees and elbows must be covered at all times and that a high collar is required.

Dining and entertaining

Across the Middle East, hospitality is a means of demonstrating generosity, power, and wealth. As a result, Jewish and Arab hospitality sometimes appear extravagant to Americans. Accept the inevitable, and enjoy the prodigious feast to which you will be hosted. You will never eat better, or more!

In Muslim countries:

- ✔ Eating with your left hand is symbolically dirty.
- ✔ Asking about your host's wife or daughters, who you are unlikely to see, is rude.
- ✔ Publicly holding hands with, or kissing anyone of, the opposite sex is offensive.

Gifts

In Jewish homes, a gift of flowers to the host is preferred. But gifts to the host are frowned on in Muslim homes. And under no circumstances, should you give a Muslim a gift of alcohol, a picture of anyone or any animal, or anything made from pigs.

Social taboos

In most of the Middle East, it's bad manners for an outsider to discuss politics or religion. Showing the soles of your shoes or feet is rude in Turkey and in the Arabic countries, as is openly disagreeing with someone. And in Turkey, first names are used only when you know the person very well.

The thumbs-up sign is rude in Muslim countries.

Africa

Africa is so huge, so diverse, so complicated, and so rich that almost nothing can be said about shared etiquette across the continent. A few general things exist that we can point out. The northern countries bordering the Mediterranean are Islamic, and you can expect that the kind of lavish generosity, indirect business discussions, expansive sense of time, and second-class citizenship status for women found in the Arabic countries is found here too.

In the countries with colonial pasts, inroads of European etiquette have occurred. Not surprisingly, these inroads follow the particular country's colonial affiliation. One sees some English manners in Kenya and Nigeria, for example, Dutch manners in various places in South Africa, and Portuguese manners in Cape Verde. But beware! Countries with colonial histories are often ambivalent if not hostile about past control by Europeans. Some countries have, since the demise of the colonial system, engaged in systematic eradication of its residues.

Meeting and greeting

Across Africa, you will rarely find hostile greetings between men. Indeed, the opposite is closer to the truth — greetings are usually ebullient, confident, and quite lengthy.

Handshakes

Soft handshakes are common across Africa. In countries with large post-colonial populations, such as Kenya and South Africa, you can expect European style handshakes from the white people you'll meet. In South Africa, handshakes between whites and whites, on the one hand, and whites and blacks, on the other, differ. Although white people shake the hand of another white person in much the same way as in northern Europe, whites and blacks shake hands with an additional flourish. After shaking the full hand, they grasp thumbs and then return to a full handshake.

In the Muslim countries of northern Africa, you may find men holding handshakes so long that they become a handhold. Do not be offended. This is common practice.

Names and titles

You can never go wrong by using last names and titles when you first meet. Academic titles often add a great deal of luster.

Business attire

Conservative is the keyword. In particularly hot countries, some easing up on the dark business suit is permitted. And, of course, your host will not be bound to Western dress. He may show up in dressy traditional attire.

Dining and entertaining

Africans are justly famous for the pleasure they take in eating and entertaining and for their generosity. If you're invited to someone's home almost anywhere in Africa, be prepared — your host will go all out to impress you and to please you. In many countries, you will find no utensils of any kind and will be expected to eat with your hands. Remember, in Muslim countries, not to eat with your left hand, which is symbolically tainted. Watch your hosts in other countries for similar taboos. When in doubt, do as your host does.

India

India is a country composed of a multitude of religious cultures coexisting side by side. The dominant religion is Hinduism, but significant numbers of Muslims, Buddhists, Sikhs, Jains, Jews, and Christians also live in India. Onto this religious diversity is grafted a layer of British formality and good manners, resulting across the country in a population that is as polite as it is distinctive.

Indians of all religious backgrounds are wonderful speakers and take great pleasure in discussing their beliefs eloquently. Business is no different — you can expect a great deal of discussion of the details of a business deal. Add to this love of discussion the pleasure most Indians take in bargaining and you have the makings for some long business meetings.

Meeting and greeting

In general, Indians are formal upon first meeting. Elders are respected and deferred to in many situations, business ones included. Caste rankings still play a role in a wide variety of social and business interactions, although they're not as pervasive as they previously were. You may see an Indian bow slightly to another — that is either a show of respect for age or a show of respect for someone higher in rank.

Handshakes

Handshakes between Indians and Westerners, women included, are the norm for most of the cosmopolitan areas. However, in areas of the country where religious traditions are still strong, Indian men may only put their hands together and make a slight bow to a woman.

Business cards

Business cards are presented without great ceremony. But present your card with your right hand.

Names and titles

Use last names upon meeting someone for the first time and mention any higher academic or other titles.

Business attire

India is hot and the clothing is casual. Suits are rarely seen, although a light jacket with a shirt and pants is a standard outfit for businessmen. Women wear slacks and a jacket or long dresses.

Dining and entertaining

Business lunches are common in India, and it's perfectly appropriate to discuss business at lunch. Dinners at Indian homes are bounteous and delicious. It's rude to show up on time, but you should be no more than half an hour late either. When you eat, do so without using your left hand. As in Muslim countries, the left hand is symbolically unclean. And don't thank your host at the end of the meal.

Don't make these mistakes:

✔ Putting your hands on your hips is rude.

✔ Touching someone with your foot is rude, as is pointing with your foot.

Asia

We cover India and the countries of the Fertile Crescent in the section before this one, leaving China, Japan, Malaysia, Hong Kong, Vietnam, South Korea, The Philippines, and the other countries on the Pacific. These countries often have radically distinct cultures with radically different etiquette. In the case of Asia, more than any other region, it's best to consult country-specific books.

However, some similarities do exist. The Pacific Rim countries — China, the Koreas, Japan, Vietnam — have ancient cultures that are heavily influenced by the social and political views of the Chinese sage, Confucius. Even where Confucianism is not official state philosophy, many of its tenets are so deeply ingrained in the character and comportment of people that it serves as the basis of behavior.

Confucianism is an entire worldview — part philosophy, part religion, part etiquette manual, part political template, part economic treatise. It emphasizes respect for superiors and piety toward elders, love of family, duty to one's immediate society (village, town, region), loyalty to friends and family, hard work, wisdom, courage, humility, and unfailing courtesy to all. The person who can embody these characteristics is a person of *jen*, the Confucian superior man.

You are less likely to be the jingoistic American if you recognize that some of the cultural traditions of the Pacific Rim countries are more than 2,000 years old and are sedimented so deeply into a person's behavior as to be almost involuntary, like eye color. Expecting a businessperson from Japan or China not to bow when meeting you is a little like expecting an American businessperson not to shake hands.

Meeting and greeting

Greeting ceremonies are encoded in Confucianism and are therefore pretty standardized across the Pacific Rim (exceptions are The Philippines, which is predominantly Catholic, and Indonesia, which is predominantly Muslim). You can expect a bow, a ritualized exchange of business cards, last names, and titles, and a pretty high degree of formality.

Handshakes

Americans routinely mangle Asian handshakes. It's quite simple, actually; when you are in China, Hong Kong, Japan, Indonesia, Malaysia, Singapore, Vietnam, or South Korea, you can shake hands. But avoid direct eye contact during the handshake, and don't shake very hard or very long. Your host may bow to you. The more senior you are, the deeper the bow. You may also bow, but don't make an ass of yourself by making a great show of it. The bow is a sign of mutual respect, not an opportunity for you to expose yourself as a buffoonish American.

The Philippines is the exception here. Don't bow, but do make direct eye contact.

Business cards

The exchange of business cards must be made properly. The story still circulates that a major computer manufacturer blew a $30 million deal because, when presented with his Japanese host's business card, he just stuffed it in his back pocket.

Business cards should be printed in English on one side and in your host's language on one side. In China, the card should be printed in black or gold ink. You should always present only pristine cards.

When you present your card, you do so with both hands, native language side up and readable to your host. When you receive a card in return, study it, thank the person, and place the card gently in your jacket pocket.

Under no circumstances should you put your counterpart's business card in your wallet and then put your wallet in your back pocket.

Names and titles

Last names and professional titles are used across Asia. Don't be afraid to say that you're a professor if you are one.

Meetings

Meetings begin more or less on time in Japan, China, Hong Kong, South Korea, Thailand, and in the Chinese population of Indonesia. In Malaysia, Vietnam, and The Philippines, meetings are less likely to start punctually.

In China, some of your junior Chinese business associates will arrive early. You do not have to start the meeting ahead of time. They are there in case you need them for anything.

Meetings in most Asian countries are softly choreographed and sometimes long, with business meals thrown in to break the day up.

In most Asian countries, the beginning of the meeting follows a definite pattern. The top person from your host's country will come in at an appointed position in the flow of people. Normally, meetings have a brief prelude during which people get to know each other.

In virtually all Asian countries, the conduct of the meeting will be fairly structured. Enthusiastic sales jobs are out of place — speak slowly, precisely, and give your host every opportunity to participate. Avoid saying *no* directly. Plenty of qualifiers exist that you can use; emulate the way your hosts disagree without disagreeing.

Remember that in Asian countries, additional deference to elders is expected. Never interrupt the senior member of the delegation. And don't try to hurry the meeting up. It takes as long as it takes, and there's nothing you can do to change it.

Business attire

Your default business wardrobe is conservative business dress, with suits, ties, and tie-up shoes for men, and conservative suits and dresses for women. Because of their warmer climates, some leniency in dress is to be found in Vietnam, Malaysia, The Philippines, Singapore, and Hong Kong. But even in these countries, be conservative and avoid flashiness of any kind.

Dining and entertaining

Though business lunches are quite common, it's the events that occur after work that are famous. You'll find that Asians love to entertain in restaurants and bars and that the food is exquisitely flavored, prepared, and presented.

In China and Hong Kong, expect a banquet — a long meal with innumerable courses served one after the other. Arrive on time and get ready to eat. Take something from every serving dish, even if it's only a little amount. But never clean your plate — symbolically, the munificence of the meal means that you can't finish it.

In Japan, you will be hosted to an evening of eating and drinking. Let your host order and enjoy something from each platter. Don't refuse to eat sushi or sashimi (both of which involve raw fish) — you'll insult your host. Drink your beer or sake slowly — your host will fill your cup every time it's empty.

Koreans entertain both at home and at restaurants. Arrive on time if you're going to a private home, and bring a small gift. If you're invited out to a night on the town, be appropriately grateful, for your host is probably planning to spend a lot of money.

The Filipino style of entertaining is to invite you to a private home, where you and a gaggle of the host's relatives and friends will enjoy a lavish meal.

Gifts

Gifts for the hosts are expected in Indonesia, Japan, China, Hong Kong, The Philippines, and South Korea. They are not expected in Vietnam.

Gift-giving in many Asian countries extends far beyond a gift to your host. In most Asian countries, gifts of some kind are appropriate even for a meeting. They should be well thought out — ask someone who knows your host what is appropriate. The gift should be beautifully wrapped, but never in white paper.

Be ready to accept a gift from your Asian host. In most cases, these gifts will be professional gifts. When accepting a gift, attend to the proper etiquette. In China, for instance, politely refuse the gift, at first, and then accept it grudgingly. In Japan, the gift must be accepted with both hands and opened only after the giver has left the premises. In Indonesia, you open a gift in front of its giver if you are urged to do so, otherwise you open the gift alone.

Social taboos

Most Asians are uncomfortable with close physical contact. So, after your handshake, avoid slapping your colleagues on the back or getting too close when you're talking. An exception is Indonesia, where it's not uncommon to see male friends holding hands.

You will be hard-pressed to ever hear anyone say *no,* and you shouldn't break the silence by making a habit of it either. No, you don't say *no* either.

Putting your hands on your hips is aggressive in The Philippines.

Australia and New Zealand

Australia is a casual country and its people are friendly and open. You will find overt formality in only the most rarified circles of Melbourne and a few other cities. New Zealand, on the other hand, is more like Great Britain, with greater formality and less instantaneous camaraderie.

Handshakes

Australian and New Zealander handshakes are firm and quick. Don't grasp the other person's hand with both of yours, and don't keep shaking. Women typically don't shake hands with one another in Australia, but typically do in New Zealand. And in both countries, it's expected that women extend their hand to men.

Business cards

Business cards are exchanged, but little or no ceremony is attached to the exchange.

Names and titles

Australians and New Zealanders dislike pretense. Although you should call someone by their last name when you first meet them, this will not last long — especially in Australia, as you will probably soon be invited to call your host by his or her first name. New Zealanders are more reserved when you first meet them, but they, too, will quickly warm to you. Announcing your title when you meet is offensive because it's perceived as showing off.

Meetings

Meetings start on time and get to the point at hand without a great deal of preliminaries in both countries. In fact, in New Zealand, arriving a few minutes early is polite.

Business attire

Typical business attire is so similar to American business attire as to not require separate discussion.

Dining and entertaining

Lunch can be a business affair, but both the near-obligatory call in at the pub and evening dinners are social events. Arrive on time in both Australia and New Zealand.

Gifts

Bringing a bottle of Australian wine, a box of chocolates, or some other small item to your host's evening dinner party is expected.

Social taboos

Being overly demonstrative with another man is a taboo for men in Australia and New Zealand. And trying your hand at "G'day, mate" is more likely to result in offense than anything else.

The V for Victory sign is given palm out. If given palm in, it is offensive.

Latin America

Latin America stretches from the Texas border to the tip of Tierra del Fuego. With the recent passage of NAFTA (North American Free Trade Agreement), business between the United States and Latin America is intensely active.

Latin America is predominantly Catholic among its Spanish and Portuguese speaking populations and primarily non-Catholic among its native inhabitants. The culture is predominantly patriarchal in nature. Rigid divisions between work and home life exist: Men are in business and women are at home with the family. As a businesswoman traveling to many locations in Latin America, you should be aware up front that this insistence on strict gender roles can sometimes be jarring and can sometimes be directed toward you.

Anyone going to Nicaragua, Guatemala, El Salvador, Colombia, Chile, or Peru should know enough about the current political climate to avoid discussions that might skewer business dealings. These countries have faced serious political upheaval in the last quarter century, and, even where the wars are over, the scars are very deep.

Meeting and greeting

Latin Americans are, in general, very friendly, very physical, and very good hosts. You will first get to know each other and *then* do business — normally. In fact, you probably won't get any business accomplished during your first meeting and you may not get much done on your first trip. But you will stay up late for dinners and parties.

Handshakes

Handshakes are firm and relatively brief. Constant eye contact during a handshake is crucial in Mexico and Argentina. Men shake hands with men, and women shake hands with women in most countries. In Brazil, Peru, and Mexico, men and women also shake hands, with the woman extending her hand first.

Male friends hug each other upon seeing each other. Female friends kiss each other on each cheek and touch each other's arms. And throughout Latin America, expect your conversational partner to stand close to you and to look you in the eyes. Don't move back and don't waver in your eye contact.

Business cards

Business cards are exchanged. Your business card should be printed in both English and Spanish.

Names and titles

When you meet for the first time, use your last name and whatever titles you have.

Latin American surnames are composed of both the paternal name, which comes first, and the maternal name.

Meetings

Meeting times are set but not respected. You're expected to arrive in a timely manner, but your host is not. And the more important he is, the later he will be. Meetings themselves follow the pattern of most Spanish speaking countries, with lots of preliminary discussions designed to establish rapport. Business discussions occur only after rapport is established. And, once they start, business discussions are comparatively disorganized and prone to interruption. Decisions are typically not made during first meetings.

Latin Americans are proud of Spanish and aren't particularly eager to use English. You do yourself a favor by knowing Spanish and, if you don't, by bringing an interpreter.

Business attire

You won't go wrong by dressing conservatively: suits and ties for men, unrevealing business suits and long dresses for women. Argentina is probably the most formal of the Latin American countries and Brazil the least formal. Venezuelans enjoy expensive accessories, so long as they're in good taste.

Dining and entertaining

Business lunches are common throughout Latin America, and usually long, from 1:00 or 2:00 p.m. until 3:00 or 4:00 p.m. Dinner is a purely social event, and can occur very late; it's not unusual to sit down to dinner at 10:00 or 11:00 p.m. throughout Latin America. In general, you should keep your hands above the table at all times while eating, and pass food and drink with your right hand.

Gifts

You may be a few minutes late for dinner across the region, but you should never be early. Small host gifts are accepted in most Latin American countries. Venezuelans do not entertain at home very much. It's an unusual honor to be invited, so make sure the host gift is something special.

Be aware that the following gestures can cause problems:

- ✔ The sign for "OK" formed by your forefinger and thumb is offensive in Brazil.

- ✔ Putting your hands on your hips is a gesture signaling a challenge in Argentina, and putting your feet on a table is rude.

- ✔ Raising your fist to head level is a gesture associated with Communism in Chile.

- ✔ Putting your hands in your pockets is rude in Mexico.

Special Advice for Women Travelers

While not as many as there used to be, differences in the appropriate behavior and dress between men and women for conducting business around the world still exist. Sadly, women are also advised to be on guard for their own safety while traveling, whether in the United States or internationally.

In general, no reason exists to be routinely afraid when traveling in a foreign country. Being open to new experiences and meeting new people are part of making yourself a successful international businessperson. On the other hand, while travelers of both sexes should always be aware of their surroundings, women do need to be slightly more cautious. This section is intended not to scare you, but to remind you of ways to keep yourself safe at all times while still having an enjoyable and productive trip. Even if you're a guy, it couldn't hurt to keep reading.

If you ever feel unsafe, there's probably a good reason. Follow your intuition and do something to address your fear: Change your route, get into a taxi, go into a shop where lots of people are, or get off the elevator at the next floor if someone is making you uncomfortable. Don't let anyone tell you that you're being silly or overreacting.

Staying safely at hotels

Safe travel begins during the planning process back home. If you're at all concerned about taking a taxi in your destination country, you or your travel agent should arrange for a car service to pick you up at the airport and take you to your hotel. Your peace of mind is worth the extra expense. Your choice of hotel is also important, because your hotel is your home away from home and you should feel comfortable there. A larger hotel that caters to business travelers will probably be safer than a smaller hotel. At least on your first trip to a place, until you become more comfortable there, you should err on the side of safety. Here are a few tips to keep in mind:

- ✔ The hotel should have a bellman on duty at all hours to assist you with hailing a taxi or finding your way. Tip generously to ensure attentive service throughout your stay.

- ✔ When you're checking into the hotel, other guests should not be standing close enough to hear your conversation. Many hotels will write your room number on the key envelope instead of saying it out loud. If someone at the front desk ever says your room number loud enough that it can be heard by others, explain that you would like that information kept private and ask for another room assignment.

✔ Especially in a very large hotel, ask for a room near the elevator so that you won't have to walk down a long hallway by yourself. You should also avoid rooms on the first floor.

✔ Find your key while you're in the lobby, and keep it in your hand while you walk to your room. Having it in your hand prevents you from having to fumble for it in your purse while standing in front of your door.

✔ If you're nervous for any reason about walking to your room, ask for an escort. Again, generous tipping will ensure service with a smile.

✔ When you get to your room, lock the door immediately, and don't open it without looking through the peephole first. If someone claims to be from room service, but you haven't ordered anything, don't open the door.

✔ If you will be using gym facilities or a parking garage, make sure that an attendant will be there at night. Be sure to park in a well-lit area and look around you before you get out of the car. Before you get in the car, check the back seat to make sure there's no one in it. Of course, you should always lock your vehicle, even if you're leaving it for only a moment.

Many hotels catering to business travelers are especially attuned to the needs of women. Some offer *concierge floors,* which not only provide extra services like breakfast and evening cocktails, but also require a room key to exit the elevator on that floor. This amenity is well worth the extra money if it puts your mind at ease.

You shouldn't travel with jewelry that could be stolen — if you won't be wearing it every day, don't bring it. If you do have other valuables, however — including your passport and other important papers — lock them up in the hotel safe. That probably isn't a workable solution for protecting your laptop computer, but you should lock it in your suitcase when you're out of your room. At a minimum, don't leave it sitting out on the desk where it presents an obvious temptation.

Moving around the city

If you were a mugger or a professional con artist, who would you look for — a confident, professional woman with spring in her step, or someone who looked like she just fell off the turnip truck? Even if you feel uncertain, you can't let it show. Better yet, you should take the time to learn what you need to know so you'll look, if not like a native, at least like someone who can take care of herself. If you'll be walking somewhere, check the map before you leave, and confirm your route with the concierge. That way, you'll be able to walk confidently and look like you know where you're going.

A wireless phone, either your own or a rental, has become a real traveler's friend over the past few years. If you get lost, help from someone you trust is just a phone call away. Keep important numbers — your hotel, the colleagues you are visiting, your credit card company — close at hand. If you need to make a call, step into an unobtrusive (but not deserted) place to do so. Don't stand in the middle of the street talking on your phone. You may also want to observe how others use their cell phones in the country you're visiting. In some places, everyone has one, and they talk on them everywhere. In other countries (such as the United States!), making or taking calls during lunch, for example, is considered the height of rudeness. See Chapter 7 for more on using a cell phone politely within the United States.

Be wary of strangers who approach you on the street. While you don't want to rebuff someone who's honestly looking for directions, you also don't want to seem overly friendly. If you feel uncomfortable for any reason, don't stop to speak with that stranger who's trying to get your attention.

Occasionally, another American or other visitor may ask you for directions. Congratulations! You must look like you know what you're doing. If you don't know the directions, simply say that you don't know — without explaining that you are only visiting yourself. You never know the other person's intentions for sure, and you don't know who might overhear you.

Become familiar with the local currency as soon as possible so you'll seem confident when tipping or paying for incidentals. (A credit card is preferable for larger purchases, such as meals.) If possible, get some of the local currency while you're still at home so that you will be comfortable with it by the time you leave for your trip.

Ask the concierge how you can identify a legitimate taxi. In many countries, you could end up getting in the car with a perfect stranger who isn't licensed with any authority. The cab may end up being perfectly safe, but you shouldn't take the risk. If you're taking a taxi and the driver asks what route you prefer, never say, "You pick — I don't know where I'm going." Instead, say something like, "Since you're the expert on driving in this area, please take whichever route you think is best." If the driver seems to be going around in circles, ask him what he's doing, and ask him to stop and let you out if you think he's truly taking you for a ride! (Of course, you only want to get out in a busy area where you can easily find another taxi.) Stay in the cab while paying your driver — you don't want to be half in and half out while you have money in your hand. Of course, be sure to grab all your belongings before you step out of the cab, or your driver may drive off with your purse or briefcase.

Most taxi drivers are perfectly nice people. Some aren't. Always have your wits about you when taking a taxi, and don't let anyone take advantage of you.

Understanding local attitudes toward women

Before you travel to a foreign country, you should read as much as you can about women's roles in that country. If you're going to Canada, things will be pretty similar (though there are other differences to keep in mind when doing business there). But in many countries, the roles of women and men are quite different than they are in the United States. This section covers just a few highlights.

In Latin American countries, the prevailing attitude is that men work and are decision makers in the professional world, and women take care of the home and children. While businessmen in Latin America will probably be friendly enough, they may not treat you with the same respect that they give to your male counterparts. The best way to respond is to be businesslike and professional. Try to strike a careful balance between being overly friendly, which may come across as flirtation, or overly serious, which may seem pushy and rude. Though you probably won't hear any overt come-ons from your colleagues, overt catcalls in public places are common. Simply ignore the comments, though you're allowed to be secretly flattered!

In the Middle East, the rules are very different. Research them to avoid mistakes. While male dominance is diminishing in some areas, it's thriving in others. Saudi Arabia is a particularly difficult place for American women to do business because of the strict rules regarding separation between men and women. Not only do women not participate in business, they wear veils.

In Europe, business manners often entail the same social etiquette that's used in the United States. For example, most men will wait for a woman to extend her hand first before shaking hands. European men may open doors and pull out chairs for women. Instead of being offended and feeling that these people are not taking you seriously, realize that these gestures are signs of respect.

In many cases, businessmen will view you differently than they view local women because you are an American, and people will understand your role as a professional practicing the customs of your own country. In other cases, your counterparts may expect you to more strictly follow the rules of the country you are visiting. In either case, people may view you as slightly suspect. Your strategy should be to get as much information as you can before the trip; discuss the situation with a colleague in that area, if possible, for advice; respect the rules of the place you are visiting; and always act with extreme professionalism.

Dressing appropriately

We've already talked about dress in other sections of this chapter, but the advice bears repeating. Appropriate attire is especially important for women. In addition to helping you be an effective businessperson, dressing with respect for the local culture can help you stay safe, avoid embarrassing yourself, and avoid offending others.

In all cases, you should dress on the conservative side until you're very sure that you can branch out without embarrassing yourself. The dress of other professional women in the country you're visiting should be your guide. No matter where you travel, avoid garish makeup, nail polish in startling colors, and anything too tight, too short, or too low-cut. When in doubt, you will always be correct with a skirt that falls below the knee and long sleeves. In most cases, you should wear a skirt or dress rather than pants. And even if you're sightseeing on the weekends as part of your trip, leave your shorts at home. You will be far better off with a roomy skirt in a breathable fabric.

Keep your jewelry to an absolute minimum. You should wear your wedding ring — you might consider wearing one even if you're not married to ward off potential romantic advances. (Wearing a fake wedding ring while traveling in the United States isn't a bad idea, either, unless you *like* the idea of romantic advances!) If your engagement ring is big and sparkly, leave it in the safe deposit box at home. Small gold, silver, or pearl earrings are good choices, but if you're at all nervous about attracting criminals, wear no earrings at all. The same goes for necklaces; you can easily accessorize with a scarf, which is much less of a temptation for thieves. Whatever jewelry you bring, plan to wear all of it every day. Don't leave anything at the hotel.

In Muslim countries, the rules regarding clothing are more specific. Blouses with high necks and long sleeves are a must, and hemlines should be mid-calf or lower. The rules are less strict in Israel, but if you ever visit a synagogue or a mosque, both your knees and your elbows must be covered.

Both for professional reasons and for your comfort, shoes should be low-heeled and close-toed. Never wear a brand-new pair of shoes for travel, and never wear tennis shoes (even black ones!) unless you're on your way to the gym. Bring plenty of hose with you, because you may have trouble finding what you like in a foreign country with unfamiliar brands.

While you should avoid looking too much like a tourist, pouches that fit underneath your clothes can be very handy for your passport and cash, though you will also want some cash easily available. Fanny packs are not acceptable business wear. Instead, use a purse with a long strap. That way, you can wear it across your body, which makes it more difficult to grab and also saves wear and tear on your shoulder and neck. When you actually arrive at your meeting, switch your purse to the more traditional and professional over-the-shoulder position. Make sure that your purse has at least one zippered compartment for cash and credit cards.

Part VII
The Part of Tens

The 5th Wave   By Rich Tennant

"As a team you've done a crackup job collecting body parts. There's just one thing, and maybe I wasn't clear enough about this, but I notice you're all bringing me the SAAAME body part."

In this part . . .

We first provide ten tried and true communication tips as well as business dining tips. We then present etiquette advice from ten executives who know what they're talking about.

Chapter 24

Ten Tried and True Communication Tips

*T*hough volumes have been written about the etiquette of communicating, many of the worst offenders don't seem to be listening. Are you one of them?

Few skills are more appreciated than the ability to make conversation. The person who is able to draw people into conversations, introduce interesting topics, and make everyone comfortable is valued in all situations, business and social. Conversing is an art — but it's also a skill that can be honed.

Getting people at ease, conversing well, and keeping everyone interested may seem daunting tasks at times, but here are a few tips that may help:

✔ Make sure the tone of your conversations is positive. The person who goes from cubicle to cubicle complaining and putting down other people won't go far. Enter into a conversation wholeheartedly and listen to what is being said. Leverage a good sense of humor and tell stories well.

✔ Make good eye contact. Doing this lets the other person see that you are open, friendly, and genuine about getting to know them. Eye contact also makes it easy for them to respond.

People who look away, sideways, down, or up when talking to another person are seen as shifty, or rude, or not really interested in the other person.

✔ Be certain that your verbal and nonverbal messages say the same thing. You show that you're attentive by your body language. That means you neither slump in your chair nor sit rigidly without moving. You should watch the face of the person speaking and not let your eyes wander all over the room. And you should sit comfortably without shifting every few minutes.

✔ Ask questions of others and really care about their answers. Remember that people like to talk about themselves. Questions, unless they are too personal, are a great way to help quiet or reserved people open up. Try to include everyone in the group in the conversation by asking various people questions and drawing out their opinions.

✔ Do not swear or tell off-color jokes, and avoid questions about religion, income, or political preferences. Don't bring sexual topics or overtones into your work discussions. If you have proper manners, you will make a conscious effort to speak inclusively, without letting sexist terms creep into your vocabulary. Listen for the things that slip out of your mouth without your thinking about them, and try to make sure that even these flippant comments are polite.

✔ Pay attention. Think about what you want to say and don't interrupt, whisper, walk away, or start doing something else while someone is still speaking to you. Likewise, sense when you are boring people by their body language.

✔ Show that you're a team player. Use *we* when referring to work done by your team. Acknowledge your coworkers' contributions by using *we* instead of *I* and *our* instead of *my.* Be sure to ask for the other person's opinion rather than only giving your own.

✔ Listening well means more than just sitting quietly. A payoff exists for listening well: You'll remember all the major points of the conversation, including any actions that are your responsibility. You'll be able to ask intelligent questions during, and at the end of, the conversation. And who knows — you might even learn something.

✔ Repeating back what you think you're hearing, particularly when dealing with bosses or clients who are giving you instructions for work to be done, is always a good idea. Your good listening can create clarity for everyone.

✔ Quickly discern potential topics of interest to any given group and steer the conversation in that direction. Sense how to step in to fill an embarrassing void in conversation.

When you've mastered the skills in the list, you have our permission to consider yourself a true artist of conversation.

Chapter 25

Ten Executives Talk about Etiquette

● ●

In This Chapter

▶ Practical advice and smart ideas from executives

● ●

*W*e interviewed a number of executives, from a wide range of companies and locations, about etiquette. We asked them: How important is etiquette for success in business? Can etiquette make or break a deal? Does it affect the bottom line? What role does personal behavior play in our technology-driven economy? What else would you like to say about etiquette in business? We received a wide variety of answers and include them for your benefit.

Harvey Mackay

I'd like to start a campaign to return good manners to business. Exhibiting good manners does not make a person appear to be weak or wimpy. Rather, it demonstrates that person's maturity and ability to appropriately respond to business situations. Who would you rather have working for you — the sales rep whom customers look forward to dealing with or the bulldozer who'll stop at nothing to get the order? Bad manners are bad business.

— Harvey Mackay, Chairman
Mackay Envelope Corporation
www.mackay.com
Minneapolis, MN

Reprinted with permission from nationally syndicated columnist Harvey Mackay, New York Times bestselling author of Swim With The Sharks *and* Pushing The Envelope.

Ranjini Manian

In India, having your arm around a person of the same sex on the street is completely acceptable, while public displays of affection to the opposite sex are a no-no. At first, many Indian professionals landing in Silicon Valley do not understand the quizzical looks they get but then learn how the perception is drastically different in the West.

Etiquette across cultural boundaries has to be a subtle and sensitive adaptation to the local culture rather than a patronizing and obvious attitude. Training in etiquette coupled with showing common courtesies, care, and concern for others will make good cultural ambassadors of you for your country. Class can be learned and cultivated and pays rich dividends when it shows.

— Ranjini Manian, CEO
Global Adjustments
Relocation Services and Cross Cultural Trainers
www.globaladj.com
Madras, India

Lynne C. Lancaster

With today's employees sporting everything from neckties to tie-dyes and addressing one another as everything from "sir" to "dude," at-work etiquette has become a corporate conundrum. Inviting four diverse generations of employees to convene around the same conference table is often an open invitation to frustration, bad feelings, and dissent.

At BridgeWorks, we've observed firsthand the fall-out from this interpersonal free-for-all. Organizations are grappling with how to set standards for professionalism while allowing for generational differences. Individuals are struggling to express themselves, yet want to know how to fit in. And customers are confused when their expectations about etiquette go unmet.

Understanding how the generations perceive aspects of etiquette such as language, clothing, and behavior is becoming one of the sharpest tools for cementing key relationships, whether with clients or coworkers. Organizations that can preach and teach effectively on this topic will truly be able to build bridges, not gaps.

— Lynne C. Lancaster, President
BridgeWorks
www.generations.com
Mill Valley, CA

Dominic Gallello

With software, a developer is like a parent and the program is the child. If a customer tells a programmer face-to-face that the "baby is ugly," I guarantee by the next morning that the developer will be showing the customer a much prettier baby!

Remember these simple customer courtesies:

✔ When customers come to visit, start the meeting by having the customers present their objectives and pain points. Make sure all members of senior management are present. Never miss this chance and NEVER miss this chance for an internal meeting instead.

✔ When customers leave your facility, always walk them to the door or the elevator. Make them feel like they are the most important people on earth.

✔ Check in with important customers. An e-mail or a phone call to find out how things are going is worth a lot.

✔ When a customer is in pain because of our products, we communicate, visit, investigate, communicate, resolve, and communicate. Customers understand that things may not be fixed overnight, but they want to know that you are feeling their pain and doing as much as you possibly can about resolving the issue.

— Dominic Gallello, CEO
RedSpark, Inc.
www.RedSpark.com
San Francisco, CA

Sonja Hed Brown

As CEO of an Internet publishing company producing products for children, I want to emphasize the importance of doing all we can to create a culture of respect and civility for our kids.

Walk down middle school America and you're likely to be assaulted with cursing and pushing. It's a race for position without concern for anyone else. School violence is rising and is a national concern. Evidence shows acts of violence and disrespect occur when students don't have basic skills of etiquette. This makes sense. How often will students be shoved, before they shove back? Training students with, at minimum, simple everyday manners can go a long way in improving the environment of our schools.

Students want a safer, more pleasant school environment, but on their own can make little change. As business leaders, we must model respectful behavior in our workplaces. We all have an important role to play in making the world a kinder place.

— Sonja Hed Brown, CEO
Myschoolbooks.com
Minneapolis, MN

Don Welshon

In today's business world, with communications via Internet and e-mail, it has become easy to fall into the trap of complacency. This does not go unnoticed even though not much is said about it. Practicing modern etiquette enhances the trust and faith in the business decision stream of information. In our ever-widening global economy we regularly deal with individuals halfway around the world and from entirely different cultures. We may never meet them face-to-face, and good etiquette, up front, tuned to blend both cultures, will prove invaluable for all involved.

Avedon is a manufacturer: We're bricks (actually plastics) but use clicks, too. While many companies are competent and proficient with their products, and with electronic interface, etiquette is evident in action. The organization that presents itself best with respect for others will ultimately win in the crucial long-term business relationship.

— Don Welshon, Vice-President
Avedon Engineering, Inc.
www.avedon.com
Denver, CO

Marcia Sterling

In the past, people thought about good manners in terms of some pretty silly protocols for proper social behavior. But in today's business world, good manners have a lot more to do with having the right attitude about partnering to achieve a win-win result.

— Marcia Sterling, General Counsel and
VP of Business Development
Autodesk Inc.
www.autodesk.com
San Rafael, CA

Michelle Burke

Consulting in various organizations across the country allows me to observe and train employees in the areas of accountability and effective communication. The difference between good manners and bad manners is how a person is remembered. In each moment, a person can either build their credibility or chip it away by a simple word or act.

With the mad rush to be first in everything, the lack of time seems to have impacted our ability to be kind and courteous when interacting with others. We have yet to see the long-term ramifications of this behavior. However, what I'm hearing from participants is that it directly affects their ability to be more productive and motivated on the job. I believe any CEO would want to know if a lack of civility exists in his company and take action immediately to correct it. After all, this impacts the bottom-line of any business.

— Michelle Burke, CEO
Executive Counterparts
Author of *The Valuable Office Professional*
www.executivecounterparts.com
San Francisco, CA

Larry Tesler

I am known more as a technologist than as a business leader, but etiquette can be critically important for someone entering the business culture from engineering or academia. Treating others with respect and consideration is a great technical skill, too.

— Larry Tesler, President
Stagecast Software, Inc.
www.stagecast.com
Redwood City, CA

Thomas Conner

Now, more than ever, good manners, respect, and civility make communication in business easier for closing the gap between traditional business and the e-model of today. It doesn't matter where you are or what your company does — we can all show consideration for others.

— Thomas Conner, CFO
MonsterLabs.com
Nashville, TN

Index

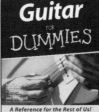

 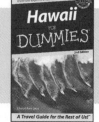 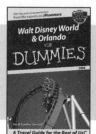

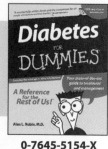